IT'S A FUNNY GAME

It's a funny game . . .

BRIAN JOHNSTON

BOOK CLUB ASSOCIATES
LONDON

TO PAULINE

a second offering with all my love

Contents

Acknowledgements   9

Preface   10

FIRST OVER
'As I was saying . . .'   11

SECOND OVER
'A life full of moment'   23

THIRD OVER
Down YOUR Way   38

FOURTH OVER
Nice people   52

FIFTH OVER
All's right with the World Cup   69

SIXTH OVER
Alarums and excursions   85

SEVENTH OVER
The sun shines sweetly on cricket 1976   94

EIGHTH OVER
Captains courageous   108

NINTH OVER
Out of the mouths . . .   124

TENTH OVER
Sadness and joy   127

ELEVENTH OVER
Dear Sir, I want to be a cricket commentator   139

TWELTH OVER
It's the Ashes! It's the Ashes!   146

THIRTEENTH OVER
In the box   161

FOURTEENTH OVER
Horse d'oeuvres   174

FIFTEENTH OVER
Packer up your troubles!   187

SIXTEENTH OVER
I can't help laughing   195

LAST OVER
or Who's been a lucky boy, then?   213

Index   225

Acknowledgements

My grateful thanks to all of the following:

Les Bailey for his streaker poem – Mrs Alan Hamilton for her late husband's poem *The Cricketer's If* – *The Times* for the reproduction of an article by Michael Leapman – an unknown lady for her parody of the Crispin Day Speech from Shakespeare's *Henry V*. And to my daughter, Clare, Linda Green and Wendy Wimbush for their skill in deciphering my writing.

Preface

I have been put into bat again – I have been asked to follow on. Any person who writes *two* autobiographies must be egotistical. But any person who refuses when graciously asked has to be pretty strong-minded. If Jim Swanton had not pinched the title first I might even have called this book *Follow On*. But I have chosen its present title because so often in the commentary box I have found myself saying: 'It is impossible to forecast what will happen. CRICKET IS A FUNNY GAME.' In fact, this is the most common of all cricket clichés – or *clish* as that great man Ernest Bevin used to call it. But as cricket is a way of life for me, so I feel that the phrase can equally well be applied to life itself. So for those of you who are not cricket fanatics, there is no need to despair. There is more than just cricket in this book, which takes up from where I left off at the end of 1973 in my first autobiography *It's Been A Lot Of Fun*. I only hope that *you* will think that It's *STILL* a Lot of Fun.

St John's Wood
Christmas 1977

First Over 'As I was saying . . .'

It was that great *Daily Mirror* columnist Cassandra who, on restarting his column at the end of the war, began: 'As I was saying when I was so rudely interrupted . . .' I have no such excuse for starting to write another book. Except perhaps for two things. A number of people after reading *It's Been a Lot of Fun* assumed that I had retired. No such luck for the listeners! I *did* retire as a member of the BBC staff in September 1972 but have continued to work as a freelance ever since.

The other thing became obvious to me on 25 January 1975 – that in spite of my career as a broadcaster for thirty years I was still not as well known as I had thought. This was brought home to me when flying back from Australia. Our aircraft had stopped at Bahrain to refuel at about two o'clock in the morning. I was pacing up and down the transit lounge to get a bit of exercise when an Englishman in an elegant overcoat approached me. Why he was wearing an overcoat in Bahrain where the temperature was in the nineties I don't know. Anyway, he came up and said, 'Excuse me, I think I recognise you.'

So I put on what I thought was a friendly smile at that hour of the morning and began to reach for my pen. 'Who do you think I am, then?' I asked him. 'Tell me,' he said, 'did you ever drive a bus in Watford?' I gasped out a firm '*No*,' and he went on, 'Well, you are the dead spit of a chap who did.' With that he turned and walked off without another word. I am convinced he was not joking nor had done it for a bet.

This lack of fame was further emphasised a few months later at Euston Station – of all places. I had come down on the sleeper from Manchester and at 7 am was walking up the cold dark platform, not looking my best I must admit after a night on the train. I heard footsteps behind me, and soon a man drew level with me. He gave me a good hard look then said, 'Do I know you?'

'I don't know,' I replied, 'who *do* you think I am?' 'Aren't you Alan Dixon?' he asked. Well, poor Alan, who was a BBC sports commentator in North Region, had died about six years before. So I said, 'Alan Dixon? But he's dead.' 'Yes,' replied the man. 'I know he is!' To this day I still cannot work out what he meant!

Anyhow, with *Down Your Way* as a weekly basis, life in my 'retirement' in the autumn of 1973 was as busy as ever. I went up to Manchester to record two programmes of *Call My Bluff*, something I had always wanted to do. I was in Paddy Campbell's team and although I did not do too badly, I could not match the skill and ease with which Paddy and Frank Muir played. We recorded the two programmes during the evening in front of the same audience. We changed our ties, shirts and coats before the second one but kept on the same trousers.

I expect that, like me, you imagined that the panel made up their own meanings of the words. This was, I believe, tried originally, but now the *True* or *False* explanations are cleverly composed in advance and typed on to little cards. An hour or so before the show you are 'summoned' to the Captain's dressing-room where, after consultation, he allots you your cards, either *True* or *False*. You then learn these and have them in front of you during the programme. You can vary them to suit your own particular style. Much of the art of winning the game depends on the selection by the Captain of the right person to give the *True* version of a particular word. A deadpan face and the ability to lie convincingly are essential ingredients for the contestants. It's certainly as much fun to do as it is to watch, but alas I have not been asked back (yet!).

In November 1973 the Lord Mayor's Show came round again for TV and this has become a hardy annual ever since. The timing has always been dicey, the ideal being for the Lord Mayor's coach to pass our commentary position opposite St Paul's about a minute before the end of our broadcast.

But this is the longest *unrehearsed* procession in the world and I regret that on two occasions we have missed the Lord Mayor before we had to hand back to the studio. But in 1976 we achieved perfection with the Lord Mayor reaching us on the dot, and what is more, for the first time ever he surprised viewers by speaking a message to them from the window of his coach as it passed our cameras. The secret was that our engineers had been along early to the Mansion House before the Lord Mayor got dressed in all his finery and robes, and had 'wired' him up with a small microphone and pocket transmitter.

I had often been to the Festival of Remembrance at the Royal Albert Hall but 1973 was the first year I had commentated on it for radio. Previously I had resisted doing it as I feel that this service and the Two-minute Silence are very personal matters for people who, like myself, lost many friends during the war. But it went all right – unlike the Two-minute Silence service broadcast once by a West Indian radio station. The programme was being recorded in the main square of the town and at about five minutes to the hour the engineer in the control room sat listening to the hymns and the bands playing. He then unfortunately dozed off, but awoke a few minutes later and to his horror heard nothing coming over the air. Thinking that there had been a breakdown he automatically went into his emergency drill and put on a record of martial music. Result – the Two-minute Silence was shattered. So was the poor engineer when he realised what he had done.

At about this time I was a member of the panel on another sporting quiz, *Sporting Chance*, which is always fun to do and keeps one informed about sports other than cricket. One of my friends who heard the programme was inspired to send me a rude postcard which showed a quiz master putting a question to a panellist.

QUIZ MASTER   What did Eve say to Adam the first time she saw him?
PANELLIST (*After a long pause*) Ah – that's a hard one.
QUIZ MASTER   Quite right – two marks!

In mid-November 1973 there was Princess Anne's wedding

to Captain Mark Phillips and as usual the BBC went to town and pulled out all its ceremonial stops. I had previously been a commentator for TV for King George VI's funeral, the Coronation and Princess Margaret's wedding. But this time I was selected for radio and had a superb position on the corner of the Mall and Horse Guards Parade. I had to describe the procession on its way to and from the Abbey, and also did some interviews with the crowd. I was lucky enough to be one of the few to go to Buckingham Palace the evening before to see the wonderful collection of wedding cakes which had been sent to the Princess. There were dozens of them, many with horsey motifs, and it was nice to learn that they were all being sent off to hospitals. We were also shown the seating plan for the wedding breakfast – round tables for about ten people each – and a preview of the menu and wines. I can assure you they were mouth-watering and I thought of them as I munched a ham sandwich in my car as I rushed off to Shropshire to do a *Down Your Way*.

Our daughter Clare flew back from Australia and we had a very happy family Christmas at our cliff house in Swanage. As usual, all seven of us opened our stockings together early Christmas morning on Pauline's and my bed. I love Christmas but must admit that a well-known vicar got the retort he deserved when he said in his sermon: 'Christmas is a time of great and enduring joy for all of God's two-legged creatures.' One of his parishioners was heard to say in a loud voice, 'Try telling that to a turkey'!

The year 1974 started off with a quick trip to West Germany to record some quizzes with the forces, one of which took place in an RAF hospital. I was told that the Queen Mother had been there six months before and as usual had gone round all the wards talking to the patients. She came to a man who was writhing with pain in his bed. 'What's wrong with you?' she asked sympathetically. 'Oh, Mam,' replied the man, 'I'm in great pain. I've got an awful boil on my bum.' 'Oh dear, very painful,' said the Queen Mum, not batting an eyelid. 'I do hope it gets better soon.'

She passed down the ward and when she had left the sister

came back and gave the man a terrific rocket. 'How dare you mention a word like that to Royalty – or to any visitor for that matter. Make something up. Say you've sprained your ankle. But never use THAT word again.' The man said he was very sorry and quite understood and promised never to do it again.

Three months or so later, Princess Margaret came out to Germany to visit one of the Highland Regiments of which she is Colonel. She came to the same hospital and like her Mother talked to all the men in the wards. Eventually she came to the man with the boil (he was still there), and asked him what was wrong. Remembering the sister's instructions he replied: 'I'm in great pain, Mam. I have a badly sprained ankle.' 'Oh,' said the Princess with some surprise, 'so the boil on your bum is better, is it?'

I hope the story was true. But I doubt it!

Most of January and February 1974 was taken up with launching my autobiography *It's Been a Lot of Fun*, and all the publicity connected with it. Radio did us proud and I appeared on most of the programmes such as *Today*, *Open House*, *Be My Guest*, *Jack de Manio Precisely*, *Desert Island Discs* and quite a bit of local radio round the country. Television was not so generous, only *Pebble Mill* in Birmingham giving me a spot. I had long wanted to receive the accolade of appearing on *Desert Island Discs*, the longest running programme on the BBC. Roy Plomley not only thought up the idea during the war but has presented it ever since, and is a most friendly and sympathetic interviewer. My selection of eight records was a fair reflection of my tastes and was as follows:

1 *Eton Boating Song*   sung by Eton College Musical Society
2 *All the things you are*   sung by Hutch
3 *We'll gather lilacs*   sung by Vanessa Lee and Bruce Trent
4 *Double Damask*   A sketch by Cicely Courtneidge
5 *Strolling*   sung by Bud Flanagan
6 Elgar's *Enigma Variations*   played by Philharmonia Orchestra conducted by Sir Malcolm Sargent
7 *Tie a yellow ribbon round the ole oak tree*   sung by Dawn
8 *End of the party*   Composed and sung by Barry Alexander (my eldest son so called because there was already another member of Equity named Barry Johnston)

The book I chose to take with me was John Fisher's *Funny Way to be a Hero*. It is an analysis of British Music Hall with biographies and routines of all the great comics and comedy acts.

My book was published in the middle of February 1974 and I'm happy to say received a very kind press. Unfortunately we had to battle with the three-day week and the General Election, so that when the first print sold out there were long delays before more books could be got to the shops. So we lost some of the impetus of the early publicity but in the end my book did quite well and at the final count had sold over fifteen thousand copies. Not in the David Niven class, of course, but not too bad. I suppose I should have put in some of my early sexual experiences, though I'm afraid they would not have been as amusing as his undoubtedly were!

Our publication date was also not too cleverly timed, as the following week Pauline and I flew off to Barbados for a long-planned holiday – thanks to *Down Your Way* allowing me to pre-record three programmes. The main idea was to see the Third Test between England and West Indies at Bridgetown. It was strange to sit in the stand and just watch the cricket *without commentating*. I must confess that at the end of the day I was far more exhausted than if I had been working.

England, already one down in the series, managed to draw the match after being put into bat by Kanhai. They got off to a terrible start but were saved by Greig (148) and Knott (87) who took the score from 130 for 5 to 293 for 6, England finally making 395.

West Indies replied with 596 for 8 declared, of which Lance Rowe made 302, the highest innings by a West Indian batsman against England. It was the third score of over 300 which I had seen in a Test and I must admit I'm not too keen to see another. The other two were 311 by Bobby Simpson at Old Trafford in 1964, and 307 by Bob Cowper at Melbourne in 1966. Rowe's was the most entertaining of the three but however good the batsman, it's rather like a brilliant after-dinner speaker going on too long.

England, thanks to a not out hundred by Keith Fletcher,

drew the game, which was remarkable for the fact that altogether ninety-nine no balls were called – seventy-nine not being scored off by the batsmen. This is a record but not one to be proud of, although of course with the present front foot law it is not as easy as it seems. However, I am always surprised that even the greatest bowlers – including slow ones like Underwood – give so many runs away simply because they fail to put their front foot in the right place during their delivery stride.

This Test was the turning point of the tour for England. They batted well in a rain-spoilt match in Guyana and then went on to win a thrilling game in the Final Test at Port of Spain, winning by 26 runs with one hour to spare, and so squaring the series. It had been a triumph for Dennis Amiss who, in the Tests, scored 663 runs with an average of 82.87 and 3 hundreds. Tony Greig also emerged as a formidable all-rounder with 430 runs and 24 wickets, mostly taken by his off-spin which was helped by the bounce in the wickets.

It was Mike Denness' first tour as captain and he grew in confidence and tactical skills as it progressed. But it was difficult for him initially, as at least six of the players had played in more Tests than he, and naturally he felt he had to make his mark as a leader. He tried to do this by largely going his own way and not often seeking the advice of his more experienced players. But as his confidence grew he became more receptive to their opinions and, in the end, although not up to his best form with the bat, came out of the tour with the credit of having led a happy and not unsuccessful team.

Back in England after three glorious weeks of sunshine, I appeared in Derek Nimmo's chat show, *Just a Nimmo*, which was great fun. The theme of the programme was sporting commentary and the others on the show were Cliff Morgan and Jimmy Hill. I had often seen Derek do his 'toe twiddling' act, which he performed goodness knows how many times during the long run of *Charley Girl*. He had evidently heard that I can tuck my ears in, and quite out of the blue without previous warning, he asked me to do it during the show. So for the first time after nearly thirty years on TV, I tucked my ears in for millions to see. It caused some hilarity and had an amusing sequel a few weeks later.

We were doing a *Down Your Way* in Kirby Lonsdale and had got lost in the dark on our way to interview someone just outside the town. I spotted a lane leading up to a farm, so we drove up and I knocked on the door.

After some delay, a woman came to the door and peered out into the gloom. Her face lit up when she saw me and her first words were: 'Can you really tuck them in?' Only after proving that I could did she say, 'Good Evening, Mr Johnston', and showed us the right way to our prospective victim.

He happened to be a prosperous farmer and as we sat in front of a crackling log fire, I learnt a very good tip from his wife. They had some beautiful carnations in a vase, and when I admired them, she said they were over a fortnight old. I asked her how she kept them so fresh, and she explained that instead of putting them in water, she always used fizzy lemonade. I have tried it ever since and I can assure you it works – they really do stay fresh for far longer.

Incidentally, while recalling the farmer's wife who asked me to tuck in my ears, I couldn't help thinking of the stupid story of a man who also called at a house late one night. He was telling a friend about it and said, 'I knocked and a woman opened the door in her nightdress,' and the friend remarked: 'What a funny place to have a door'!

After commentating on the 1974 Boat Race from Chiswick Bridge for radio, and the Battersea Easter Parade for TV, I introduced a charity concert at Welwyn for my friend Martin Gilliat. It was a serious musical occasion and I was taught an object lesson of when not to try to be funny. The lady accompanying the singers at the piano was a Miss Nunn, and although her name was in the programme I thought I ought to give a verbal credit, so I said: 'And now, ladies and gentlemen, I am sure you would like to show your appreciation of the lady at the piano. Before the show started I was talking to her and asked her what her name was. And answer came there Nunn!' And deservedly, except for a loud guffaw from Martin in the front row, laughter also came there none!

It was a wet summer for the double tour of India and Pakistan. England under Mike Denness beat India easily three–nil and so avenged their defeat at the Oval in 1971. As so often happens over here, the Indian batsmen could not cope with the England fast bowlers and seamers. This time Old, Hendrick, Arnold, Willis and Greig took all the wickets except for four by Underwood, who was the only spinner selected by England for any of the six Tests during the summer. The famous trio of Indian spinners, Bedi, Chandrasekar and Prasanna, came off just as badly and the England batsmen made a packet of runs against them. The England batting averages were remarkable and must be a record for any top six batsmen for any country in a Test series. Here they are:

David Lloyd	260.00
Keith Fletcher	189.00
John Edrich	101.00
Mike Denness	96.33
Dennis Amiss	92.50

and Tony Greig a comparative failure with only 79.50.

Wadekar on his second tour to England as captain had an unhappy time not only as captain but also with the bat. I felt especially sorry for him because, as a leg-puller myself, I appreciated the time he pulled *my* leg in 1967. And what's more he did it in front of the TV cameras.

It happened one Sunday at Southport when BBC 2 was covering a match between the Indians and Lancashire, the Indian tourists including their captain the Nawab of Pataudi and Wadekar himself. I have discovered since that a conspiracy took place between Pataudi and Desmond Smith who was the PRO for Rothmans at the time. They saw that instead of commentating as I usually did, on this particular Sunday I had the job of interviewing batsmen as they returned to the pavilion. It's a dicey job at the best of times as no one who has just been bowled by a full pitch, or caught off a dolly, relishes being asked what happened. You know – ask a silly question . . .

Anyway, I was sitting in a deckchair in front of the pavilion when I saw that Wadekar was out. So I got up and with my microphone went out to meet him. We had become good friends on the tour and I always called him Wadders and he called me Johnners. So it was with some confidence that I approached him and in front of the cameras asked him, 'What happened Wadders?'

Instead of the smile I was expecting I noticed that his face was completely blank, so thinking he had not heard me over the applause of the crowd, I repeated the question. To my utter surprise he said in broken English – 'Sorry, I no speak English, not understand' and continued on his way to the dressing-room. 'But Wadders,' I gasped, 'we've often talked together on the tour – surely you understand. How did you get out?' But it was no good, he brushed me aside murmuring: 'Me no speak English – sorry' and disappeared into the pavilion.

Was my face red as I turned to face the camera! I tried to laugh it off – not very successfully – and hurriedly handed back to the commentator. I wasn't really angry – just embarrassed and nonplussed, but couldn't help laughing when I hurried into the dressing-room to find all the Indians, including Wadekar, in fits of laughter. I had to admit it – in front of several million people I had been well and truly done!

Pakistan were a tougher nut to crack and all three Tests in 1974 were drawn. Rain interfered with the first two at Leeds and Lord's. No play was possible on the fifth day at Headingley with England needing 44 runs to win with 4 wickets in hand, Fletcher being 67 not out and Old not out 10, with Arnold, Underwood and Hendrick to come. It could have been a very close thing either way. At Lord's, Pakistan had all the bad luck with the weather and leaking covers, Underwood having a field day with 13 wickets in the match. But once again there was no play possible on the last day when England only needed 60 to win with all their wickets in hand. So this time it seems certain that *they* would have won.

There was quite a hoo-ha about the covers – or lack of them as the Pakistan manager Omar Kureishi thought. In an official protest he accused MCC of 'an appalling show of negligence and incompetence in not covering the pitch adequately'. Strong words, but as MCC Secretary Jack Bailey pointed out, the slope at Lord's makes it extremely difficult to prevent water from running down from the grandstand side. It's difficult to believe but the level of the boundary at the Tavern side is seven feet lower than the grandstand boundary, a big drop when you consider that the ground is only 144 yards across.

The Third Test at the Oval was a very different affair. The sun shone and both sides made gigantic totals on a slow, easy pitch – Pakistan 600 for 7 declared; and 94–4, England 545. For Pakistan, Zakeer Abbas, spectacles gleaming in the sunlight, played superbly for his 240, his first Test hundred since his 274 on his Test debut against England at Edgbaston in 1971. For England, Amiss scored his eighth Test hundred and as usual did not give up after reaching three figures, going on to make 183. Both he and Fletcher had a splendid summer but with the Australian tour coming up the England batting still lacked a consistently successful opening pair. They were far too liable to early collapses with someone like Knott or Old having to come to the rescue later on.

We had our usual number of amusing incidents in the commentary box. In the First Test against India at Old Trafford there was no play on the Saturday until 1 pm. I was due to begin the commentary at 11.30 am when play should have started. But it was a cold miserable day with rain and dark clouds, and the Indian spectators were sitting miserably huddled together in one of the stands. I heard my cue from Radio 3 in my headphones '. . . and so to find out the prospects of play, over to Brian Johnston at Old Trafford'.

'It's raining here,' I said, 'and there certainly won't be any play for some time yet.' I then meant to say, 'There's a dirty black *cloud* here.' Unfortunately, what I *did* say was, 'There's a dirty black *crowd* here!' Collapse of everyone in the box, including the former Maharajah of Baroda – or Prince as we called him – who was one of our summarisers throughout the series.

Then, during the Second Test at Lord's against Pakistan we pulled off a leg-pull on Henry Blofeld. There were a lot of interruptions for rain on the Saturday, and whenever it does rain we do our best not to return to the studio for music. Instead we try to fill in the time by answering listeners' letters, interviewing people or just discussing current cricket topics. We were doing just that early in the afternoon when there was no play. We were all in the box and took it in turns to introduce some new subject.

Henry – who when he gets excited talks very fast and hardly draws breath – got stuck into some topic in which he was passionately interested. Looking straight into the microphone he talked at a great pace completely ignoring the rest of us. After two or three minutes he still had not brought any of us into the discussion. So we all quietly left our seats and got our producer Peter Baxter to slip a note in front of Henry. All it said was, 'Keep going until 6.30 pm!'

This momentarily stopped Henry in his tracks. You should have seen his face as he saw the rain pouring down outside with little prospect of play, and realised that we had all deserted him. But he carried on gamely, and we soon had mercy on him, and slipped back into our seats . . .

Second Over   'A life full of moment'

During my September 1974 holiday in Swanage I caught a bug – and still have it. Golf. As a boy I had played the occasional nine holes with my old Mum, but never seriously. Most of my shots sailed over extra cover with the usual crick-eter's slice. After that, with a family of five and generally working for the BBC every Saturday and some Sundays, I never seemed to have any spare time. Whenever I did, in the summer I played cricket, and in the winters on tours with MCC was quite happy to go to the beaches.

I am a very bad golf player, and still have no handicap except for my slice and my swing. But my friends have been incredibly kind and patient, and allow me to play with them: we normally play a greensome in which all four of us drive off and then each partnership chooses which of their drives they wish to play. This is not always the longest drive, as if mine has gone a reasonable distance and is fairly straight, it is good tactics for my partner to play the second shot. In this way a bad player like myself can have some slight influence on the result of a game. But with a four-ball I trail miserably behind, and it virtually becomes my partner versus our opponents.

I have worked out my own philosophy of golf. During a round – if lucky I may play as many as six reasonably good shots. Afterwards it is these that I cherish and remember and forget all about the many bad ones. My friends on the other hand are all pretty good average golfers. So they play many good shots and only a few bad ones. But judging from their conversation it is these latter that they remember and worry about, so that I often end up happier than they do.

Now that I play I appreciate golf on TV all the more and

try to discover its secrets by watching the masters. I am encouraged to see that even they play a few slices or hooks, but am immediately depressed by the ease with which they invariably get out of trouble. Mind you, they do have one advantage over me. When *they* slice, the ball often hits the long line of spectators, and bounces back on to the fairway. But nobody comes to watch *me*, so that my slice disappears into impenetrable undergrowth.

Inevitably I suppose, I have begun to collect golf stories which make a change from cricket. It's interesting that quite a few of them have to do with death, starting with that oldest of chestnuts:

Two golfers were putting on a green by a road, when a funeral procession went slowly by. One of the players took off his cap and stood reverently to attention. His opponent remarked on this unusual display of respect for the dead person. 'Well,' said the player, 'it's the least I can do. I was married to her for forty years.'

Then there was the very bad golfer with a terrible slice which always went into the rough. When he died his will requested that his ashes be scattered on the fifteenth fairway. So after his funeral his friends took the urn up to the course and as requested emptied it out on to the fifteenth fairway. But unfortunately a strong wind was blowing and blew the ashes straight into the rough!

There was also the elderly golfer who was worried whether he would get any golf when he died and went to heaven. So he found a crystal gazer and asked him about the prospects for golf in the after-life. The crystal gazer looked into his crystal ball for a few moments and then announced that he had two bits of news, one good, one bad. The golfer asked for the good news first. The crystal gazer told him he could see a beautifully laid out course with perfect fairways and smooth lush greens. The golfer was delighted but said he supposed he had better hear the bad news, too. 'Here it is,' said the crystal gazer. 'I am sorry to tell you that I can see you driving off the first tee at 9.30 am next Thursday!'

On a slightly more corny note there was the golfer who always carried a spare pair of socks in his bag – just in case he ever got a hole in one.

And then there was the long driver of the ball who regularly hit it two hundred and fifty yards or more. But gradually over a period of a few months he found that he was beginning to hit the ball shorter and shorter distances. From two hundred and fifty yards he went down to two hundred and twenty-five, then to two hundred, and a hundred and fifty until in the end he couldn't hit it more than a hundred yards. So he decided to go to his doctor to find out if there was anything wrong with his health. The doctor examined him thoroughly and then told him he had two things to tell him, one good, one bad. 'Let's have the bad first,' said the golfer. 'Okay,' said the doctor, 'stand by for a shock. You are gradually changing into a woman.' The golfer turned pale and croaked out, 'Come on, quick, give me the good news.' 'Right-ho,' said the doctor, 'from now on you'll be able to drive from the ladies' tees!'

Jimmy Tarbuck tells a lovely story of the golfer who was always accompanied by his dog when playing a round. Every time the golfer made a good shot or sank a long putt, the dog would stand up on his hind legs and applaud his master with his front paws. A friend asked him what the dog did when the golfer landed in a bunker or missed an easy putt. 'Oh,' said the golfer, 'he turns somersaults.' 'How many?' asked the friend. 'It depends on how hard I kick him up the arse,' was the reply.

And finally what about the unorthodox golfer who, like Brian Close, could play equally well either right- or left-handed. His opponents never knew which it would be until he drove off from the first tee. One of them asked him how he decided which way he would play. He replied that if, when he woke up in the morning, his wife was lying on her right side, then he would play right-handed. If she was lying on her left side, then he played left-handed. 'But what happens if she is lying on her back?' asked the opponent. 'In that case,' said the man, 'I ring up the club to say I will be an hour late!'

In between learning golf my September holiday was twice interrupted. First I went to Manchester to record *Reunion* for BBC TV. This was a series where three people who had been at school together met to discuss their schooldays and the paths which their lives had taken since then. My old school chums were William Douglas-Home and Jo Grimond. We had been at Eton and Oxford together and before the war had occupied the same house at 35, South Eaton Place. It was kept by a lovely couple called Mr and Mrs Crisp. Since then, William had become one of our most popular and prolific playwrights with an unerring touch for dialogue and light comedy. At the time of our recording he had had sixteen plays in the West End averaging three hundred and fifty performances each – not bad! Jo had been leader of the Liberal party from 1956–1967 and was – and still is – the father figure of that party. My favourite remark by a Liberal was attributed to that great character Lady Asquith. When asked what she thought of the two-chamber system she is said to have replied: 'I personally couldn't do without it. You see, my husband is a liberal peer.'

Anyway, under the tactful and friendly chairmanship of Brian Redhead, William, Jo and I were given our heads and encouraged to talk non-stop for about forty minutes – not something which any of us found very difficult to do! But somehow we each managed to get a fair share of the conversation. We came to no very profound conclusions except that Eton was the best trades union in the world and that all three of us had been very lucky in the jobs we had chosen to do.

Towards the end of September 1974 I flew off to South Africa for a week as I had been asked to share the commentary with my old friend Charles Fortune on the Datsun International Double Wicket Competition. I wonder what Lord Harris would have had to say about a Japanese car firm sponsoring cricket matches! Anyway, it is a splendid form of cricket consisting of two-a-side, with a maximum of 8 overs an innings – and each team playing the others once in a one-innings match.

It must have been an eye-opener to those who still belittle what South Africa is doing to try to integrate her sport – especially cricket. There in Johannesburg playing together, staying in the same hotels, attending receptions together, and sharing dressing-rooms were teams from South Africa white, South Africa black, England, Australia,

New Zealand, West Indies and Pakistan. They were all perfectly happy and thoroughly enjoyed the experience, which of course would not have been possible a year or two earlier.

The big crowds enjoyed it too, especially as Eddie Barlow and Barry Richards won it for South Africa white, but only after a tough fight against South Africa black. What a turn-up for the books that would have been had the latter won. But the success of the competition bore out what I have always felt. It is grossly unfair to punish cricketers for apartheid by cancelling their tours, and with boycotts and demonstrations. It is not *their* fault. Blame the politicians but leave sport alone. In the end I am sure it will be the best means of achieving unity between whites, coloureds and blacks – all over the world.

In October I was paid a wonderful and much appreciated compliment by those friendly and generous cricket fanatics – The Wombwell Cricket Lovers Society. They gave a special dinner in my honour and presented me with the 1974 Denzil Batchelor Memorial Award for 'Services to Cricket'. It was totally undeserved because, as I have said so often, I have been lucky enough to earn my living from what is really my life's hobby. But it was a delightful occasion with some excellent speeches by the Bishop of Wakefield and the President of Yorkshire, Sir Kenneth Parkinson.

I have known the latter since before the war, when on my various visits to Yorkshire he used to entertain us at parties with his conjuring tricks. He tells an amusing story of how as an average club cricketer he was called on to open the batting to that very fast bowler the late Father R. P. H. Uttley of Hampshire. Both the first two balls which he received pitched on his middle and leg, and with a loud click the balls shot off to the fine leg boundary. On each occasion there were loud appeals for LBW, but the pace was a bit too fast for the elderly umpire to follow the ball. So hearing the sound of a ball on wood he signalled a four to the batsman each time. A few balls later a very fast yorker from Uttley spreadeagled Kenneth's stumps, and he retired to the pavilion to considerable applause for those two finely executed leg-glides. How was the umpire, or the unsuspecting crowd, to know that Kenneth had a *wooden* left leg which now had two large dents on it the size of a cricket ball!

This reminds me of the batsman who *did* glide a ball off his legs down to long leg. But the bowler appealed for LBW, and when the batsman trotted confidently down to the other end, he saw to his horror that the umpire's finger was up. 'You can't give me out LBW,' he said, 'I hit that ball hard.' 'I know you did,' said the umpire thinking quickly, 'I am merely signalling byes.'

My health at the dinner was proposed by Trevor Bailey, who over the past few years has added much wisdom and caustic wit to our ball by ball commentaries. He tells a splendid story against himself. In 1954 in the First Test at Brisbane, Australia were put in to bat by Len Hutton. They had scored about 300 for 2 when Trevor came on for a final spell. Hot and tired, he ran up to bowl but the ball stuck in his hand so that although he went through his bowling action, he did not actually deliver the ball. 'That's the best bloody ball you've bowled today, Biley!' shouted a barracker.

Anyway, the dinner was a lovely occasion for me, and Les Bailey, the Society's Poet Laureate, wrote these kind words on the back of the menu.

> *A life full of moment, bonhomie and cheer*
> *From Eton to Oxford to a young Grenadier.*
> *BBC Outside Broadcasts and pastures quite new*
> *Where he even survived being once sawn in two.*
> *Now a rich sense of humour, an eloquent style*
> *Has added to cricket a reason to smile.*
> *And all the world over where the great game is played*
> *The sunshine of commentary is the memory he made.*
> *At Cricket, Monte Carlo, or just* Down Your Way
> *We'll remember him always – till the last close of play.*

In December 1974 we had a rather unique gathering of past and present Grenadiers – officers and senior NCO's – to say goodbye and thank you to our much loved Colonel of the Regiment, General Sir Allan Adair. It took the form of a mixed cocktail party in the Banqueting Hall in Whitehall, and there must have been at least a thousand people present. So as you can imagine, there were plenty of reminiscences!

Among these was the tale of a very gallant and distinguished ex-officer who had won the Victoria Cross in Italy. A friend of mine who served with him out there was censoring the letters of the men in his company and one of them wrote: 'Captain —— has just been awarded the Victoria Cross. If he was as bloody to the Germans as he is to us he thoroughly deserves it. P.S. Let them keep their f . . . . . . medals. The only cross I want to see is Charing Cross!' When my friend finished this story someone else asked if we knew that old Major X (a very ugly officer) had been attached to the French in 1940, and had done so well that he was recommended for the Croix de Guerre. Unfortunately they couldn't find a French General who was prepared to kiss him!

But the star of the party was Mr Harold Macmillan, who had served with the Regiment in France during the Great War. He made an excellent speech in praise of Sir Allan and told this story about the war in the trenches.

He and some other officers were sitting in a dug-out near the front line. They were drinking port although their Commanding Officer, Colonel 'Ma' Jeffries, strongly disapproved of drinking and discouraged them from doing so. They had several bottles open on a wooden table when to their dismay they heard footsteps approaching along the trench, and by the voices realised it was the Commanding Officer making an inspection. They hurriedly got some candles, stuck them in the half-filled bottles, and managed to light them just before 'Ma' Jeffries entered the dug-out. They all got up and stood to attention, and the Colonel seemed quite pleased with all he saw, and after a short chat went on his way. Much relieved, they quickly removed the candles and went on with their drinking.

About six months later one of them met Colonel Jeffries in the Guards Club in London. 'Would you like a glass of port, Colonel?' asked the officer. 'I think I'd prefer a small brandy if I may,' replied the Colonel. 'The port might taste of wax.' I was lucky enough to be introduced to Mr Macmillan later in the evening and he assured me that the story was true.

But I didn't dare ask about the one told me about him by Lord Carrington, who was in the 2nd Battalion Grenadier

Guards with me throughout the war. He was known as 'the small peer', and behind his spectacles and mild expression, he's a very determined character. Not only is he extremely brave and strong-minded but also has a lot of talent, something a stranger would never suspect on first meeting him. It was his platoon of Sherman tanks who took Nijmegen Bridge in Holland in September 1944 and for which action he was awarded the MC. In addition to his political career in this country he was possibly the ablest and most popular High Commissioner Britain has ever had in Australia. He has a wonderful sense of humour and was highly respected by everyone in Australia. I think it's no secret that they would have liked him to be their Governor-General, but it would have meant his being away for five years from the centre of the political scene, and would also have involved a large financial sacrifice.

Anyhow, he told me this story of Mr Macmillan who visited Australia on a Commonwealth tour during the peak time of his 'Super Mac' reign as Prime Minister. He was given a great welcome wherever he went by British immigrants who gathered at airports or outside his hotels to see and cheer him. He sensed their homesickness and desire for news from home, so made a habit of giving a little speech which always started with the phrase, 'I bring you greetings from the Old Country'. He did this hundreds of times, always accompanying it with a little circular wave of the right hand.

One day, he and Lord Carrington were sitting in the back of a car on their way to some place in the outback, miles from anywhere, and passing through desolate countryside. They were naturally discussing political business as they made their way along the dusty road. Every half-mile or so Mr Macmillan would break off the conversation and wave out of the window with his right hand and mutter, 'I bring you greetings from the Old Country . . . !' his only audience being the odd kangaroo or wombat! I told you that Lord Carrington had a sense of humour!

I had a bit of bad luck myself over the question of drinking in the Grenadiers. When I first joined the 2nd Battalion at Shaftesbury in June 1940 I took with me a dozen bottles of

Perrier-Jouet champagne, as I thought I might as well drink it while the going was good. I put it in charge of the mess-sergeant and thought no more about it. One evening one of the officers who had just returned from Dunkirk decided to throw a birthday party and asked one of the mess-waiters to bring in some champagne. This he did, and everyone including myself drank large quantities of it and remarked on its excellent quality – far better than the usual cheap brand we usually had. It soon ran out and yes, you've guessed it. It was *my* precious case which we had been drinking, as revealed by an apologetic mess-sergeant when he returned from an evening out.

Even in retirement I still seemed to be flying all over the world, and after Christmas and New Year's Eve in St John's Wood, I flew off to Australia on the first day of 1975. The excuse was to try and push sales of my book in Australia but I must admit that the main reason was to see another Test at my second favourite cricket ground, Sydney (Lord's must be No. 1). Christopher Martin-Jenkins was now the official BBC Cricket Correspondent and so was covering all MCC tours as I had in the past. So it was just a holiday for me and we pre-recorded three *Down Your Ways* to enable me to be away for nearly four weeks.

While in Australia I appeared on quite a few TV and radio chat shows to talk about the book plus some fruitful interviews with the Press. I stayed with my daughter Clare in a house she shared with some other girls in the pleasant Woollahra district of Sydney. As usual I had a marvellous time with lots of parties, bathing, harbour cruises and trips up country.

Clare and I gave a small party at her house for friends and some of the MCC party and their wives. We adjudged it to have been an unqualified success when in the early hours of the morning the distinguished cricket correspondent of a top London daily bade us goodbye and instead of leaving by the front door, tottered up the stairs and disappeared into a cupboard!

When I arrived the tour was not going well for Mike Denness and his team. They were having a torrid time against the tremendous pace of Lillee and Thomson. They had lost the first two Tests at Brisbane and Perth, but had managed to draw the third at Melbourne thanks to a great innings of 90 by Amiss, some fine fast bowling by Willis and the usual good-all-round performance by Greig. It was in fact a most exciting low-scoring match with Australia eight runs short of victory with two wickets standing, and England might well have won it had Hendrick not pulled a hamstring after bowling only fourteen balls in Australia's first innings.

Poor Mike Denness was getting the blame for everything and with Test scores of 6, 27, 2, 20, 8, 2, he decided to drop himself for the Sydney Test. But to be fair he was not the only one who was failing, and after seeing Lillie and Thomson bowl at Sydney I was convinced that no team in the world – not even the South African or West Indies stars – would have done any better. This was borne out the following year when the West Indies lost five of their Tests.

The Australian opening pair made a fearsome sight. At one end there was the long classical run up and action, the speed, accuracy and variations in pace of Lillee. At the other the thunderbolts of Thomson delivered off a shortish run with a slinging action and the right arm coming over *at the very last moment* from right behind his back. Much of his lightning speed was generated by his tremendously powerful shoulders. The Sydney pitch had pace, and even more important, bounce. They did not *have* to bowl short to get the ball to rise, though of course they unleashed a number of bouncers, one or two from Thomson soaring over Marsh's head, although he was standing at least twenty-five yards back. A good length ball from them was sufficient to force the batsmen to play almost every stroke chest or head high. Batting became a matter of self-preservation.

It might have been possible just to stay there by ducking and swaying out of the way. But runs had to be scored *somehow*. It was all very well for the critics from the safety of the stands to say 'get behind the line of the ball'. But what in fact could this have achieved? What scoring stroke *can* you play against a good length ball coming straight at your head if you are dead in line? So the temptation was to try the occasional injudicious hook or to run or steer the ball towards third man, sometimes deliberately over the slips, with body well away from the bat. Remember that in 1932–3 the great Don Bradman had the skill and quickness of eye and foot to step back towards square leg and play Larwood's leg-side attack into the vacant spaces on the off-side. He was heavily criticised at the time for doing so, but managed to score 396 runs and average 56.57 in the series, though of course for him this was comparative failure.

In spite of everything, England nearly saved this Sydney Test thanks to some typically plucky batting by John Edrich, who after a sickening blow from one of the few balls that didn't rise went off to hospital. But he returned to block for two and a half hours and made 33 not out. Due to him and the tail-enders Willis and Arnold, there were only five overs and three balls left when Australia won, and so regained the Ashes which had been won by Ray Illingworth's side on the same ground four years before.

Remarkably, a record Sydney crowd of 178,027 watched the match. I say remarkably because just as this type of blistering attack is dangerous and unpleasant for batsmen, it is also unpleasant and boring for the cricket-loving spectator. No one, except those who would have got a kick out of the gladiators of ancient Rome, can really enjoy watching batsmen literally fighting for their lives or at best preventing serious injury.

An even worse effect is that it limits the number of strokes which it is *possible* to play in front of the wicket, however good the batsman may be. In this match for Australia, there was a classic 144 by Greg Chappell and some solid batting by McCosker (80) and Redpath (105). And for England there was just one innings which the connoisseur of stroke play could appreciate. That was an astonishing 82 by Alan Knott who played every known stroke in the book and a good many which are not and never will be in it! He is a wonderful improviser on the basis of a sound technique, and on this occasion, he slashed, lashed, hooked, dabbed, steered, glided, cut, drove and any other word you can think of ! He played with such success that he actually made 56 in an hour after lunch off his own bat – amazing going against that pace and the inevitable slow over-rate.

Final proof for me of the pace of Lillee and Thomson were

the hands of Rodney Marsh. He showed them to me and they were puffy and badly bruised. To protect them he had wound bits of plaster round each finger. I told him it reminded me of an old BBC radio show – *Much Binding ON the Marsh!* Unfortunately he had never heard of Kenneth Horne and Dicky Murdoch's show, so my joke (?) fell a bit flat!

Incidentally, if any young wicket-keeper finds that his hands are getting bruised, I strongly recommend something which I always used, and I'm glad to say Alan Knott does as well today. Place a thin layer of plasticine inside the inner gloves. It's amazing how it helps to absorb the shock of the ball thudding into the gloves. But I *don't* recommend the method used by George Duckworth when his hands took such a battering standing up to Maurice Tate on the fast Australian pitches of his day. He placed a thick piece of raw steak inside his gloves, and as you can imagine, at the end of a long hot day in the field, he was given a wide berth by his team-mates in the dressing-room!

I was back in England when Mike Denness led his side to victory in the final Test at Melbourne, and was delighted for his sake that he made his highest first-class score – 188. Admittedly Thomson was not playing and Lillee only bowled 6 overs because of an injured foot. But losing the series 1–4 was better than at one time looked likely.

Nowadays on tour MCC travel mostly by plane with the occasional coach journey to an up-country match. They rarely if ever go by train, unlike the old days, when they used to travel right across Australia for days on end. The trains even had a lounge with a piano to help while away the time. I don't know any modern player who plays the piano but in the past Ewart Astill of Leicestershire and Dick Pollard of Lancashire were expert ticklers of the ivories, as of course was Don Bradman. He even made a gramophone record when he was over here in 1930. It may also surprise some people to know that that man with flair for so many things – Ted Dexter – plays the organ and piano extremely well. The Warden of Radley College once told me that often after scoring one of his many brilliant hundreds for the school, Ted would take off his pads and relax by going across to the chapel to play a few fugues!

But back to the trains – because there has long been a story told about an MCC player on tour, though no one seems to know for certain which player it really is. I have heard it told about at least half a dozen. Anyway, let's call him Smith and what is said to have happened is this. A girl was nursing a baby in a carriage, the only other occupant of which was a man who kept staring at the baby. He couldn't take his eyes off it, and the girl became more and more embarrassed and annoyed. Finally she could stand it no longer and asked the man why he was staring so. He replied that he would rather not say. But when the girl persisted he said he was sorry but he was staring because the baby was the ugliest which he had ever seen in his life. This naturally upset the girl who broke into floods of tears and taking the baby went and stood in the corridor.

She was still crying when the MCC team came along the corridor on their way to the restaurant car. They all passed her except Smith, who being a decent chap, stopped to ask her why she was crying. She told him that she had just been insulted by a man in her carriage. So Smith said: 'Well, cheer up. I'll bring you back a cup of tea from the restaurant car. That should make you feel better.' So off he went and returned in about five minutes. 'Here's your cup of tea,' he said to the girl, 'and what's more I've also brought a banana for the monkey!' What happened then is not related!

While in Sydney I discovered an interesting story about women's cricket from my daughter, Clare, who was working as sales representative for the New Caledonian Tourist Office in Australia and New Zealand. New Caledonia lies 1,150 miles in the Pacific north-east of Sydney and, said Clare's brochure '. . . is a tropical paradise of blue waters, white sands and lazy hot days and balmy evenings'! Captain Cook found and named New Caledonia in 1774. By 1853 it had become a small French colony and in 1946 was promoted to be a French overseas territory.

The brochure goes on to reveal that 'cricket is played on this small piece of the south of France with the flavour of Paris'. That is unexpected enough. But it becomes even more remarkable when one learns that only WOMEN play. The reason for this seems obscure. It could be that the men consider it too 'cissy' but seeing the tough way in which the women play, that seems unlikely. What *is* certain is that cricket was started by English missionaries in the nineteenth century and that there are now fourteen teams in the capital, Noumea, and three from the adjoining groups of islands, Ouvea, Mare and Lifou. These teams play for a cup awarded annually on 24 September – the anniversary of French occupation – and they practise every Saturday 'with ardour'.

Although the laws and conditions are somewhat eccentric, to say the least, the game is definitely recognisable as cricket, and bears no relation to the French cricket which we all used to play as children. The matches take place on any available land, but usually on a slag pitch, because any grass is reserved for baseball and football. The pitch is sixty-two feet long, the stumps twenty-seven and a half inches high and there are no bails (our pitches are sixty-six feet and the stumps are twenty-eight inches high). Instead of our bowling and popping creases there is a three and a quarter foot square marked out around the stumps in which the batswoman or 'joyeuse' must stand. The bat can be thirty-nine inches long (our maximum is thirty-eight inches) and only three inches wide (ours is four and a quarter inches). So it looks rather like a baseball bat and can be of any weight. The ball – called '*la boule*' – is made of dried sap and bounces, even on a slag pitch. The bowling actions vary from a blatant chuck to a good old-fashioned lob.

The ladies are dressed in gaily-coloured floral smocks called Mother Hubbards – possibly because they are bare underneath! They wear no pads, batting gloves, thigh pads or indeed any other sort of protection so far as can be seen under the smocks. Runs count as in our cricket but are called '*pines*'. There are no boundaries and the batswomen must run up and down the pitch barefoot until the ball is returned to the wicket-keeper. It is therefore not surprising that the laws allow a 'tired' batswoman to be replaced by the next on the list, or to call for a substitute to run for her. Each run is greeted by shrill tin whistles and a hand-clapping version of the Melanesian Pilou-Pilou war song.

The bat must rest on the shoulder and it is forbidden to

hold it in the air or to let it touch the ground. If a player drops the bat she must stay in the square until given another one. Incredibly there is only one ball per over, so there is no over-rate problem in New Caledonia!

And now, in case the whole thing smacks of women's lib, here comes the rub. Both the umpires and the scorer must be MALE. They are considered to be fairer and to have more authority in a dispute, and more capable of breaking up a scrap when the women get excited and fight – as they often do. Here are one or two of the laws these male umpires must enforce.

It is forbidden for players to throw insults (modern Test players please note), nor must any player enter the field in a state of drunkenness. And here is something which might well be introduced to Test Cricket – the umpire has the right to send a player off after a warning. Finally, further proof that the males are really in complete charge of the game – neither the players nor the spectators are allowed to look at the score until the game is over. There are no time limits and the game goes on until the umpire declares one side the winner. The losers then have to fork out about five pounds to give to the winners.

So far our women cricketers have never visited New Caledonia, but I know that Rachel Heyhoe-Flint would just love to take on these besmocked Amazons!

Third Over Down YOUR Way

As soon as I had returned to England at the end of January 1975, I began to hear rumours within the BBC that *Down Your Way* (from now on *DYW*) was to be taken off the air. For reasons of economy the BBC were having to make cuts and this meant that Radios 3 and 4 and Radios 1 and 2 would have to share programmes at certain times of the day. So something had to go, and it was no secret that Tony Witby, controller of Radio 4, did not wish to lose a particular favourite of his called *Celebration*. He looked at the tempting time of 5.15 pm on Sundays and decided that it was the right slot for his programme, and that *DYW* would have to be sacrificed.

The news was officially broken to me by producer Richard Burwood as he and I travelled by car during a *DYW* at Sedgefield in County Durham. Even though I had been forewarned, now that it was definite it came as a bit of a shock. The weekly commitment had become very much part of my life.

The news was given to the Press the following week and I must say they really went to town on our behalf. For a thirty-year-old steam radio programme to hit the headlines in this telly age was a rare and unexpected event. There really was a tremendous outcry against the decision. Somehow the BBC had underestimated the affection with which the programme was held. Not only the nationals but all the provincial papers led the protests and the BBC itself was inundated with letters and phone calls from many devoted followers. The director-general, Sir Charles Curran, was brought into it when on a phone-in he turned down the suggestion that *DYW* should continue but be presented by the twenty local BBC radio stations.

The real reason for taking it off was never given officially, except to say it was for economy. Some of the Press took this to mean that the programme itself was too expensive, with a producer, engineer and myself travelling to places all over the country every week. But in terms of cost per minute this made no sense at all. With the repeat on Tuesdays, Radio 4 was getting eighty minutes of air time for about a hundred and thirty pounds – mere chicken-feed compared with most other similar programmes. In fact, when I read it I immediately told my bosses that I would take a cut in my fee if it would be of any help. But they refused to accept this offer and confirmed to me that there was no question of the programme itself being too extravagant or expensive.

The protests continued to pour in – I admit to soliciting a sister, a brother, an elderly aunt and a couple of cousins! – and some of the letters we received were most touching and rewarding. Many felt they were about to lose an old friend and it was nice to have such proof that we evidently provided some innocent pleasure for so many thousands of people.

Quite a few letters of protest were sent to the newspapers and one of the very nicest was written to the *Daily Mail* by comedian Norman Vaughan. He wrote: 'I don't mind things being changed so long as they remain as good or better than they were before. But *Down Your Way* was as gentle and honest as Sunday cricket on the village green.' Alongside that letter was one from another comedian and friend of mine – Dickie Henderson: 'I'm all for change, but why change something which is successful? I found *Down Your Way* not only interesting but educational.' Gentle, honest, interesting, educational – four very welcome adjectives to have applied to our programme.

The last programme was to come from Painswick in Gloucestershire on Sunday, 20 April, but even before then the planners had gone some way to mollify the protestors. It was announced that *DYW* would return temporarily for six programmes on Saturdays in July/August during the usual repeat time of *Any Questions* which was taking its annual six weeks' holiday. But unknown to us even more was going on behind the scenes. The pressure from listeners had

impressed Clare Lawson-Dick, the new controller of Radio 4.
The first I heard about it was a telephone call from Anthony
Smith, the BBC's radio outside producer from Bristol. I
knew him well as I had worked with him for many years
contributing cricket reports into his Saturday night sports
programme from West Region. I was surprised and
delighted with what he had to tell me. He said he had just
been stopped in a corridor by his immediate boss Michael
Bowen, of *Any Questions* fame. Michael had asked Tony
whether he would like to produce *DYW*, which was coming
back in October on the same regular basis as before, but
would in future be produced and run from Bristol. Tony had
rung me immediately before I heard it from anyone else, as
he wanted to assure me that I would still be the presenter – which was very thoughtful of him.

The announcement in the Press came a month
later – appropriately on my birthday, 24 June. In a state-
ment Clare Lawson-Dick said: 'Fans of the programme
wrote to us in large numbers asking for it to be restored. We
were also greatly touched and influenced by letters from
blind and disabled people who were unable to travel and
said that *Down Your Way* had been their only means of getting
to know Britain.' I think the BBC deserves credit for admit-
ting that their previous decision had been wrong. By so
doing they showed that they *do* try to give listeners what they
want. It was quite an exercise for the Press office who told me
that it was the first time that the BBC had *publicly* admitted
to bowing to public pressure on behalf of a programme.

But amidst all our jubilation there was one person in
particular for whom I felt very sorry – Phyllis Robinson.
With Richard Burwood she had produced the programme
from London for the past thirteen years. It had become very
much her 'baby' and part of her life, since her associations
with it started far earlier than that.

DYW began in December 1946, produced by Leslie
Perowne and John Shuter, with boxing and ice hockey commentator Stewart Macpherson as the presenter. The very
first one came from Lambeth Walk and for the first ten
programmes it came from various parts of London. It was all
very free and easy with no preliminary research. Stewart just

went along with a recording car, knocked on people's doors and interviewed them there and then. It was naturally very much hit and miss in more senses than one. Not only did Stewart have no prior knowledge of the person he was going to interview, but on one occasion he was actually hit under the chin by a man who came to the door and mistook Stewart for someone who had been molesting his wife! Shortly after this Stewart said he had had enough and that he felt that the programme wasn't 'him'.

Lionel Gamlin then took over for half a dozen programmes until the BBC found that one of their war-time reporters was 'available'. In fact he was virtually unemployed. So they booked him in the early spring of 1947 for a trial six programmes. His name was Richard Dimbleby and he (naturally!) did so well that he continued to do it till 1953, when after exactly three hundred and fifty editions he found that his family newspaper at Richmond, and his growing TV work, made the weekly *DYW* assignment too much of a burden. Phyllis Robinson had started with him as a recorded programme assistant, and then took over as producer towards the end of Richard's time. In those days the programme was occasionally done 'live' from places like the Hebrides, Shetland Islands and the Channel Islands. During the six years Richard only missed one programme when he caught chicken-pox from his eldest son David and then Wynford Vaughan-Thomas deputised for him. He did however have to link the two hundred and fiftieth from his Surrey home because he had broken a rib falling off his horse.

For some reason *DYW* was rested for two years but returned in 1955 with Franklin Englemann (Jingle) to present it. Previously all the interviews had been recorded on to discs but now the era of the tapes had arrived and they have been used ever since. The first of the new *DYW*'s came from Crewe – the theme being all change, with Richard making a typical gesture by going up to Crewe to introduce Jingle. From then on Jingle became *DYW*, and *DYW* became Jingle. People will always associate his strong but friendly personality with the programme. Like Richard, he only missed one between 1955 and 1972. He caught 'flu and as it was coming from Cardiff, Alun Williams was able to deputise for him at the last moment.

Jingle had just recorded his seven hundred and thirty-third programme when he died suddenly in March 1972 and I had to take over from him at short notice, and except for two breaks have done it ever since. As this book goes to press I am 255 not out. The two breaks were during the summer of 1972 when because of my duties as BBC cricket correspondent Roy Trevivian, Geoffrey Wheeler, Alex Macintosh and Paddy Feeney took over for four weeks each. The other was for four weeks in January 1973 when I went to South Africa as PRO for Derrick Robins on his cricket tour out there. My place was taken by that fact-seeking Scotsman with the querulous plaintive voice – Fyfe Robertson – a complete contrast to me in accent and pace of delivery.

The format of *DYW* has changed from time to time, but has always had the basic idea of a certain number of people being interviewed about their town or village and then each being asked to choose a piece of music. For the first two years after Jingle took over it only ran for six months each year, but then settled down to a steady pattern of ten months a year, with Jingle doing *Holiday Hour* in January and February. For ten years the programme lasted for an hour with nine people being interviewed. But ever since I have been the presenter it has lasted for forty minutes with six interviews. In Richard's day the emphasis was very much on the music with short interviews but ever since Jingle took over the interview has invariably been longer than the music. Nowadays the average is something like four and a half minutes of interview and two and a quarter minutes of music.

The choice of music is left entirely up to the person interviewed, with two provisos. It must not have been chosen the week before and obviously it has to be available – either in the BBC Record Library or obtainable in the shops, or perhaps the person interviewed has a private recording. At one time, because the programme goes out first on a Sunday, much sacred music was chosen especially in Scotland. I think people possibly thought that this type of music was what the BBC wanted them to choose. Though there *was* proof in 1958 that even in London the Sunday Puritan spirit

still existed. When *DYW* visited Oxford Street the proprietor
of an umbrella shop forbade any of his staff to take part
because it *did* go out on a Sunday.

Over the years the choice has broadened. Although we
still get the inevitable favourites, nowadays we do have a few
requests for something in 'the charts'. But there *are* some
regulars which continually crop up. In Richard's day it was
Bless this House and *Now is the Hour*. With Jingle, *Jerusalem* and
Stranger on the Shore were top favourites. Among our most
popular ones today are Handel's *Hallelujah Chorus*, Verdi's
Hebrew Slaves Chorus, the theme tunes from *Love Story*, *Dr
Zhivago* and *The Onedin Line*, and the music from Gilbert and
Sullivan. And of course there's our distinctive signature tune
which most people know so well but of which they frequently
ask the title. It's *Horse-Guards Whitehall*, by Haydn Wood
played by the Queen's Hall Light Orchestra.

People also often ask us how we choose the places which
we visit. As we are now approaching our fourteen hundredth
town and village, this is getting a little bit harder every year.
Stick a pin in a map of the United Kingdom to represent
each place and you would find that there's not much space
left. But the producers who actually choose the locations
follow certain basic rules. First of all we never (with excep-
tions in Northern Ireland) visit a place twice. Then we must
distribute our visits equally over all parts of the country, and
ensure that we have the right proportion of big and small
towns, villages and industrial, residential or agricultural
districts.

Luckily our files are still full of invitations from people
asking us to visit them. So once the area is decided, reference
to a file usually produces a place within it where we have
been asked to go. There are by now very few big towns
unvisited by *DYW*. Since 1972 the only really large place I
have been to is Blackburn with just over 100,000 inhabitants, and I think the next largest is Harpenden with about
30,000. Our present average is something between 2,000 to
5,000. Sadly, since I took over we have only been to Northern
Ireland three times, though since 1947 there have been
thirty-nine visits altogether. But with a non-controversial
programme like ours it is practically impossible to talk to

people about their town or village and ignore all the terrible things that are going on around them. It would put me in the position of being completely insensitive, and out of touch with their real problems, and to appear to be asking inane and pointless questions.

DYW at one time went abroad mostly to Europe, often to fit in with a Trade Fair or an event like the Olympic Games. But now, except for a short cruise on the S.S. *Canberra* in 1976, we stay at home, though we are hoping to go abroad again. In addition to geographical locations (as they say in *Twenty Questions*) there have been a number of 'one-offs' such as exhibitions, institutions, hospitals, theatres, schools, charities, museums, the three Services, stations, airports, zoos and even an oil rig.

Most of what success *DYW* has depends on the selection of the right six people and this is entirely the responsibility of the producer. There are certain obvious ingredients needed to achieve a properly balanced programme – i.e. one person who can tell the listener as much as possible about a place in as entertaining a way as possible. There must be someone to talk about past events and the history of the place. If it is an industrial town then we probably look for someone from one of the factories, or if it is agricultural then a farmer or a shepherd or someone connected with the countryside. Many places have some sort of traditional ceremony, such as an annual traction-engine fair or a pancake race, and a person is needed to explain these. There is the social side of a town with its clubs, institutions, sports complex, and also the 'do-good' side of a community which is so essential to the happiness of a place. But more important perhaps than any of these, the producer is always on the look-out for a 'character', or the man or woman with an unusual job or hobby. If they have the local dialect and accent so much the better.

We are very conscious of the fact that the majority of the people we interview are on the elderly side. This is inevitable as in general they know far more about a place and its customs, simply because they have lived there longer. 'Characters' too develop the older they grow. So whenever possible we do try to include at least one young person to represent the youthful side of a place – this also helps to liven up the choice of music! There is also the need to get as fair a balance as possible between the sexes, though in spite of Women's Lib I would say we still average four men to two women per programme – it just seems to work out that way.

One of the producer's difficulties is to avoid any similarity with the programmes which have gone out in the previous few weeks. For instance, however old or beautiful a church may be, vicars have to be rationed out, so do farmers, good ladies who run Women's Institutes, Old People's Homes or Meals on Wheels. Everyone naturally wants to mention *everything* which goes on in their town and naturally feels that theirs is better than anyone else's. Quite often we get somebody writing in after a programme asking why we did not include old so and so who is a real character and known to everyone as Mr Whatever the name of the place is. What they don't realise is that the producer has probably visited the person but found that he or she is stone deaf, has a slight stammer or even that we interviewed someone in the same trade or profession only the week before. They may even have refused to take part though this very rarely happens, and when it does it is usually because of excessive modesty or shyness.

How then does the producer make his or her choice? After selecting the place we are to visit something like two or three months in advance, a letter is written to the local town clerk (or his equivalent in these complicated days of council re-organisation) saying that we would like to visit the town and asking the clerk to prepare a list of likely people to interview who can best put the town on the map. Any list they send is of great help but the producers will also have read every guide book available about the place to find out about its industries, history and customs. This will give them a clue as to the type of people they must look for on arrival, when they will not only call on the town clerk, but meet the local press and pick up valuable information in the pubs – often the best sources of all. The producer is also often helped by the original letter suggesting our visit which may include some possible names.

The way we record the programme has changed since it has been produced from Bristol. When it was centred in

London Phyllis Robinson or Richard Burwood used to leave on Sunday night and spend Monday and two-thirds of Tuesday in research and selection. The engineer and I joined them at tea-time on the Tuesday, in time for me to have a quick look-round armed with my guide book which is always sent to me beforehand. After a short briefing about the place and the people selected, we would then do one or possibly two interviews that evening. On Wednesday we would do the remaining four plus my 'top' and 'tail' – or introduction and close, usually finishing mid-afternoon.

To be courteous and polite we have always allowed up to one hour for each person so that we don't appear to rush in and out. This still applies today and Tony Smith and I purposely don't look at our watches until we get up to go and it's amazing how often we find that we have taken between fifty-five and sixty minutes. The producer has of course already met the person to be interviewed, but although he has briefed me beforehand, I always spend the first twenty minutes or so over a cup of tea or coffee getting to know them, finding out about their family and interests – in fact gaining their confidence and making friends. I then know roughly the sort of question I will have to ask to draw them out and get the information which we want in a relaxed way. We then record possibly up to seven minutes depending on the interviewee's ability and clarity in answering my questions. We then have time to play back the interviews so that a husband or wife who has been sent out of the room during the recording can hear the result. We find that most people are far less inhibited if they have no one else in the room except for the producer, the engineer with tape-recorder and myself. Sometimes when a wife is the domineering type, if present she can be tempted to prompt her husband with stage whispers – very offputting! Because some of the people interviewed are busy they can only see us in their factory, office, shop or home at a certain time. So we don't necessarily record the interviews in the exact order in which they will finally go out on the air.

Phyllis Robinson and Richard Burwood used to go back to London and on the Thursday and Friday edit the interviews and time the music before slotting it in between each interview. Every producer makes sure the music *is* available by ringing the Gramophone Library from the location. But if there is any doubt then I put the question about the choice of music *twice*, so that the person interviewed can give an alternative choice.

You may wonder about the editing of the interviews. This is done first of all to 'tidy' up, removing the occasional 'ers' and hesitations, or something which the person regrets having said and would like removed. Or again if the answers given to me are rather monosyllabic it means I have to prompt and encourage the interviewee with a number of supplementary questions. The whole thing then ceases to be a conversation and becomes just a series of questions and answers. But in the editing it is often possible to take out some of my questions so that the answers are joined up to make a more comprehensive reply.

But basically, it's all a matter of the timing and as I've shown, unless the person is outstanding the average interview has to be cut down to just over four minutes. One other thing which has *not* changed is that we choose and interview six people *only* and those are the ones who go out on the air. Some other interview programmes record a number of people and then finally select a few of them. But we don't think that is fair and anyone whom we have interviewed can safely tell his or her friends: 'Listen to me next Sunday at 5.15 pm – I'm on *Down Your Way.*'

But to go back to the way the editing has changed. The programmes from London, once edited on the Friday, used to go out two days later on the Sunday. It is difficult to believe it now but there was *never* a spare programme in reserve in case of an accident to me or the producer or engineer, or even in case the tape got lost or destroyed by mistake. Phyllis backed her luck and with Richard and Jingle only missing one programme each out of more than a thousand and with me luckily fit, she was proved right. But it was a terrific gamble and I often implored her to record at least one in reserve. But she felt that she gained from the topicality and avoided the risk of any of the people interviewed dying if the programme was recorded too far in advance. But of course this policy was the reason for the hurried selection of myself to replace Jingle. He died on the Wednesday night after recording a programme, which with the consent of his widow went out on the following Sunday and Tuesday as usual. But the show had to go on – hence my first *DYW* only six days after Jingle's death.

Partly to avoid this risk but mainly for reasons of time and money there has been a change since we went to Bristol. We now record two programmes in the first week of the month and two in the second, leaving the last fortnight free for editing, in which, by the way, I have no say. I am never present in the studio when it is done. This I think is a good idea as I am too close and involved, whereas the producer has been able to listen to and judge each interview impartially as it's being done. Each pair of programmes are recorded within an area of about sixty square miles to save mileage and time, but they are not put out on the air in successive weeks. For instance, if we record a pair in Oxfordshire and Northants, two programmes, say from Scotland and Wales, would be put on between them.   Our recording timetable has also been altered. Tony Smith (or the producer who deputises for him about twelve times a year) now leaves Bristol on a Monday, vets one town from Monday evening to Tuesday evening and then travels the sixty miles or so to the next place. By the time the engineer and myself have arrived on Wednesday evening he has made his selections. We sometimes do one interview that night and five the next day before setting off for the first town which Tony vetted on the Tuesday. We finish sometime on Friday afternoon ready for a nice peaceful weekend.

It's a tightly-timed but well-organised timetable and we still find that each place takes around six hours to do, though the kind hospitality of people does sometimes mean that we get behind the clock. It's not unusual to be offered tea or coffee, biscuits and home-made cakes at all four houses or offices which we visit in a morning. We have learnt to say 'no thank you' politely but sometimes when the tray is laid out ready we don't have the heart to do so, no matter how much our stomachs complain. We appreciate that although it's just another pleasant day's work for us, *DYW* only visits a place once in a lifetime, so in a small way it's quite a big day

October 1975: The first *DYW* on its return from exile. The village is Lacock in Wilts.
B.J. and 'victims' are outside the fifteenth century inn, the Angel.   (Copyright *Radio Times*)

B.J. chats with a Romany in his caravan. (Copyright *Kent Messenger*)

All at sea aboard cruise ship S.S. *Canberra*. Left to right: Douggie Barnes, engineer, B.J., Commodore Frank Woolley and Anthony Smith, producer.

A slice of country life discovered at Conisborough in Yorkshire.

Well played, sir! B.J. bats at Standish C.C. (Lancs) with chairman Guy Hisley (l.) and vice-president Fred Bazley (r.) in the slips.

B.J. tries out a boneshaker with owner Peter Shirtcliffe at Downham Market, Norfolk.
(Copyright *Lynn News & Advertiser*)

'Birdman' Henry Douglas-Home (second left) looks pensive after an interview in the woods at the Hirsel – home of Lord Home.

Say neigh! B.J. chats with Joanna Vardon and friend. (See p. 55)

B.J. interviews playleader Tricia Barnes at the Jonathan Page adventure playground, Aylesbury. (Copyright *Bucks Herald Aylesbury*)

Madame, will you walk and talk with me? One of B.J.'s 'victims' at Stow-on-the-Wold. (Copyright *Wilts & Glos Standard*)

What's yours? B.J. talks to Christopher Sykes at Woburn about his collection of pub signs. (Copyright John J. Walker)

Good morning, Your Grace! B.J. greeted by the Duke of Marlborough on the steps of Blenheim Palace (note eggs).   (Copyright The British Tourist Authority)

for the 'victim'. Luckily I have never had the same experience as Richard Dimbleby who once had to squeeze in three interviews in one evening. As a result in each house he visited the table was laid either for high tea or supper and he bravely did justice to all three! But he did have more room for it than me!

It's the same everywhere we go. We invariably get a very warm welcome and this really does make my job rewarding. I was, however, once slightly surprised by a greeting from an effusive and friendly lady. She flung open her front door and said: 'Oh, Mr Johnston, how nice to see you. I have always wanted to meet you. And do tell me – how big is your apparatus?!!' I can only think that she was referring to our engineer's equipment – if you see what I mean!

As you can imagine, *DYW* involves a lot of travelling and I usually go by car except to Scotland when I either fly or use the train. Trains have a funny effect on me. I hope I am a fairly gregarious and friendly person but once inside a railway carriage I shut up like a clam. Even if there's only one other person I never say a word but just slump behind my newspaper. It sounds dreadfully unfriendly but I find there are quite a few people who do the same. At any rate the late Lord Justice Birkett – the best after-dinner speaker I have ever heard – once told a lovely story which bears it out.

He was speaking at the 1953 Cricket Writers' Dinner to Lindsay Hassett's Australian Touring Team. He said how delighted everyone was to see them and told them what a great welcome they would get wherever they went all over the country. But he did give a slight warning. 'Don't be put off,' he said, 'by the apparent aloofness and reserve of the British people. We are not really cold and unfriendly but just hide our feelings. Indeed, we treat each other in exactly the same way, so there is no need for you to worry.'

Lord Birkett then went on to tell the following story to prove his point. One day as the Flying Scotsman left King's Cross on its non-stop journey to Edinburgh there were four people sitting in one carriage, each in a corner seat reading his newspaper. There was complete silence, except for the slight rustle of paper, as the train glided swiftly through the Hertfordshire countryside. After it had passed through

Hitchin about thirty-two miles out of London, one of the men could bear it no longer. He put down his *Times* and said: 'Look, this is ridiculous. We are going to be alone in this carriage non-stop for four hundred miles. Let's get to know each other and have a chat. This silence is unbearable. I'll start off by telling you something about myself. I'm a Brigadier. I'm married and I have one son who is a solicitor.'

The man sitting opposite him put down *his Times* and said: 'This is an amazing coincidence. *I'm* also a Brigadier. I'm married and I also have one son who is a banker.'

The third man then put down his *Times* and he said: 'This is ridiculous. You'll never believe this. I'm also a Brigadier. I'm also married and have one son who is a schoolmaster.' All three of them looked at the fourth man who was still sitting quietly behind his *Daily Mirror*. 'Come on,' they said to him, 'join in and tell us something about yourself.' A gruff voice from behind the paper said: 'Sorry, I'd rather not,' and then silence reigned again. So the other three ignored him and chatted among themselves for about half an hour and then decided to try again. 'Come on,' they said, 'be a sport, do join in.' 'Oh well, have it your own way,' said the man as he reluctantly put down the *Daily Mirror*. '*I* am a Regimental Sergeant Major. I am NOT married. I have three sons – and they are, all three, Brigadiers!'

While on the subject of trains there was the bishop who was sitting in the corner seat of a crowded carriage doing *The Times* crossword puzzle. He seemed to be getting on pretty well and filling in a lot of the answers. But he began to look puzzled and putting down his paper asked the other passengers: 'Could any of you kindly help me? I want a four-letter word with female affiliations ending in UNT.' There was a slight pause and then a young man suggested: 'What about AUNT, sir?' 'Ah,' said the bishop with relief, 'that's it. I thought I must be wrong. Have any of you got a rubber?'

But, as usual, I have digressed, and now a final word about *Down Your Way*. It is a wonderful programme to do and as with so much of my life I have been unbelievably lucky to get the job. We are unashamedly square and uncontroversial. We go to a place to find out the good things about it, and never look 'under the carpet' for the sort of things which hit the headlines in the popular press. We just try to find nice people who will reflect all these good things. It is one of the satisfying features of *DYW* that there *are* so many nice people about. We are told *ad nauseam* of the terrible things which go on in our society and how mean and self-centred people are. Up to a point this is obviously true. On the other hand you come round the country with me and it really will cheer you up to meet so many people who are devoting so much of their lives or leisure time to helping others. Call them do-gooders – or what you like. But their numbers are legion and they are the salt of the earth. I like to think that they are the true heart of Britain. It all sounds terribly old-fashioned and patriotic – but I *do* mean it. In addition of course I learn a little about a lot, and discover old buildings, customs and traditions which have been in existence for centuries. There's also the joy of journeying all over Britain which in spite of the growth of towns and the spreading tentacles of industry still remains to me the most beautiful country in the world.

Fourth Over Nice people

The most important part of *Down Your Way* to me is the memory of the people whom I have interviewed. By now they number fifteen hundred, so I can obviously only mention a fraction of them. I suppose pride of place must go to the only centurion whom I have so far interviewed in the programme – Mrs Emma Brewster of Radcliffe on Trent. She was as bright as a cricket and looked wonderfully fit and alert as she sat in her armchair by the fire. She had goodness knows how many great-grandchildren and was lovingly looked after by one of her granddaughters. During the interview I asked her whether she had received a telegram from the Queen on her hundredth birthday. 'Oh, yes,' she said, 'I did, but I was very disappointed. It wasn't in her own handwriting. I think she must be getting old and bored with doing it so often. I know I would be!'

Then there was the vegetarian from Usk in Wales who during the war was sent out to India to run the mule transport. Knowing he would be short of the green stuff out there he took with him a lot of mustard and cress seeds. Each night at the end of a hot sticky day he would take off his wellington boots and plant some seeds inside them. By next day he had some fresh(?) mustard and cress to eat with his curry for lunch.

Talking of wellies – when we went to Presteigne in Powys a young farmer called John Davies, who was a champion sheep shearer, told us about an unusual competitive sport which was very popular in those parts. It was welly-wanging, and it used to take place at all the local fairs and fêtes. It is very similar to throwing the javelin except that you hurl a wellington boot instead. The good throwers get quite a good distance – something in the region of forty yards. John told us with delight that the ladies also ran a competition and that the local lady welly-wanging champion was a Mrs Woolley from Willey!

There was a lovely old lady of well over eighty in the small town of Penkridge in Staffordshire. She was a farmer's daughter and still delivered milk round the town each day. She lived in her father's old house where she had been born. It had been a farm but was now a terraced house in a street. The remarkable thing she told us was that in all her life she had never spent *a single night away from the house*. She had been to London for the day and on several coach trips to the seaside, but had always returned at night to sleep in her own house. The only concession she made in this extraordinary tale was that she had not always slept in the same room. I found it very difficult to take in when I thought of the many hundreds of nights I myself have spent away from home either on my job or on holiday.

When in Buckfastleigh for *Down Your Way* I was told the following story of a new vicar at the parish church on the top of the hill above the town. He was being taken round the churchyard by the verger who was giving him a potted history of the various people buried there. When they came to one tombstone the verger said: 'This was Harry – I warned him but he wouldn't listen. I told him that the cider would be the death of him and would get him in the end. And it did. He went on drinking it in spite of all my warnings.' The vicar stooped down to read the writing on the tombstone, and read: 'Harry——, who died aged 96 years on——.'

In St Davids Dyfed – the smallest cathedral city – we came across the local baker, a great talker and character called Dai Evans. He kept a donkey which drank beer and was famous for miles around for his homemade bread and cakes. Inevitably he was called Dai The Crust. His greatest triumph was on a visit to the district by Prince Charles. Dai had the honour to present one of his special loaves personally to the Prince of Wales. From then on he assumed the title of Dai the *Upper* Crust!

Anthony Beard was a young farmer at Widecombe-in-the-Moor in Devon, of Uncle Tom Cobley fame. He did a milk round in the local villages, and incidentally used plastic instead of glass milk bottles and so saved himself the time and labour of having to collect and wash them. In his spare time he was an entertainer singing West Country songs and telling stories in the Devonshire dialect. He even yodelled and composed his own songs. One of the stories was about a farmer who often milked the cows in the open fields to save bringing them back to the farm. One summer evening he was milking away when a holidaymaker leant over the hedge and asked him if he knew the time. The farmer put his hand under the cow's udder and replied: 'Ten minutes to six, mister,' and went on with his milking.

The holidaymaker was amazed and rushed off back to the village to fetch his wife to see this extraordinary countryman who could tell the time by putting his hand under a cow's udder. The couple came back in about twenty minutes and found the farmer milking another cow at the same spot by the hedge. The holidaymaker persuaded his wife to ask the time. Once again the farmer put his hand under the cow's udder and replied: 'Just on ten minutes past six.' The couple thanked him and went off dumbfounded at what they had seen. In explanation Anthony added: 'What the farmer didn't tell them was that each time he lifted the cow's udder, he could see the clock on the church tower.'

When we visited North Berwick – that mecca of golfing – Mrs Doreen Stevenson told us about the old professional, Ben Sayers, renowned maker of golf clubs and with a great reputation as a teacher. At one time North Berwick was very fashionable with politicians who came there to breathe the invigorating air and of course to play golf. Lord Balfour and Sir John Simon were frequent visitors and one day Ben was partnering Lord Balfour in a foursome. They were playing on the No. 1 links which runs along by the sea and on which in the old days the local farmers had grazing rights.

At one hole Lord Balfour drove off and his ball went straight down the middle but landed slap in the middle of a juicy cow pat. Lord Balfour thought this was very funny and laughingly apologised to Ben, but said it was his shot and that he would have to 'get out of the mess'. But the wily Ben took a mashie and after taking deliberate aim played a complete air shot. 'I'm sorry, m'lord,' he said with a cunning smile, 'I'm afraid I got a fly in my eye, which made me miss it completely. Now it's *your* turn to get it out!'

One of the most cheerful people I have ever met in *DYW* was Syd Hart who had spent most of his life in the Cheshire Home at Ampthill suffering from multiple-sclerosis. In spite of all his trouble life seemed to be one big joke to him, and he apologised during our interview for not speaking too clearly. He explained that in his hurry to get ready he had put in someone else's false teeth by mistake!

Then there was Arthur Roland of the little village of Alston in Cumbria. He kept – of all things – a bottle shop. Just rows and rows of empty bottles – eight thousand of them, of all shapes, sizes and colours. Some were worth twenty pounds or more and people from all over the world descend on Arthur to add to their own collections. The surprising thing about Arthur was that he did not drink anything except tea.

In Ruthin, North Wales, we discovered a young girl called Patricia Evers-Swindell who remarkably painted on *cobwebs*. She lived in an old house with some old stables attached. She collected the cobwebs from these, some still with the spider and dead flies in them. She then covered them thinly with milk to take some of the stickiness out of them and then painted on them with ordinary brush and paint. Dogs' heads were her speciality and by framing the web between two pieces of glass she obtained an excellent three-dimensional effect.

The great thing about doing *DYW* is that we are always learning something new. I personally had never heard of a Foaling Bank but we came across one in Newport, Shropshire. It had been started by Joanna Vardon as a completely new idea, and was the only one in the world. It was really a sort of swap shop. All over the country a number of mares die giving birth to their foals and so leave orphans to be looked after. Alternatively a number of foals die at birth or are stillborn, leaving an unhappy mother with lots of milk and no foal to drink it.

So Joanna Vardon had what was really a very simple idea,

but a very difficult and complicated one to carry out. She thought what a waste it was of foal-less mares and mother-less foals. So why not bring the two together? This she has done in a remarkable way and people from all over the country – and even from abroad – arrive at all times of the day or night with horse-boxes – or even a mini in the case of one tiny foal lying on the back seat! Speed is the essence of the operation as a mare's milk dries up in about twenty-four hours if there is no foal to suckle her. There is also the problem of a mare accepting a foal which is not her own. Joanna found that she had to skin the dead foal and wrap its skin round the orphan foal before the mare would accept it. A rather gruesome business but carried out cheerfully by Joanna Vardon and her band of lady helpers. It should also be pointed out that the whole scheme is non-profit making and people pay what they can afford. Since the bank started in 1966 Joanna and her staff have dealt with well over five thousand cases.

At Budleigh Salterton we had the pleasure of meeting 'Golden Voice' – alias Stuart Hibberd, the first ever BBC radio announcer. Now aged eighty-four he was amazingly hale and hearty and entertained us before the interview with songs and recitations without any music or notes. He re-called the early days at Savoy Hill when all the announcers had to change into dinner jackets at 6 pm. At first he wore a stiff shirt but the engineers complained that it made crack-ling noises into the microphone, so from then on he had to wear a soft one.

He denied making some of the well-known gaffes which are generally attributed to him, such as:

'There'll now be an interlush by Ernest Lude';

'We are now going over to the bathroom at Pump';

'You will now hear the bum of the flightelbee.'

But he *did* admit to two. During a weather forecast he once said that there would be 'heal and slate' instead of 'sleet and hail'. And when introducing a programme of American music he announced that the next piece would be *The Star Bangled Spanner*!

He made one amusing slip during our interview. I said that I understood that he still played a part in the life of the church at Budleigh. 'Yes,' he said, 'I still read the news – hmm lesson, every Sunday evening.'

At Goring on Thames I interviewed the wartime Commander-in-Chief, Bomber Command, Marshal of the Royal Air Force, Sir Arthur Harris, nicknamed Bomber. I was a bit apprehensive as I had never met him before and outwardly he had always seemed to be a tough stand-no-nonsense sort of character. He had certainly had to fight hard throughout the war on behalf of his Bomber Command, and had a reputation of speaking his mind, with no fear of anyone. Anyway, we thought we must make sure to be punctual for our interview and so get off to a good start.

As a result, we were in fact a few minutes in advance of the time arranged. After we had rung the bell of his charming riverside house, the well-known figure opened the door and in a gruff voice barked out: 'You're early,' in such a way that it appeared to be a bigger crime than being late. However he soon smiled and welcomed us and we spent a delightful hour with him in his study. There were pictures of all types of aeroplanes dating from the early days of the 1914 war and signed photographs of all the great war leaders, from Sir Winston and General Eisenhower downwards. There were letters and memos written on paper with headings of No. 10 Downing Street or SHAPE headquarters.

There were war mementoes everywhere, and the one he said he treasured most was a half-smoked cigar lying proudly in a glass case. He had attended Sir Winston's farewell dinner as Prime Minister which he gave at Chequers in 1953. Sir Winston had insisted that he smoke one of his famous torpedo-size cigars. Unfortunately, Sir Arthur was a non-smoker and admitted that after a few puffs he had had to leave the room in a hurry! But he kept the cigar and it was obvious that he worshipped Sir Winston and was grateful for all the support and help he had received from him.

Many people – MPs and other commanders in the services especially – were constantly sniping at Sir Arthur and making life difficult for him. I asked him why Bomber Command never got the full appreciation and recognition which it undoubtedly deserved. He thought that it was because people, having been bombed themselves, disliked bombs.

The public also never saw the direct results of his bomber's work whereas the more glamorous Fighter Command could be seen in action in the skies defending our homes. I also asked him why he was not given a peerage like all the other war leaders. He said that after the war Winston had said he would ask Mr Attlee to give him a peerage but that he, Sir Arthur, had refused and was content to accept a baronetcy in 1953. But he seemed to have no bitterness and to be living a happy and contented life among the friendly people of Goring. He had obviously lost none of his guts and determination because on the day before I saw him he had judged the local Jubilee Baby Competition in the town – and that *does* take courage.

Incidentally, Sir Arthur was not like Monty, who during a battle went to bed as usual at 10 pm and woe betide anyone who disturbed him. Sir Arthur admitted that whenever his bombers were out, except for the odd cat-nap he never went to sleep and was available for instant decisions at any time of the night. He was never made into a war hero like some of the others, but after meeting him I am convinced that Bomber Command and the nation owe him much gratitude and possibly a slight apology for the somewhat churlish way he was treated.

At Coldstream in Berwickshire I interviewed Henry Douglas-Home, brother of Lord Home and a well-known ornithologist and broadcaster in Scotland. In fact he is known up there as the Birdman and I talked to him in a glade of a wood on the Hirsel Estate – family home of the Homes. It was from here that he used to compete with *his* birds against me with *my* birds from a wood at Hever in Kent. These friendly competitions were great fun to do and were done 'live'. We both had microphones placed strategically throughout our woods to catch the song of as many birds as possible. Percy Edwards was the judge and noted down all the different birds he heard, each side taking it in turns to broadcast, and the one with the most species of birds heard was the winner. The results were always very close, though on one occasion Henry did accuse me of cheating! I must say I was once very suspicious of him too when, with the scores level, we suddenly heard a cuckoo from his wood – a most unlikely bird to hear at the time of the year when we were broadcasting. There is in fact the hoot of an owl in the archives in Scotland which Henry recorded, saying it was the most perfect reproduction he had ever heard. It was only years later that his brother William admitted that it had been him hooting behind a bush! No wonder I was suspicious about that cuckoo!

Henry told us two delightful stories about the Home family. On one occasion he and his two brothers, Alec and William, were turning out things in the Hirsel cellars when they came upon a large stuffed crocodile with wicked gleaming eyes. Their Aunt Olive was coming to lunch so they thought that they would play a trick on her. William took the crocodile and placed it on a rock in one of the streams running through the Hirsel grounds. After lunch he took his aunt for a walk, and led her to a bridge crossing the stream. Suddenly William gave a shout and pointed: 'Look, Aunt Olive, quick, we'd better run. There's a crocodile down there on the rock.' But instead of screaming or running for her life, Aunt Olive kept completely calm. 'Really,' she said, 'I didn't know that they came this far north!' But was she pulling William's leg or did she mean what she said?

The Homes had a wonderful Jeeves-like butler called Collingwood, and one day before the war someone said to the old Lord Home: 'I'm sorry to tell you, m'lord, but I think Collingwood is going mad. Early this morning at 7 am I saw him walking over a ploughed field in full butler's rig. Black coat, striped trousers and all, talking and singing to himself.' On investigation Lord Home discovered what had happened. His youngest son, George, was a very keen bird-watcher and used to go off at 5.30 am to a hide to watch the birds through binoculars. But he found that the birds, having seen him arrive, were aware of his presence, and stayed quietly out of sight. So George persuaded Collingwood to go with him one morning, much against Collingwood's will. He finally agreed but said he would have to come fully dressed as he had to be back in time to take up early morning tea to Lord and Lady Home. The idea was that the birds would see George and Collingwood go together into the hide, and that after a short time Collingwood would ostentatiously leave

it, singing and talking to himself to attract the attention of
the birds. The hope was that the birds would be fooled into
thinking that the 'enemy' had now gone, not noticing that
although two had arrived only one had left. Anyhow, that
was the explanation of the singing butler.

One of the most unusual and eccentric people I have ever
interviewed was Richard Booth of Hay-on-Wye. He was
unusual because he has turned Hay into a book town. He has
six second-hand book shops with over two million books on
about fifteen miles of shelving. His object is to have as many
books as possible on each subject, so that someone who is,
say, interested in bridge or gardening can go to Hay and be
directed to shelf after shelf on his or her subject. In no other
bookshop in the world would it be possible to find such a
concentration of books on so many different subjects. Visitors come to Hay from all over the world and there is an
annual book week with lots of celebrations.

Richard buys his books in vast quantities, and when I
went to see him he was just back from America where he had
bought up a hundred thousand second-hand books. Just
think of the job of sorting that lot, and then the even more
difficult task of deciding on the right price for each one after
buying them in bulk. He admitted that he must sometimes
unknowingly buy up a rare first edition and let it slip through
his fingers.

He was eccentric because on 1 April 1977 he declared
Hay-on-Wye independent and indeed I received an invitation to the opening ceremony. He was also in the process of
appointing his own ambassadors to various countries.

It was as you can imagine a fascinating interview to do
and it had a most surprising and hilarious ending which alas
the listeners never heard. When I asked Richard for his
choice of music I caught his eye and for some unknown
reason he got the giggles – or in theatrical language he
'corpsed'. So did we all, but luckily the engineer kept recording and I often play the tape when I want a good laugh. It's
quite hysterical. He was laughing so much that to start with
he couldn't get a word out. So I kept on repeating my
question in between my own laughs. Gradually through his
chokes and sobs he managed to blurt out that he wanted
Golden Years or anything by David Bowie.

I must have asked him at least ten times for his music before his answer was considered good enough to go in the programme. Although they did not hear the laughing tape on *Down Your Way* listeners did hear it at the end of a programme I did with producer Michael Craig called *It's A Funny Business*. I explained what had happened and then we just played the hoots of laughter. Jimmy Tarbuck told me sometime afterwards that he was motoring along listening to the programme, and began to laugh so much that he had to pull into the side of the road until it had finished.

And then there was a young chap called Chris Fleming at Wem in Shropshire. He played a big part in organising activities in the town and also ran a disco. He advertised it as 'the most boring disco in the world', chiefly because his Shropshire customers demanded a squarer type of music than is normally played in discos. He wore an earring on his left ear. I asked him why only *one* earring and not one on his right ear. 'Well,' he replied, 'I would look an awful fool if I wore two, wouldn't I?'

Jack Pharoah of Ravenglass was an amusing character and one of those people who seem to be able to turn their hands to anything. When I interviewed him he had a cobbler's shop and kept a garage. But he had been a fisherman, a ferryman and a guide to the local bird sanctuary, among other things. He was not above a bit of subterfuge to help to boost trade. As a ferryman he used to ferry visitors across to the sanctuary. But at low tides it was just possible for them to walk across if they so wished. So to discourage them he used to get his son to walk across the sands in full view of the visitors. Then suddenly his son would pretend to be sinking into the sand and mud, as if caught in some quicksand. Naturally enough after that, most visitors opted to go across by boat!

Jack also once worked quite a clever trick on the owner of a Rolls-Royce. The man drove up in his Rolls and asked Jack to fill it up, while he went across the road to get some cigarettes. He was in such a hurry that he left the engine of the Rolls running. When he got back he asked Jack how many gallons he had put in. 'Seventeen, sir,' said Jack. 'But,' protested the Rolls' owner, 'the car only holds fifteen gallons.' 'I know,' said Jack, thinking quickly, 'but as you left the engine running it used two gallons while I was filling the car up!'

We received a double bonus when we visited Harpenden in the shape of Lord Hill and Eric Morecambe. Lord Hill, Cabinet Minister and, uniquely, chairman, in succession, of both ITA and BBC, is still best known to many people as the war-time Radio Doctor. He told me how he was the first man ever to mention the word 'bowels' on the air with that deep bedside voice of his. His philosophy in his radio talks was to give confidence to his listeners and discourage them from worrying about their health. 'Leave it alone. It won't get better if you pick it,' was a typical bit of advice.

As for Eric, what a lovely person he is. Modest, kind, friendly, a great worker for charity but perhaps most important of all, a naturally funny man. He doesn't have to try to be funny. He just is. Jokes come automatically to him no matter to whom he is talking. During our interview, which was completely unrehearsed, I asked him why he came to live in Harpenden. 'Oh, we came here one day to sell my mother-in-law . . .', or again when I asked him about the running 'feud' between him and Des O'Connor, 'Oh, we're great friends really. He even came to my daughter's wedding – he wasn't asked, but he came.' Eric is a keen ornithologist, so I asked him if he went out walking with big binoculars. 'Oh, no,' he said, 'I leave Big Binoculars behind. He's not too keen on birds.' And so on.

Eric is a most rewarding person to talk to, and genuinely fond of Harpenden and its inhabitants. They all know him by sight of course and he enjoys going shopping and talking to them. 'It's only when I go to Luton that I put on dark glasses and a limp . . .'

One of the joys of doing *Down Your Way* is the chats we have with people both before and especially after the interview. Afterwards they are always relaxed and come up with some splendid gossip and stories about their town or village. In one Yorkshire town which we visited one of our 'victims' told us about a local lady who was well known for never giving anything to charity if she could help it. However hard people tried to persuade her she used to invent all sorts of excuses, one of her favourites being that she was deaf and couldn't hear what was being said. Not knowing this, one evening a man walked up her drive and rang her front doorbell. After some delay she came to the door and asked him what he wanted.

'Well, madam,' he said, 'I apologise for troubling you but I wonder if you would be generous and help a good cause. I am collecting on behalf of the Brighouse and Rastrick Band Instrumental Purchase and Repair Fund.' 'It's no good,' she said with her voice raised, 'I can't hear a word you are saying. Please shout it louder.' So the man repeated his request at the top of his voice. But it was still no good, and the lady shook her head, cupping her hand behind her ear.

Once again the man tried, as loud and as deliberately as possible. But the lady said, 'It's no good. I still can't hear a word. You'll have to go away.' The man looked very disappointed and muttered quietly under his breath: 'Stuff her, the stingy old bitch' – at which the lady said: 'Yes, and you too can stuff your Brighouse and Rastrick Brass Band Instrumental Purchase and Repair Fund' – and slammed the door in his face.

Inevitably, as I've said, we tend to talk to a good many elderly people, and a friendly colleague warned me of one pitfall into which he had fallen. He was interviewing a very old lady who was ill in bed. Sitting by her bedside he asked her. 'Have you ever been bed-ridden before?' 'Yes, young man,' she replied, 'I have many times. And I've got ten children to prove it!' So that is *one* question I never ask!

And another warning to would-be interviewers. Never judge people's age by their appearance, as a mythical broadcaster is 'reputed' to have discovered to his cost! He was visiting an old people's home to find out why some people live to such a ripe old age. He picked out the three oldest men he could see, and asked each one the same questions. How old are you, and to what do you attribute your old age?

The first old man said he was a hundred and two and had never smoked in his life, had always gone to bed at ten o'clock every night and had been happily married for sixty-five years.

The second said he was a hundred and six, had never

drunk, took a long walk every day and although a bachelor had enjoyed a healthy sex life as a young man.

The third old man looked particularly frail and wizened. He said he had never gone to bed before 2 am, drank at least two bottles of whisky and smoked sixty cigarettes a day. But most important of all he had enjoyed sex at least three times every night with any woman he could find.

The interviewer was flabbergasted as he gazed at the wrinkled old face ravaged by time. 'Well,' he said, 'I don't know how you've done it. Remarkable. But I don't think you said how old you are.' 'Twenty-eight next birthday,' replied the 'old' man.

All this travelling round the country staying in different hotels can have its complications – as my friend Henry Blofeld, the cricket writer and commentator, once found to his cost. He was reporting a county match at Nottingham and for the first night stayed at the Bridgford Hotel. But because they were booked up he had to move to the Albany Hotel for the next two nights. He had a good dinner with a few aperitifs and a bottle of wine and then went up to his room for an early night feeling 'nicely thank you'.

As he always does he slept in the nude, and woke at about 2 am wanting to spend a penny. So in a sleepy, bemused state he got out of bed, groped his way round the room and found a door which he thought was the bathroom. He went through it and it shut with a click behind him. He then looked for the loo but to his horror found he was standing in the brightly-lit corridor outside his room, without a stitch of clothing on and without his key. He was by now wide awake and quickly spotted a tray on the floor outside the next-door room. He whipped the paper napkin from under the plates and held it in front of his vital parts.

He realised that he must get hold of the night porter to open his door for him with a pass key. So he crept along the deserted corridor to the lift, which to his relief started coming up when he pressed the button. When it arrived he got in and pressed 'Ground Floor', intending when he reached there to call out to the night porter for help. The lift began to descend but to his alarm he felt it slowing up as it approached the second floor. Someone had obviously pushed the button and sure enough as the lift stopped at the gates there waiting to get in was a party of men and women in evening dress, laughing and joking after what had obviously been a very good evening.

The laughter stopped for a second as they saw Henry crouching at the back of the lift desperately clutching the inadequate napkin against himself. Then of course there was uproar, with roars of laughter, and a few shrill squeaks from the ladies. Luckily they had not opened the gates so Henry quickly pushed the ground-floor button again and the lift shot down out of sight of the party. He explained what had happened to a surprised night porter, not used to seeing naked men approaching his desk in the middle of the night. He gave Henry a pass key and saw him into the lift, which luckily raced up past the party on the second floor still recovering from shock. So Henry slunk back to his room and ever since has made sure that he knows the geography of every hotel room before he goes to sleep. A lesson for us all!

Luckily I don't often have to travel by tube – at least during the rush hour. Unlike a friend of mine who had to travel to and from the City every day. He was once standing in a crowded carriage with bodies pressed closely together. He suddenly realised to his embarrassment that he had left his trousers unzipped and was in danger of exposing himself. So, hoping no one would notice, he surreptitiously managed to get his hand down and slowly pull up his zip. He then relaxed and looked about him pretending that nothing had happened.

When the train stopped at the next station (which was not the one he wanted) he found himself being drawn mysteriously towards the sliding doors, following very closely behind a very attractive blonde. He tried to stop but was dragged on to the platform and as she made her way to the exit, he realised that he was attached in some way. He desperately tried to explain to her as she snapped at him to leave her alone and stop following her. Finally she tried to turn round but found that she could not do so. They then both found out what had happened. His zip had got caught in the back of her fur coat and a lot of fiddling had to go on before he could free himself by undoing the zip. Quite a crowd had gathered round them, as he apologised profusely to the blonde, who in the end saw the joke. But as he did himself up blushing like mad, my friend there and then decided to have fly buttons on his next pair of trousers.

Whether out of kindness or not I don't know, but within a few days of learning that *Down Your Way* was coming off, I was asked to become a member of a new *Twenty Questions* team. This, too, caused quite a furore as except for Anona Winn all the members of the old panel were to be discarded. It seemed bad luck on them, especially Joy Adamson who had been on the panel for twenty-five years and Norman Hackforth who for eighteen years had been either the mystery voice or one of the panel. The new question-master in place of Peter Jones was to be Terry Wogan, and in addition to Anona and myself our panel was completed by humourist William Rushton and a charming actress Bettine Le Beau.

But of course as a professional broadcaster one must accept any opportunity which is offered, without allowing one's feelings to interfere, and I'm sure the old panel understood this. Anyway, we were on a hiding to nothing because in fact *Twenty Questions* is not an easy game to play. In order not to waste questions team spirit is essential and this can only develop after several series together. There is the knack of knowing the right questions to ask early on to establish in which area the object is. For instance, if it is Animal someone must ask: 'Is it human?' If so, then: 'Alive or dead? Fact or fiction? Are there lots of them? Only one,' etc.

If it is *not* human then: 'How many legs? Domestic or wild? Do you eat it? Is it something made from an animal?' For Vegetable you obviously start with: 'Can you eat it? Is it a growing plant? Can you wear it? Is it wooden, rubber etc?' And for Mineral you have to establish whether it is wet or dry, metal or stone, natural or handmade. That leaves the hardest of them all, Abstract, which can be almost anything and the recognised first question here is: 'With what sense do you recognise it?' After that the best of luck! It's hit or miss.

So you can realise that there is a lot of skill needed which is only acquired by practice and knowing what the other team members are thinking. Plus of course that unbelievable intuition with which Anona Winn seems to be gifted. Willie

Rushton proved to be a splendid guesser, keeping quiet for possibly two-thirds of the questions and then suddenly popping up with the correct answer – which proves the value of listening carefully to the answers given by the questionmaster. Bettine with her broken accent and innocent charm managed to inveigle far more helpful answers from Terry than any of us.

We did thirteen programmes altogether, recording two in an evening or at lunchtime in front of an invited audience at the old Playhouse Theatre near the Embankment. In case you have never been one of these audiences the procedure is for the mystery voice (tucked away somewhere in the bowels of the theatre) to give the object to the listeners unheard, of course, by the panel. At the same time as he is speaking two brown-coated attendants carry a board across the front of the stage with the object printed on it for the audience to see. But again, of course, the panel are not in the know. It is all absolutely above board and I am convinced that no producer has ever divulged the answers or even given hints to the panel beforehand.

We recorded the programmes throughout the summer and not surprisingly in my opinion we were nowhere near as good as the old panel, which I hope was some small comfort to them! We got a little better the more practice we had, but our producer, Alastair Scott-Johnston, did not make it easy for us. He had a special delight in giving us the dreaded Abstract objects so that our percentage of victories over Terry was not as high as it should have been. Just to show what people thought of us, two old ladies were leaving the Playhouse after two of our recordings. Someone heard one of them ask the other: 'Did you enjoy it dear?' 'Yes, I did,' the other replied, 'very much indeed. But you know I *still* prefer *Twenty Questions!*'

But it was all great fun to do and under Terry's cheerful guidance we were a very happy team. The only thing I did *not* look forward to was the solo spot which really was rather frightening. You are out on your own with no help from the rest of the team. Often your mind goes a complete blank when it is quite obvious to everyone else what the object is. For instance, for one of my solos, the object was Animal or

Vegetable. By the applause and laughter of the audience when they read what the object was, I suspected it would be something personal. After a few questions I established it had to do with cricket but failed to get it in twenty questions. I could have kicked myself afterwards. The answer was – a bat.

Fifth Over All's right with the World Cup

The year 1975 was a great summer for cricket. The sun shone, there was the first ever World Cup Tournament, the Prudential Cup, and the added bonus of a four-match Test series against Australia.

The Prudential Cup was an unqualified success. Eight countries took part and during an unbelievable fortnight of uninterrupted blue sky there were fifteen matches played of one innings each with a maximum of sixty overs. Naturally the two junior members of the International Cricket Conference – Sri Lanka and East Africa – were outclassed, but there was some thrilling cricket watched by large crowds everywhere.

The teams were divided into two groups, A and B. In Group A England and New Zealand got through to the semi-final, and in Group B West Indies and Australia. But West Indies only just beat Pakistan in the closest match of the competition, winning by one wicket off the fourth ball of the last over. But they had a surprisingly easy victory over Australia by seven wickets thanks largely to a sensational innings of 78 by Kallicharran who scored 35 off his last ten balls from Lillee.

In the semi-finals, England, top of Group A, played Australia, the second team of Group B. On a green pitch England were put into bat and found the fast left-arm deliveries of Gary Gilmour unplayable. With a devastating late inswinger he took 6 for 14 and England could only make 93 off 36.2 overs. But Australia found the conditions just as difficult and lost six wickets with Gary Gilmour top scorer with 28 not out before they won by four wickets.

In the other semi-final West Indies beat New Zealand

easily by five wickets which meant they would meet Australia in the final at Lords. And what a match it proved to be, watched by twenty-six thousand with the gates closed. It continued uninterrupted except for the intervals from 11 am to 8.43 pm. This made it probably the longest-ever day in cricket of this class. The famous Gillette semi-final between Lancashire and Gloucestershire at Old Trafford in 1971 started at the same time and didn't finish until 8.50 pm. But this included an hour's delay because of rain at lunchtime. But luckily the Prudential final was on 21 June – the longest day in the year – so the light held and Prince Philip presented the Prudential Cup to the worthy winners – West Indies. Thanks almost entirely to a superb innings of 102 by their captain Clive Lloyd they made 291 for 8 off their 60 overs. In reply Australia were 274 all out off 58.4 overs, but when all seemed inevitably lost nearly brought off a dramatic victory thanks to a last-wicket stand of 41 between that dynamic speed duo Lillee and Thomson. It really was a wonderful match and set the seal on the competition, which was such a success that there was universal clamour for a repeat as soon as possible. It also gave me an opportunity for a nickname which I could not resist. Eighteen-year-old Javed Miandad just had to become Javed Mumandi.

After the severe drubbing which England had received during the winter in Australia, not even their most optimistic supporter could have expected them to win the four-match Test series against Australia, which had been laid on at short notice to fill the gap after the Prudential Cup was over. In fact Australia only won 1–0, and their victory in the First Test at Edgbaston was largely due to Mike Denness' decision to put them into bat when he won the toss. Poor Mike! He had seemed to have salvaged some of his reputation as a captain and player after England's Test victories at Melbourne and Auckland, to which he contributed scores of 188 and 181. But the morning of 10 July at Edgbaston was dull and grey, and Mike after consultation with his team took a gamble and lost. It is now known that it *was* a team decision though of course the responsibility was Mike's. But Snow and Arnold especially fancied their chances against the Australian batsmen, expecting that the damp heavy atmosphere would give them movement in the air and off the pitch. At the same time the most cynical of the pundits thought that the decision might have been slightly influenced by the wish to avoid meeting Lillee, Walker and Thomson in conditions which should favour the bowlers at least before lunch.

As it turned out, the England bowlers got no movement off the pitch nor in the air, though at one time Australia, at 186 for 5, were struggling a bit. But thanks to some solid and consistent batting (Marsh's 61 was top score) they reached 359. Not a winning score and one which Denness might well have settled for at the start of the match. But the gods don't like captains who put the other side in. As soon as Edrich and Amiss opened for England so did the heavens for Australia, and a terrific thunderstorm flooded the ground. Edrich (34) was top scorer, the next highest being Knott with 14 and England were all out for 101, Lillee and Walker getting unpleasant lift and movement out of the damp pitch. England following on 258 runs behind were 93 for 5 at the close on Saturday night. After further thunderstorms on Monday they were all out 173 – beaten by an innings and 85 runs with a day and a half to spare. Mike Denness of course became the scapegoat and the media brayed for his blood. In fact by the Friday evening he had already told the selectors that he was ready to stand down in view of what had happened.

Naturally the statisticians had a field day. At least so far as England is concerned W. G. Grace seems to have been right, when he once said, 'After winning the toss, by all means think about putting the other side in. Then think again and invariably decide to bat.' Including Edgbaston, England captains have put Australia in to bat on eleven occasions, and have only won once – in Melbourne under J. W. H. T. Douglas in 1912. They have lost eight times, the three which perhaps most of us remember being Len Hutton at Brisbane in 1954, Peter May at Adelaide in 1959 and Tony Greig in the Centenary Test at Melbourne in 1977.

Australia's captains have done a little better after putting England into bat on twelve occasions. They have won three and lost five. If you were to ask Richie Benaud today I'm pretty certain he would give you much the same advice as W.G. But he himself did in fact win two out of these three victories, both at Melbourne – against England in 1959, and West Indies in 1961, the other being by Monty Noble at Lord's in 1909. But I am equally sure that Richie would say that, knowing the conditions and the fine bowlers he had to take advantage of them, his two decisions were NOT gambles.

But to go back to the Edgbaston disaster. It is unfair to put the entire blame for England's defeat on Mike Denness' decision. First of all Lillee and Walker with seven wickets apiece, and Thomson with five, all bowled well except for some waywardness by Thomson in the first innings. They took full advantage of the conditions and were backed by superbly aggressive fielding. It was also obvious that some of our batsmen were still shell-shocked from the battering they had received in Australia. For instance, poor Dennis Amiss, whose last three Test scores against Australia had been 0, 0, 0, made 4 and 5, also suffered a sickening blow on the left elbow.

The other disappointment was a 'pair' for the twenty-one-year-old Essex batsman Graham Gooch, playing in his first Test. Only the week before at Lord's he had made a fine attacking 75 against the Australians. But this time he received an unplayable ball in the first innings, pitching on a good length middle and off and leaving him late off the pitch. He snicked it to Marsh and brought forth the inevitable cliché from all of us in the commentary box that a less gifted batsman would not have been good enough to touch it. Cliché maybe, but true for all that.

But whatever the excuses or reasons, no one could deny that England had got off to a disastrous start and that changes including the captaincy had to be made. So for the Second Test at Lord's Tony Greig was appointed captain, and the selectors decided to try batsmen known to be good against fast bowling – somewhat obvious perhaps! Anyhow in place of Denness and Fletcher, Barry Wood and David Steele were brought in, plus allrounder Bob Woolmer in place of Chris Old. Wood is a small gutsy player at his best against speed, and the surprise selection Steele, a front-foot player with great powers of determination and concentration. But more of him when we get to Lord's.

Before leaving Edgbaston I must relate an amusing experience we had in the commentary box there. During one of the breaks in play due to the thunderstorms, we were having one of our usual discussions in the box rather than return to the studio for music. It was a hot sultry afternoon and for some reason we were discussing how cricket seemed to run in families. I suggested that this was often due to an enthusiastic mum who was prepared to play cricket in the garden with her sons. I quoted Penny Cowdrey, whose three boys are all following in Colin's footsteps. I said that only the week before she had taken five wickets against the Junior Boys XI of her youngest son Graham's preparatory school at Broadstairs. I then added mischievously: 'Yes, they tell me that on that day her swingers were practically unplayable.'

As I had suspected, this remark started everyone in the box giggling. Under some difficulties we continued the discussion and mentioned Vic Richardson's daughter who for years bowled for her three sons Ian, Greg and Trevor Chappell. Don Mosey said Trevor was having a wonderful season in the Lancashire League and that people were saying he would eventually be better than either Ian or Greg. I added that he had already played for South Australia but that I thought he had lost his place in their side last season. 'Anyway,' I went on with confidence, knowing that Alan Mac-Gilvray was at the back of the box, 'we've got just the chap to confirm this. Alan . . .'

I turned round and saw that Alan was fast asleep, chin resting deep on his chest, with a slight whistling sound coming down his nose. This set us all off laughing again, but to cover up and save Alan any embarrassment I managed to blurt out: 'I'm sorry, I'm afraid Alan must have left the box.' With that Alan woke up with a snort and a start and said: 'What's going on? What do you want to know?' But by then we were helpless with laughter and couldn't tell him. All the listeners could hear was a gentle hissing and sobbing as we tried to stem our laughter. Nobody spoke for at least ten seconds, and that is a long time on the air. Don Mosey, who is the worst giggler of the lot, managed to make a bolt for the door, and collapsed outside, leaving me to hold the fort.

When I was able to talk I came clean with the listeners and admitted that Alan had indeed been caught napping! This so far as I am concerned has been the only occasion in thirty years of broadcasting when I have seen a box of commentators silenced by their laughter. The only other similar occasion – which I have described before – was when I was doing a radio broadcast at Hove on a match between Sussex and Hampshire. Henry Horton was playing for Hampshire and he had this funny sort of stance at the wicket with his bottom stuck out. I thought I ought to explain this to the listeners so said: 'Horton has a funny sort of stance,' and then *meant* to say – 'it looks as if he's sitting on a shooting stick.' BUT I got it the wrong way round! Then although I myself managed to keep going, for the first and only time I saw a scorer – Michael Fordham – having to leave the box because he was so hysterical with laughter.

To get back to the Second Test at Lord's, Tony Greig personally got off to a great start in his new role as England's captain. After four wickets had fallen to Lillee for only 49 runs, he made an aggressive 96. His first partner in this rescue act was the newcomer David Steele. With his grey hair and steel spectacles he was a most unlikely figure to bat No. 3 for England, and to have to face the speed and fire of Lillee and Thomson. But in addition to his normal forward defensive stroke, he attacked anything short with superb hooks and cuts. He made a fine 50 before being bowled by Thomson, and the crowd rose to him. They had taken him to their heart and in this one short innings he suddenly became a national hero – the plain Mr Everybody who dared to stand up to Lillee. People felt they could identify themselves with him, since in his appearance he was more like someone you'd expect to see in a solicitor's office than a Test cricketer.

More support came from Alan Knott with a typical 69 and England made 315. Snow then bowled beautifully and Australia were all out for 268. In the second innings Edrich and Wood put on 111 for the first wicket – a rare luxury for England – Edrich finished with 175 – the second highest innings against Australia at Lord's. England batted with far more assurance and confidence and Greig was able to declare at 436 for 7 setting Australia 484 to win. All except poor Dennis Amiss (10) made useful scores and Steele once again played bravely and sensibly for 45. In the end Australia by dogged batting reached 329 for 3, but it was an honorable draw, and a match which Greig could look back on with great personal satisfaction. It was not just his own scores of 96 and 41 but his flamboyant captaincy seemed to give new spirit to the England team.

This, alas, was to be the end of the road – temporarily only as it turned out – for Amiss. He obviously needed a rest from the battering of Lillee and Thomson who always seemed to keep something especially nasty up their sleeves for him. Equally sad was that Graham Gooch in spite of 31 in the second innings was dropped by the selectors for the Third Test – yet another case of a young attacking batsman being shed after far too short a trial in Test cricket. Shades of Colin Milburn!

It had been mighty hot at Lord's with the temperature in the nineties. In the Long Room of the Pavilion even the most traditional members removed their jackets and ties, much to the 'distress' of the Secretariat. But they did not go quite as far as a gentleman in front of the Tavern. For a bet he removed all but his plimsolls and socks and 'streaked' on to the field during a break in play. He ran across towards the grandstand, and then turned right-handed and ran down the length of the pitch towards the Nursery End, doing the splits over both sets of stumps. It was of course a 'first' at Lord's which was the last place one would have expected it to happen. I suppose I should have disapproved but I must admit I thought it gloriously funny and that it fitted into the gala atmosphere of the packed, sun-drenched Lord's. The streaker did it very delicately and no play was interfered with. The police led him gently away to loud applause and much laughter from the huge crowd.

The next day, the magistrate fined him the amount of his bet which left him with a small profit from what he got out of interviews with the Press. They splashed his photograph across their front pages, showing his backside as he cleared the stumps. In private I was shown the full frontal photograph which the Press did NOT publish! Alan Knott was batting at the time and standing down by the stumps at the Nursery End. He told me later that as the streaker ran towards him it was the first time he had ever seen *two* balls coming down the pitch at him! Needless to say my poet friend Les Bailey of Wombwell turned up trumps and sent me this poem:

> *He ran on in his birthday attire*
> *Setting the ladies aflame with desire.*
> *But when he came to the stumps*
> *He misjudged his jumps –*
> *Now he sings in the Luton Girl's Choir!*

In between the Tests I took part in two unusual events. First of all Guinness sponsored a competition for throwing the cricket ball, which was televised by London Weekend. It took place after a day's racing in front of the grandstand at Sandown Park. A number of first-class cricketers and club cricketers took part, and the object was to see if anyone could beat the ninety-one-year-old record made by Richard Percival in 1884. He threw a ball 140 yards 2 feet – an incredible distance, and funnily enough he also did it on a racecourse at Durham.

Everyone had three throws but no one got anywhere near the record. The winner was John Lever of Essex with 107 yards 8 inches, second was Majid Khan 106 yards 1 foot 3 inches and third Keith Boyce 106 yards 1 foot 1 inch. Boyce in one of the practice throws the competitors were allowed before racing began actually threw 120 yards but possibly the long wait affected him and the others. But whatever the reason I was surprised that no one could get nearer than 34 yards to the old record. In almost all other athletic sports such as running, jumping, swimming and so on there has been regular improvement in performances, with records being smashed year after year. Perhaps – dare I say it – Mr Percival's record was not made under such close and careful scrutiny as we had at Sandown Park.

There is one other possible explanation. Our short boundaries of about 75 yards mean that our cricketers are not required to throw long distances. One day cricket has improved the speed and accuracy of throwing beyond belief but not the distance. Unfortunately no member of the Australian touring team was allowed to compete for fear of injury to their shoulders. Otherwise someone like Doug Walters or Jeff Thomson would almost certainly have won, because with boundaries of 100 yards or more on Australian grounds they have the need to throw further, and get the necessary practice.

The other event was a nostalgic one for me and I hope for quite a few listeners too. Aeolian Hall in Bond Street, which had been the home of BBC Radio Light Entertainment for many years, was being closed down. To mark the occasion Radio 2 decided to mount a special edition of the old *In Town Tonight* programme. It was broadcast 'live' in the actual studio from which *In Town Tonight* used originally to come, and in addition there were three or four points outside in various parts of London. John Ellison – the old presenter of *In Town Tonight* – was in Piccadilly Circus doing interviews with passers-by, Pete Murray was up in Big Ben and I was in a sauna bath in Kensington. It was quite like the old days of *Let's Go Somewhere*, the spot I used to do in the programme from 1948–52. Radio 2 paid three visits to me – in the hot room, under the cold shower, and being 'slapped' on the massage table – all of them naturally accompanied by my usual giggles and shouts. It was twenty-three years since I had done a similar programme, and I must admit at least *I* enjoyed it.

At the time too it was a happy occasion for my old friend John Ellison. He had been seriously ill for the past year or two and came back especially to do this broadcast, in the programme which he had introduced for so many years. But sadly it was his last broadcast as he died a short time later. Besides being a great friend of mine, John had taken me under his wing when I first joined the BBC in 1946, and I learnt much of what I know today about radio from him, especially in the art of interviewing. He was a really professional radio performer with great charm and an ability to get on with people. Someone once described him as the commentator with the smile in his voice – a well-deserved epitaph.

The Third Test at Headingley in August made cricket history. It was the first Test ever to be abandoned because of vandals as opposed to rioters or bottle throwers. England went into the match greatly heartened by their performance at Lord's which had given their morale a much-needed fillip. The selectors made four changes, poor Amiss being spared another confrontation with Lillee and Thomson. He was replaced by John Hampshire on his home ground. He was currently in good form and always at his best against fast bowling, but lacked consistency. Even so he had been rather unfairly ignored by the selectors since making 107 against West Indies at Lord's on his debut in 1969 – since then he had only played in seven Tests.

The other batsman to be dropped was Graham Gooch, which to many seemed a cowardly and retrograde step. If he had been good enough to be chosen for the First Test it was surely much too early to discard him after only four innings. Three were admittedly failures, though his first 0 at Edgbaston was the result of an unplayable ball. But his 31 at Lord's was sound enough even if lacking his usual aggression. To replace him the selectors made the astonishing choice of Keith Fletcher – if you believe in the concept of horses for courses. Headingley had been his unlucky ground ever since he had been picked instead of Phil Sharpe in 1968 against the Australians and then promptly dropped three catches at slip, which the Yorkshire crowd thought that Sharpe would have gobbled up. As poor Fletcher followed these misses with a 0 he has not been given much of a reception at Headingley ever since!

Edmonds and Old came in for Woolmer and Lever, so unusually England went into a Test with two front-line left-arm bowlers. This time the selectors were proved right as the pitch was slow and easy paced and took a certain amount of spin almost from the start. Greig won the toss and England struggled to 288 thanks to the doggedness of Edrich (62) and that man Steele again (73). The only bright batting came from Greig with an aggressive 51. Australia could only make 135 in reply thanks to a sensational Test debut by Phil Edmonds, who in his first twelve overs in Test cricket took 5 for 17 – he finished with 20–7–28–5 compared with Underwood's 19–12–22–1.

In their second innings England managed to muster 291, thanks inevitably to Steele (92) who once again combined grim forward defence with the occasional four off the shorter balls, and once actually straight drove Mallett for 6 which shook everyone. Incidentally, his runs for England earned him a lifetime's supply of lamb chops and steaks from a local butcher who sponsored Steele with a chop for every run up to fifty, and a steak for each run after that. The failures of Hampshire (14 and 0) and Fletcher (8 and 14) confirmed that the selectors' policy of chop and change in order to follow the men in form seldom pays off. At least they could not have done *much* worse by leaving Woolmer and Gooch in the side and by so doing have given some encouragement to youth.

Australia were set the 'impossible' task of scoring 445 to win. At that time only Australia with 404 in the Headingley Test of 1948 had made more than 400 to win in the fourth innings of a Test. But thanks to McCosker (95 not out) and Ian Chappell (62) by close of play Australia were 220 for 3, and so only needed 225 with seven wickets in hand to win. One of the reasons for their success was the change in the bowling of Edmonds. His nagging accuracy of the first innings deserted him and he bowled far too many balls outside the leg-stump. At any rate the game was beautifully poised, with both sides having good reason to think that they could win.

This made the abandonment of play on the last day all the sadder at the time, though as it turned out heavy drizzle from mid-morning onwards would have prevented play anyway. The first I heard of the vandalism was when I was woken up at my hotel by a telephone call from the *Today* programme. They told me what had happened and asked me to comment. Naturally I was disgusted and angry that cricket had once again been made the scapegoat of politics. I recalled some of the other Tests in which pitches had been interfered with. There was Lord's in 1926 when a hosepipe had flooded the pitch but no one ever discovered who had turned it on or left it on. On Len Hutton's tour of Australia the Melbourne pitch was found to have been mysteriously watered when play was resumed after the weekend. I had of course also been present when play was interrupted by bottle-throwers at Sabina Park during Cowdrey's tour and for the famous Illingworth walk-off at Sydney. There were also other bottle-throwing incidents which interrupted play in the West Indies on both Hutton's and May's tours. But the only other complete abandonment of a match due to anything other than weather was the Karachi Test in 1969. Here the crowd invaded the pitch and set fire to the stands with Alan Knott 96 not out on the way to his first Test hundred. On this occasion players, Press and broadcasters had to take refuge in the pavilion, before being smuggled out of the ground – twelve to a car! We all packed our bags and flew back to England that same night.

The damage to the Headingley pitch was not severe. There was some crude oil on a good length and some holes dug with a knife near the batting crease. But it was sufficient to make play out of the question, as it would have been grossly unfair to restart the match on a newly cut pitch, unaffected by the wear and tear of four days' cricket. The culprits were caught and one of them served a thirteen-month prison sentence. Ironically, as I've said, because of rain their action had no affect on the result of the match but it did give them the publicity they wanted for their cause – the release of a colleague from prison. Unfortunately, it cost cricket at least five thousand pounds and could have ruined what was certain to be a really exciting Test.

The Fourth and final Test at the Oval also earned its place in cricket history. It was the longest game of cricket ever played in England, lasting the full six days and ending as late as 3 September – the only time I can remember a Test Match in September. Our selectors admitted their mistake at Headingley and dropped Fletcher and Hampshire, bringing back Woolmer and re-introducing Roope to Test cricket after an absence of two years. Ian Chappell won the toss for the first time in the series on what was to be a slow pitch

throughout. After being robbed of his hundred by the vandals at Headingley when he was 95 not out, McCosker made
his maiden Test century and Ian Chappell, in his last Test as
Australian captain, made a typically aggressive 192 and was
able to declare at 532 for 9. For some reason which I have
never discovered he treated the packed Oval crowd with
contempt and discourtesy, failing to acknowledge in any way
the generous applause for his hundred or the acclamation
he received on returning to the pavilion. An unnecessary
display of bad manners which would, I know, have
greatly shocked his grandfather, that great sportsman Vic
Richardson.

England as at Edgbaston got the worst of the weather, and
during their first innings of 191 had to struggle against
drizzle, interruptions, heavy cloud and bad light. Lillee (2),
Thomson (4) and Walker (4) took full advantage of the
conditions, and the inevitable Steele was top scorer with 39.
Following on 341 runs behind there was only one thing for
England to do – to get their heads down and fight for a draw.
And this, with grim determination and plenty of guts, they
proceeded to do. The newcomer Roope (77) and Woolmer
(149) justified the selectors' choice, and need I say it Steele
(66) again 'came good' and brought his final figures in his
first ever Test series to:

Inns	N.O.	Runs	Top Score	Average
6	0	365	92	60.83

Remarkable. Those two great England stalwarts Edrich (96)
and Knott (64) were other big contributors to England's
second innings' score of 538.

There were only eighty-five minutes left for Australia to
try to make 198 to win, and they made 40 for 2 before stumps
were pulled up half an hour early. The real winner of the
game was Harry Brind's pitch in his first Test as groundsman at The Oval. It was far too slow, but remained true and
showed no sign of breaking up. The short series of four Tests
had been a great success, the cricket, the crowds and the
weather all helping to make the 1975 cricket season one to
remember. Australia deserved to win the series because they
took their chance when it was offered them at Edgbaston.

England could console themselves that thanks largely to the lack of pace and bounce in our pitches they had wiped the slate clean after their annihilation in Australia, and but for the weather might have squared the series.

Just three last memories of the Oval Test. Bob Woolmer's hundred was the slowest ever by an England batsman against Australia. It took him 6 hours 34 minutes against the previous slowest 6 hours 2 minutes by Colin Cowdrey at Sydney in 1959. Secondly, on the Saturday when the light was at its worst we were all surprised that the umpires Dicky Bird and Tom Spencer did not stop play for bad light. So evidently was John Snow, who kept casting long glances at the dark clouds and making it quite obvious that he found it difficult to see out in the middle. When he realised his hints were being ignored he decided on more drastic tactics. He hit Walker over mid-off for 4, and then gave him 'the charge' and lofted him over long on for another 4. This was followed by a cross-batted stroke for 2 to mid wicket – 10 runs off the over, the most expensive of the day. Then surprise surprise, immediately it was over the umpires conferred and declared that the light was unfit! We couldn't help wondering how many runs Snow might have made had the light been good!

Finally I was given an opportunity for one of my more preposterous puns. Trevor Bailey was discussing whether England should have taken more risks in their second innings in order to score more quickly. If they did, of course, there was the danger of their losing wickets. 'It's very difficult to strike a happy medium', he said. 'You *could* go to a séance,' I butted in, ducking the sweets and bits of paper flung at me by my long-suffering colleagues.

I know that I am biased but I have always found that cricketers in general are very nice people. There's something about the game perhaps which helps to build character, tolerance and humour. The modern first-class cricketer is no exception and I am extremely grateful to them all for the way they have always given me – and continue to give – their friendship.

I have only one complaint against them. I wish they could look as if they were enjoying themselves more. How seldom do you see them smiling or laughing *on* the field. Yet I know that almost all of them love cricket and are sacrificing quite a lot of money to play it. But I fear the pressure and the pace of the present crowded season has made their cricket too much like a job of work. For them it's like going to the office or factory every morning. It's not that they really *play* too much cricket. But the constant dashing from place to place up the motorways is an exhausting business. They have to do it to fit in all the different types of competitions.

It is possible for someone to finish a three-day County Championship match on a Friday, travel somewhere to play a one-day Benson and Hedges on the Saturday and be off again somewhere else on the Sunday for a one-day John Player match.

Sometimes, if there has been rain on the Saturday, a cricketer will have to go back to finish the Benson and Hedges on the Monday or Tuesday. It could even happen that he then has to report for a five-day Test Match on the Wednesday. Four different types of cricket in one week, with of course the Gillette Cup to come later in the season. It's a wonder they know which game they are playing with all the different rules and regulations.

And of course it sometimes happens that a batsman is not out in a county match on the Saturday evening, has to play a new innings in the John Player on Sunday and then go back to continue the not out innings on Monday. However much anyone loves cricket it is not surprising that it sometimes seems too much of a good thing to the county cricketers. But of course this applies to almost everything in life. The less you have the more you appreciate it when you do have it, as this following story illustrates:

There was a professor lecturing to a group of men on the subject of sex, and he asked his audience if they would help him. Would those who made love to their wives *every* night please hold up their hands? Then those who made it every other night, twice a week, once a week, once a month and so on. Each time the men rather sheepishly held up their hands at the number which concerned them. Finally, after he had counted each category, the professor said: 'Thank you for your help. That's all.' But a small man right at the back of the hall held up his hand and with a cheerful smile said: 'Excuse me, sir, you haven't asked me yet.' 'All right,' said the professor impatiently, 'how often do *you* do it?' 'Once a year,' replied the small man still smiling. 'Well, what are you looking so pleased about?' asked the professor. 'It's tonight,' replied the small man. See what I mean?

Sixth Over Alarums and excursions

In September 1975 Pauline and I went to Corfu for a fortnight's holiday and were lucky enough to enjoy cloudless blue skies and hot sunshine throughout our stay. We went with a party organised by *Cricketer* magazine and stayed in the Cricketer Taverna situated among the olive groves and cypress trees on the west side of Corfu. It is a beautiful island, far lusher and greener than we had expected with majestic mountains and quiet secluded beaches and coves. We visited these in a caique belonging to Ben and Belinda Brocklehurst – the *Cricketer* hosts. We used to chug our way along the deserted west coast until we found a peaceful spot with not a living soul in sight.

When we were not swimming or sunbathing we went to the picturesque cricket ground right in the centre of Corfu Town. Cricket has been played in Corfu for over 160 years and was first introduced there by the Royal Navy. The ground has been greatly improved in recent years and the outfield is now of coarse grass with a matting pitch. The Greeks are up to good club standard in bowling and fielding but their batting would be no good on an English grass pitch. But out there on the matting with its bounce they get away with some crude cross-batted strokes. What they lack in skill they make up for in enthusiasm and courage, cheered on by the shouts and applause of the large crowds which sit under the trees around the ground, sipping cool drinks brought by waiters from the nearby cafés.

There are usually matches every Wednesday, Saturday and Sunday, and at the weekend there are often three to four thousand people watching. There were two local Greek teams when we were there, now there are three. Our two were Gymnasticos and Byron, who play each other and visiting teams from England and Holland, who usually spend a fortnight on the island. There are also occasional matches against BEA and the Royal Navy. Somehow there always seemed to be exciting finishes with the excitement and uproar worthy of a Wembley Cup Final. I was persuaded to play in one match for the *Cricketer* against Gymnasticos and going in No. 11 made a stylish single down to third man before being caught in the gully. But at least I can say I have played in Corfu.

Although extremely brave when batting – often without gloves – and in attempting impossible stops or catches, the Greeks tend to kick up a tremendous fuss when they *are* hurt. A batsman hit almost anywhere will lie down moaning and drumming his legs on the ground. One of their batsmen was hit in a match against the Old Wellingtonians who, with a team made up from the *Cricketer* readers, were staying at our Taverna. The bowler was their volatile captain – Christopher Brown, son of Freddie Brown and a fast and highly dangerous bowler on the matting. As usual the batsman collapsed groaning on the ground, and various spectators rushed out to attend to him. But he lay there writhing in apparent agony, so a call was made for any doctor in the crowd.

In the Old Wellingtonian party was a young medical student in his first year at a teaching hospital. He wasn't selected for this match, so got up from his deckchair in the shade and went out to try and help. He approached the injured man, knelt down and asked him where he was hurt. Between his groans the man muttered something in Greek and pointed to his left ankle, which when the sock was rolled down, was sure enough badly bruised and looking a nasty mess. But the young Wellingtonian rose to his feet without doing anything. 'I am sorry,' he said, 'I haven't got down that far yet in my studies,' and walked back to his seat.

One day, when watching, I was looking through an old scorebook on the scorers' table. You won't believe this, but I do assure you the Greeks have some rather unusual names. I found that in one match a batsman from a visiting English team was out: stumped Penis Bowled Crabsarse!

Back from our holiday in Corfu, I had a very busy
autumn. There was the new way of recording *Down Your
Way*, doing two in the first week of the month, two in the
second week, leaving the last half of the month free. There
were the usual number of talks, lectures and dinners and
commentary on the Lord Mayor's Show for television. There
was also a very special occasion for me when the Sheffield
Cricket Lovers' Soceity gave a dinner in my honour. My old
friend Don Mosey proposed my health and I still blush at the
kind tribute on the front of the menu.

To Brian
As a token of our appreciation
for the pleasure you have given
cricket lovers the world over.

Could anything be nicer than that? It did much to allay the
guilty feeling I often have that a large slice of my life has been
taken up with describing a piece of leather being hit by a
piece of wood. It also made me – a southerner – feel very
humble and grateful to my wife's home county, Yorkshire.
To date I have had two dinners given in my honour and both
have been in Yorkshire – at Wombwell and Sheffield. And,
you know, it's always rightly said that Yorkshiremen know
their cricket!

As Christmas approached we had one of those domestic
crises which crop up in every family. For about six years
Pauline had had a dodgy back and had undergone treatment
on it from time to time. At the end of November it suddenly
'went', and her specialist decided that complete rest might
stave off an operation. So for eight weeks she was on her back
in bed which, with me away so often, brought quite a few
complications in our life. But everyone rallied round and the
Red Cross did a marvellous job in helping to ferry our
youngest daughter Joanna to and from her school bus in
Islington. They were all volunteers who gave up their spare
time to help and only charged the bare minimum to pay for
their petrol.

We had also sent out invitations to a Meet the Neighbours
Party. After nearly thirty years in St John's Wood we felt we
knew many of our neighbours – some intimately, some on a

nodding acquaintance. But we wondered how many of them knew one another so we sent out fifty invitations and only had one refusal! I naturally wanted to cancel the whole thing, but Pauline pleaded for it to go ahead. So go ahead it did with Pauline holding court in our bedroom. It was voted a great success and as a result we hope that quite a few neighbours know each other better.

With three of the family – Clare, Andrew and Ian – all in Sydney, Barry, Joanna, Pauline and I – plus of course Cally and Mini – had our turkey and plum pudding round the bedside from where we telephoned the others in Australia, which cost a little matter of twenty-one pounds by the time everyone had had their say! An unusual, rather expensive but happy Christmas.

But back to backs! It's amazing how many people in all walks of life do suffer from a bad back and it is a great temptation to take their advice. They all seem to have a miracle man round the corner who has cured them by some magic manipulation. Unfortunately most people add: 'You simply *must* go to him. He's wonderful. I've been to him for years.' Not much of an advertisement for his healing powers if it means constant attendance!

But rest worked wonders with Pauline and by January she was up and about and gradually returned to normal – until that fateful Easter Saturday. It was one of those days. On the Good Friday Pauline had swung a gentle golf club and suffered no pain nor seemingly any after-effects. My son Barry was busy arranging a party for his birthday the next day. On the Saturday we were all going to the local point to point and the stew – our staple diet on these occasions – had been cooked in readiness. I woke to hear a whisper from Pauline saying that her back had gone again, and that she was in great pain and could not move. She had those old shooting pains up the left thigh and leg. I rushed out to the doctor's to get some pain-killing pills and returned to find that four out of Barry's six guests had rung to say they could not come to his party. Pauline insisted that we all went to the point to point, leaving her behind with rations for the day by her bed, though she could just stagger on all fours to the bathroom. Looking back it all looks rather heartless but it was a gorgeous spring day and all she wanted was to be left in peace to lie quietly on her back.

Anyway, we packed up the boot of my car with the stews, bottles, picnic basket, binoculars, rugs, etc, and as it was such a nice day I took off my coat and flung it into the boot which I then closed. We all got into the car, and prepared to move off. Everyone was laughing and joking but suddenly I froze in my seat and sat motionless. I suddenly realised that my ignition key was in the ticket pocket of my coat which was now inside the boot, which was self-locking. I wouldn't say that I remained calm – in fact I ran through the first few chapters of my book of expletives. But I then remembered how friendly were the Swanage police, so rang them for help. Sure enough within minutes a little white panda car came tearing up the road and a PC got out dangling an enormous bunch of car keys! Relief! Surely there must be one similar to mine among them. But try as we could, we were unable to find one to fit. We tried some of them twice but after twenty minutes or so we gave up. Then we had our first bit of luck. A friend from across the way came over and said he knew a chap in the nearby hotel who was a Ford dealer. So we went to find him and though he hadn't got any keys he told us that if you remove the back seat of a Ford it is just possible to put an arm through a narrow gap into the boot. So Barry did this and after much grunting and groaning managed to retrieve my coat. We were saved, but our troubles were not over yet. Just as we were finally about to set off the telephone rang and it was the remaining two of Barry's guests saying they couldn't come to his party. So that was off, we were leaving Pauline in pain upstairs, we were going to miss the first race and when we got there we failed to back a single winner. As I said, it was one of those days!

The next week was taken up with trying to save Pauline's back. The local GP recommended gentle physiotherapy, and before contacting her own specialist in London we decided to try one final 'miracle' man in Bournemouth, who had been recommended by friends. 'One finger on the spot and hey presto – the disc will slip back into place.' After examining Pauline he said: 'Twenty years ago I would have put you straight on the table and manipulated you. Almost certainly

I would have cured you – at least temporarily. But now I am not so impetuous. I know the risk of failure, even though it is ever so slight. So I fear that there is nothing that I can do for you.'

So off we went to London and after another examination our London back specialist said there was nothing for it but to operate, which he duly did and removed *two* discs. There followed three months or so of painful convalescence, including a stay at the delightful Osborne House in the Isle of Wight. The back seemed all right but there were still the shooting pains down the side of the leg. But the specialist was calmly confident that all would be well in the end. And touch wood, after three months of gentle exercises the pain gradually disappeared, and Pauline's back was cured. I have gone into all this with some detail to show that there is some hope for back sufferers, even if it does mean an operation in the end. But don't expect an immediate cure and try to resist the advice of well-meaning friends whose little man round the corner will cure you at a touch. I know such people exist but there *is* a risk attached to it and you could be the one for whom the magic touch does harm.

In January 1976 we had a heartening occasion involving the Metropolitan Police. At the time there were quite a few advertisements on TV encouraging children in trouble at home to dial the police on 999. One Sunday after lunch Pauline and I were drinking our coffee in the sitting-room when Cally came in and said there were two policemen walking *down* the stairs from the floor above where we and Joanna have our bedrooms.

Somewhat surprised, I went out and saw the two soft-capped policemen coming down. I asked them what they were doing and what they wanted. They were very nice and explained that they had come in answer to a 999 call from a Joanna Johnston of 98 Hamilton Terrace. They received the call when shadowing a procession which was making its way slowly down Oxford Street. So, much relieved at getting some real action, they pulled out all the stops and raced up to St John's Wood in about two minutes flat with blue light flashing and siren wailing. Before they could even ring our bell, they were admitted by our Entry-com which operates from the second and third floors.

Joanna, who had obviously been on the lookout for them, invited them in, and when they reached her floor, burst into tears. So they were coming down to find someone who could explain what was going on. We all rushed upstairs to find poor Joanna sobbing her heart out on our bed obviously overcome with what she had done. The police were wonderful. They talked quietly to her, gave her their Christian names and told her all about their car which they said was the fastest in the fleet. They went on to say that whenever she *was* in trouble it was quite right to dial 999 but if Joanna just wanted to talk to a policeman she could ring 935 1113 which was Marylebone Lane Police Station, and they would be very happy to speak to her.

Under this sympathetic approach Joanna soon perked up and explained that she had seen the TV advertisement, and wanted to see what happened. She promised not to do it again and, here comes the best part, the policemen took her down, put her in the back of their car and drove her up Hamilton Terrace and back at great speed, with siren wailing, and lights flashing. It was certainly a day which she will never forget and I wrote a letter to the Chief Superintendent at Marylebone Lane. I apologised for the trouble caused and praised the behaviour and understanding of the two officers. I added that it was so nice to be able to bowl a gentle half-volley at the police, instead of the usual bumper which they normally received from the public. He replied that he had shown my letter to the two officers and that they appreciated 'the friendly ball instead of the usual body-line, and are encouraged to return to the crease on another occasion'. Who says our policemen are *not* wonderful?

Ever since Pauline and I were married way back in 1948 we have always had a dog. We started with my favourite breed – a Sealyham with a black eye called Smokey. The last dog I had had before the war was also a Sealyham called Blob who adored cricket and used to sit on the boundary quite happily with ears pricked watching us play. Smokey was a lady and wasn't so keen. But she was a great character though not too intelligent. But she was clever enough to produce five super puppies and made a perfect mother. She had a loathing for cats. This was a pity as she was perfectly trained and would sit immediately on command except when she spotted a cat. She would then give instant chase regardless of traffic. So this unfortunately meant that she always had to be on a lead when going for a walk.

Smokey lived to the ripe old age of thirteen and we then had Bonny, a King Charles Spaniel, very highly strung and far too friendly with everyone. We sold him after a few months and he was replaced by Mini – a miniature Yorkshire terrier. Pauline saw her looking miserable in a pet shop window and took pity on her and bought her on the spot. Thank goodness Pauline did. Mini is the sweetest character, supersensitive to a change of voice and very obedient. Yorkies are very tough, will walk for miles and make wonderful companions. She delights in chasing cats and squirrels who invade the garden but never does so away from her own territory. Because she is so obedient she never needs a lead, not even in busy streets. She stays close to heel and at the word 'stay' stands rigidly still. So at a crossing she stands waiting for the word 'over' but if by chance a motorist turns across the lights another 'stay' will act on Mini like high powered brakes and she comes to a dead stop.

We haven't been so lucky with our other pets. We had hamsters who regularly used to lie down and die at the exact end of their two-year life cycle. Then there was poor old Fred the tortoise. One year as usual in late October he dug himself down in one of our flower beds to hibernate. Unfortunately January that year was freakishly hot and to our amazement one day we saw a very dishevelled and dirty Fred moving slowly across the lawn. He had mistakenly thought that spring had come. We rang a local pet shop to ask what we ought to do as we feared frost and snow would soon return and he would die of cold. The man suggested putting Fred into the fridge for a short time to make him think it really was winter and time to re-hibernate. We thought this sounded too drastic so asked the Zoo's advice. They weren't very hopeful. They recommended putting him in a basket full of straw with some food and water and trust that he would go off to sleep again. We did this, but the Zoo were right. It didn't succeed and poor Fred never went off to sleep again and died presumably of cold.

We had no better luck with two budgies who caught a chill and died, so it's just as well we were not professional zoo keepers. At a dinner I once heard a Welsh clergyman tell an unlikely story about budgies. A man had bought two from a pet shop but was annoyed that he couldn't tell which was the male or the female. So he went back to the shop and asked how he could find out.

'Oh, it's quite easy,' said the owner of the pet shop. 'Creep quietly downstairs in the middle of the night and see if you can catch them making love. When they do, seize the one on top and tie a piece of cotton round its neck. That will be the male.' So that night the man crept down to the sitting-room and after a short time he saw the two budgies 'on the job'. He quickly put his hand into the cage, grabbed the top bird and tied a piece of white cotton round its neck. The next morning the vicar called and was asked to wait in the sitting-room. The male budgie spotted the vicar's white dog collar and called out: 'Oh, so he caught you at it too, did he?' . . .

The sun shines sweetly on cricket 1976

The year 1975 had been hailed as the golden summer, with its glorious weather and champagne cricket provided by the World Cup, and the Australian tour. However, 1976 did even better. The series against West Indies inspired brilliant stroke-play and devastating fast bowling, which those lucky enough to see will never forget. As for the sunshine, the weather beat all records, and needless to say that indispensable Bible of Cricket *Wisden* gave us all the details. A spell of fifteen days in June/July was the hottest and longest over the previous two hundred and fifty years. Up to the end of August there was the driest sixteen-month period since records for England and Wales began in 1727. Whew! It makes one sweat just to think of it. But the cricketers revelled in it and cricket itself prospered as a result. There were record crowds and receipts and increased sponsorship and membership. Over £1,000,000 was distributed among the counties at the end of the season.

The four main competitions were fiercely and closely contested. Middlesex brought the Championship back to Lord's for the first time since 1949, and Kent, acknowledged masters of the limited-over game, won both the Benson and Hedges and John Player trophies – the latter by the narrowest possible margin. In fact the result was in doubt until Glamorgan had bowled the very last ball to Somerset at Cardiff on the final day of the season. Off this ball, Somerset, 188 for 8, needed 3 to tie and 4 to win the match but a tie would have been sufficient for them to win the trophy. But they could only manage 2, Dredge being run out when going for the third, which would have meant Somerset winning their first-ever competition.

What a finish, and as a result Kent with the same number of points and away wins as Essex, won the John Player by 0.42 of a run on the faster scoring rate throughout the season. You can't have it much closer than that, and poor Essex too were robbed of what would have been their first-ever win of any of the four competitions.

With finishes such as these it is easy to understand the current popularity of limited-over cricket. One of its best points is that it distributes the honours round the seventeen counties, some of whom would never have a chance of winning the County Championship. This is still the real test of which is the best county, though it's not an ideal one. First of all each county only plays twenty-two matches which means that they all play each other at least once, but only six of the counties *twice*. Some counties too, like Kent, may have to supply three or even four of their top players for five Tests and three one-day Prudential matches so that players like Knott and Underwood play only ten or so out of the twenty-two County Championship games, plus missing five or so John Player matches. I know that Yorkshire used to supply up to five players regularly for England and still ran away with the Championship year after year. But at that time Tests only lasted for three or four days. In addition the other counties had not signed up star overseas players which today means that all the counties are far more evenly matched. Up to the middle fifties there were only the 'big six' who regularly dominated the Championship, and counties like Yorkshire and Surrey during their long run of successes would reckon to win many of their matches against the weaker brethren in two days. But to prove the point that the honours are now more evenly distributed Northants won the Gillette Cup Final at Lord's, so leaving only Essex and Somerset non-winners of any event.

In the 1976 Test Matches England were outclassed and the West Indies won the Wisden Trophy 3–0. Their batting line-up was possibly the strongest I have ever seen in Test cricket and they were all magnificent stroke-players – not a dawdler among them. Just look at this for a batting order: Fredericks, Greenidge, Richards, Kallicharran, Lloyd, King or Rowe. And to support them a terrifying trio of fast bowlers

Roberts, Holding, Daniel, plus Holder for good measure. It's not surprising that this was the most successful West Indies team ever to tour England winning eighteen of their twenty-six first-class matches, including three Tests, plus all three of the Prudential Trophy matches.

England could do little to counter this great side except to bring back Brian Close in his forty-fifth year, knowing that he would present a valiant and immovable target for the West Indian bouncers. These they bowled to excess in England's first innings at Old Trafford. It made a travesty of experimental Law 46, Note 4, VI, that the two umpires did not intervene as bouncer followed bouncer, until finally Bill Alley did warn Holding after he had bowled *three in succession* to Close. The combined ages of Edrich and Close was eighty-four and their batting on the Saturday evening was the bravest I have ever seen. But what a pity that Clive Lloyd, a nice gentle character, allowed the bombardment to take place.

The First Test at Trent Bridge was drawn and from the start England's tactics showed that that was all they were hoping to achieve. After losing the toss Greig set a purely defensive field and on several occasions had there been more close fielders the West Indies batsmen might well have been caught. As it was Viv Richards played a superb innings of 232 with four 6's and thirty-one 4's, many of them sizzling drives which left the fielders standing. He and Kallicharran put on 303 for the third wicket, but one felt that Greig's tactics were at fault. He bowled Hendrick – always susceptible to injury – unchanged for two hours, but Underwood who finished with 4–82 was not brought on to bowl until 5.45 pm when the total was 235. Strange use of the greatest left-arm bowler in the world.

In reply to West Indies' 494, England batted inconsistently for 332, Steele continuing from where he left off in 1975 with a typical fighting 106 – his first Test hundred. He was well supported by Woolmer (82), Old (33) and Snow (20) but single figures from Close, Brearley, Greig and Knott showed up the fragility of the England batting. When West Indies batted again, Snow – given a more attacking field – bowled with all his old life and took four wickets.

Richards (63) again played well and West Indies declared at
11.35 am on the fifth day, setting England to get 339 to win in
five and a quarter hours – a target they were never likely to
try for. They finished up with 156 for 2, Edrich (76) and
Close (36) making sure that there was no panic after Brearley and Steele had gone cheaply.

During the West Indies' second innings there was one
rather interesting point of law. Greenidge was lame and
King – *who was not playing in the match* – was sent out as a
runner, to which England, rightly to my mind, objected.
Admittedly there is nothing in the laws to say who can or
who can not come on as a runner. All Law 2 says is 'Substi-
tutes shall be allowed to field or run between the wickets for
any player who may during the match be incapacitated by
illness or injury, but not for any other reason without the
consent of the opposing captain; no substitute shall be
allowed to bat or bowl. Consent as to the person to act as a
substitute on the field shall be obtained from the opposing
captain, who may indicate positions in which the substitute
shall not field.'

Two points here:

1. In this country at least – and I must admit I thought in
every other cricketing country – it is the custom that a runner should be someone playing in the batting eleven, and
preferably someone who has already batted. A runner who
has still to go in gets an advantage by being out in the middle
for some time before having to bat. He gets a sight of the ball,
and advance knowledge of the bowlers and pace of the
wicket.

But the West Indies' manager, Clyde Walcott, protested
when the umpires upheld the English objection, saying that
so far as he was concerned *anyone* could act as runner. This
conjures up all sorts of possibilities with professional sprin-
ters being specially employed to stand by all padded up, to
be sent out to race up and down the wicket.

2. The words 'during the match' in Law 2 are important
and recall the 'Kanhai incident' during Peter May's tour of
the West Indies in 1959–60. Kanhai had gone into the
match with a dodgy knee and during his second innings of 57
asked if he could have a runner. Peter May refused, and this

caused quite a furore at the time. But all ended happily with Peter apologising when he learnt that it was cramp at the back of the leg, and not his knee which had been troubling Kanhai. But the incident did remind people that a player should not ask for a substitute because of an aggravation of an injury which he had at the start of the match. But since the Law specifically states that permission need only be sought of the fielding captain for something *other than* illness or injury, presumably a decision about them is in the hands of the umpires.

So England got away with the draw they wanted at Trent Bridge, but at Lord's their defensive outlook probably robbed them of a win. After winning the toss they took all of the first day to score 197 for 8, though admittedly the West Indies only bowled just over eighty overs. It took Underwood the next morning with a slog of 31 to raise England's total to 250. It was to be his day because this time Greig had learnt his lesson and brought him on early. He bowled superbly taking 5 for 39 backed up by a fiery Snow (4 for 68) and West Indies were all out for 182 – 68 runs behind. Saturday alas was rained off completely with a full crowd inside the ground and thousands locked outside the gates.

But on Monday England failed to push the score along. Admittedly, Wood had retired hurt with a damaged finger and Pocock the nightwatchman and Brearley were out. But Steele (64) and Close (46) in a stand of 83 allowed the comparatively innocuous slow left-arm bowler Jumadeen to bowl nine overs for only 16 runs. England made 254 and so West Indies needed 323 in just over five hours. They finished up with 241 for 6, the match going to the last of the statutory twenty overs, with only Murray and the tail-enders between England and victory. One couldn't help feeling that had they scored more quickly on Monday, and so given themselves more time to bowl West Indies out, England might have snatched an unlikely victory. At any rate it was to be their last chance of doing so in the series.

At Old Trafford England were annihilated by some of the fastest and most dangerous bowling I have ever seen. For some reason the pitch was full of cracks and as a result was two-paced and with a variable bounce. England did well to bowl out West Indies for only 211, out of which Greenidge made a beautiful 134. Selvey in his first Test swung the ball and took 4–41. But when England batted only Steele (20) reached double figures, though extras thanks to eleven no balls contributed 19. Roberts (3–22) Holding (5–17) and Daniel (2–13) were devastating and against such frightening speed with the ball lifting unpredictably one found it hard to blame the England batsmen who were all out for 71.

West Indies went to town in their second innings with Greenidge (101) making his second hundred of the match and Richards, who couldn't play at Lord's, following up his 232 and 63 at Trent Bridge with a fine 135.

England had to bat again for eighty minutes on Saturday night and it was then that the West Indian fast bowlers seemed to go mad. They hurled bouncers indiscriminately at Edrich and Close, who resisted with tremendous bravery and somehow avoided serious injury. There was uproar in the Press over the weekend and I hope we on radio and TV spoke out against it as strongly as it deserved. Anyhow, on the Monday, although still bowling very fast, the bowlers pitched the ball up on a length and with Roberts taking 6 for 37 England were all out for 126 and so were beaten by 425 runs. A moral here surely. Good bowling will always take more wickets than the loathsome short-pitched stuff, which is not only dangerous but ruins cricket as a spectacle.

Although England lost the Fourth Test at Headingley by 55 runs – and with it the series and the Wisden Trophy – they fought back magnificently after a disastrous first day. Even in Bradman's time Headingley can never have seen so many brilliant strokes as were played by Fredericks and Greenidge. They both made hundreds putting on 192 for the first wicket, with Greenidge scoring his third hundred in succession. Nothing could stop them and at lunch West Indies were 147–0 off only twenty-seven overs – a scoring rate of over $5\frac{1}{2}$ runs per over on the first day of a Test Match! At close of play, from 330 for 2 at tea, they 'collapsed' to 437 for 9 off only eighty-three overs. So in spite of losing seven wickets after tea when the ball surprisingly began to swing and seam, West Indies kept up a scoring rate of over 5 runs per over.

It was tremendous batting with Richards chipping in with another fine innings of 66. But credit is also due to the three England pace bowlers – Snow (4–77), Willis (3–71) and Ward (2–103), who in spite of the initial onslaught never gave up.

With West Indies all out for 450 England made their usual poor start and were soon 32 for 3. But thanks to Balderstone (35), Willey (36) and a great stand of 152 between Greig and Knott who both made 116, England reached the respectable total of 387, only 63 runs behind. They then went on to confirm what an unpredictable game cricket is, by bowling out West Indies for only 196, thanks to some superb fast bowling by Willis with 5–42. This meant that England had the perfectly possible task of scoring 260 to win in roughly a day and a half. But once again the pendulum swung and England were soon 23–3. But Woolmer (37), Willey (45) and Greig (76) attacked the bowling and had anyone been able to stay with Greig, England might just have snatched a sensational victory. But the last six wickets fell for 64 runs and they were all out for 204, the three batsmen named being the only ones to reach double figures. But though they lost the match England had shown that given the right conditions to produce swing and seam, the brilliant West Indian stroke-makers could be contained and bowled out. The three successful England batsmen also showed that aggression against the battery of fast bowlers paid off better than defence.

The return of Alan Ward to the Test scene after an absence of fifty-one Tests revived the old story of how he had once gone on a club tour of Germany during which he had taken a hat-trick against a team of Germans. From then on he was known as Jerryatric Ward!

West Indies' easy victory at the Oval by the huge margin of 231 runs after declaring twice, merely emphasised what a great side they were. It also made it all the more difficult to understand how they themselves had succumbed so easily to Australia during the previous winter. Was the partnership of Lillee and Thomson on their own bouncy pitches practically unplayable? I myself suspect that it was, and that not too much blame can be attached to either Mike Denness' or Clive Lloyd's batsmen.

Anyway, at the Oval all the West Indies' batsmen prospered. Richards (291) with another superb double century was supported by all the batsmen except Greenidge and in their first innings of 687 for 8 declared there were no fewer than five innings of over 60. The incredible Richards, until tiredness overtook him, looked as if nothing could stop him beating Sobers' record Test score of 365. He finished the series with the fantastic average of 118.42 for his 829 runs. On his form of this summer he must be toppling Barry Richards off the throne of No. 1 batsman in the world. Viv has had an amazingly quick rise to the top, but I'm sure that Barry is only in danger of losing his crown because of the lack of opportunity and incentive he has had in not playing in Tests against top-class opposition.

England's reply of 435 was based on an innings of great guts and character by Dennis Amiss on his return to Test cricket. After the terrible battering he had received from Lillee and Thomson in Australia – he had four innings of 4, 5, 0, 10 against them in England in 1975, he was dropped after the Second Test. Instead of throwing in the sponge he took advantage of his absence to work out a new technique against fast bowlers. Basically it consisted of shuffling across to the off-stump or even just outside *before the bowler delivered the ball*. It looked ugly and dangerous, too, because he was nearly square on when he received the ball and so was still in trouble to any ball which left him late outside the offstump. But at least he was behind the line of the ball, though his leg stump was temptingly exposed to the bowler.

The first time he tried it out against Roberts and Holding was for MCC at Lord's when he failed in both innings (9 and 11). What was more he was struck on the back of the head turning his back on a short ball from Holding. He pluckily came back with four stitches in his head but it really did look as if his Test career was over – at least against any country with fast bowlers. I must say in his defence that I sat sideways on to the pitch on the Saturday evening of the MCC match and I have never seen faster bowling than that of Holding. A thrilling sight for the spectator with the added bonus of a flowing and balanced run-up, his feet seeming scarcely to touch the ground as he sprinted like a gazelle to deliver the ball.

Anyway after four Tests England were still unable to find a satisfactory opening partnership, the opening stands being 0, 38, 15, 29, 9, 54, 4, 5. So the selectors decided to gamble on the class which Amiss undoubtedly has and he rewarded them by making his return a dramatic success. He scored 203 out of 342 in five hours twenty minutes, hitting twenty-eight 4's. A great tribute to the determination of this nice, solid, pipe-smoking character. But to bear out what I said earlier, he was finally bowled *behind his legs*.

Although West Indies were 252 runs on Lloyd did not enforce the follow-on and once again the West Indies' batsmen showed their complete mastery of the England bowling, Fredericks (86) and Greenidge (85) putting on 182 for the first wicket before Lloyd declared, leaving England 435 to win – their total in the first innings. Needless to say they found this an impossible task against some more magnificent fast bowling by Holding, who finished the match with fourteen wickets, both he and Roberts getting twenty-eight apiece in the series. Steele made his second 40 of the match and Knott his second 50 but England were all out for 203.

So the West Indies won the series 3–0 and must rival the 1950 side as the best ever to tour England from West Indies. All they lacked from a point of view of balance was a class off-spinner or slow left-arm bowler. But with their wonderful array of fast bowlers it is doubtful whether such a spinner – however good – would have got more than a few overs in any of the Tests.

It may be many years before we shall see again such a superb combination of brilliant stroke makers and lightning fast bowlers. It may also be many years before we enjoy another such hot, dry summer, which of course was just what the doctor ordered for the particular talents of this West Indian side. As for England, they were simply beaten by a far better side in the conditions. And yet under Greig's captaincy there were new signs of a developing team spirit and an ability to fight back. But until the new generation of promising young batsmen developed it looked as if the batting would be the main problem in the immediate future.

One amusing incident occurred during the West Indies second innings. For many years now I have written short articles for the benefit brochures of players. I have naturally done it for nothing as part of my contribution to their well-deserved benefit – that is all except once. When Alan Knott had his benefit he asked me as usual to write something for him. I replied that I would be delighted but for the first time ever I was going to charge him for my work. This shook him a bit but he bravely asked me what my fee would be. I told him that my payment would be a promise from him that, if Bob Woolmer played in a Test during the summer, he would stand up to the stumps for at least one over.

This business of standing up happens to be a hobby horse of mine, since the days when Godfrey Evans stood up to Alec Bedser and kept so brilliantly. Nowadays all Test wicket-keepers stand back to every bowler other than the all too rare spinners. Farooq Engineer was an honourable exception. I think Gil Langley probably started it when he began standing back to the medium pace of Ken Mackay. Even that superb wicket-keeper Wally Grout did so too, encouraged I believe by his captain Richie Benaud.

Jim Parks stood back to Basil D'Oliveira and so did Knotty. Also when keeping for Kent he stood back to Shepherd, Asif and Woolmer. I've had a friendly running argument about it with him for years: he maintains that if he stands up he runs the risk of dropping a vital catch, and that it is not worth it for the few stumpings which might result. He and others also claim that they might unsight the leg slip who is placed there to take the sort of catch on the leg side which a wicket-keeper standing up would try for. This is possible. But I wonder whether you have noticed that with the restriction of only two men allowed behind the popping crease on the leg side, a leg slip is becoming rarer and rarer. Anyway, I feel that such a brilliant wicket-keeper as Knotty would be very unlikely to miss a chance, however difficult, and that the benefits of standing up far outweigh the risks.

First of all it exerts pressure on the batsman. With some-one breathing down his neck he has something extra to think about. He dare not risk taking up his stance a foot or so in front of the popping crease as some batsmen do to the fast medium bowler bowling just short of a length. He has to remember to keep his back foot behind the line, and if he misses the ball must not overbalance. Next it gives the bowler a target to aim at. Alec Bedser always asked his wicket-keepers to stand up, and pays tribute to 'Godders' and that much underrated wicket-keeper Arthur McIntyre for the great help they were to him. It also makes a medium or fast medium bowler look far more penetrating and aggressive when the ball goes with a thud into the wicket-keeper's hands close to the stumps. Nothing depreciates a bowler more than a ball landing with a gentle 'plop' into the gloves of a wicket-keeper standing right back.

And finally but most important these days is the increase in entertainment value of a brilliant take or stumping on the leg side by a wicket-keeper standing up. It's all very well seeing the modern-day wicket-keepers flinging themselves all over the place like goalkeepers. It's certainly athletic and results in some remarkable catches, usually one-handed, but which might in fact have been caught by one of the slips anyway. I was talking to Les Ames at Canterbury and told him that I never remembered seeing *him* hurling himself about. In fact my impression was that he always seemed to get across behind the line of the ball and stay on his feet – and the same went for Bertie Oldfield too. Les admitted that he had never flung himself to the ground and added that it was considered 'undignified' for a wicket-keeper to fall over in those days! Maybe he didn't consider as chances those wide balls at which wicket-keepers fling themselves today. I wonder!

But back to Knotty and the payment of my fee. When Bob Woolmer came on to bowl in the West Indies' second innings, Knotty turned round to the commentary box, gave me the thumbs-up and went right up to the stumps. And of course it *would* happen. Bob's first ball was a near wide outside the leg stump of left-hander Roy Fredericks. Knotty only just managed to get a right hand to it, so saving four certain byes. He turned round and gave me a 'there you are I told you so' sort of look. But he gallantly stood up for two overs and made some brilliant takes. I am sure that if he were to stand up more often he would prove that he is possibly the greatest wicket-keeper ever. It is only the lack of proof that he *can* match Evans' brilliant keeping when standing up to the quicker bowls that leaves a question mark.

By the way my TV colleagues were not in the know about what was going on, and were speculating that Knott and Woolmer were plotting some trap like a leg-side stumping. Incidents like this surely prove that even in Test cricket there is room for a bit of fun.

During the summer, 1976, I was lucky enough to be asked to commentate on one of the three Women's Test Matches in the series against Australia. It was the Golden Jubilee of the Women's Cricket Association and though the three Tests were all drawn, England won the limited-over one-day matches 2–1. Furthermore, their jubilee was celebrated by a unique and memorable occasion. The second of these matches was played at Lord's on a pitch in the centre of the ground, on a flawless day before a remarkably large and enthusiastic crowd. So after much propaganda, lobbying and arm-twisting the ladies had at last been allowed to enter the Holy of Holies even to the extent of using the dressing-rooms and baths, hitherto exclusive male preserves. So far as I was concerned as a member of MCC it was a most welcome invasion. Everyone present at Lord's on that day was, I'm sure, grateful to the good sense of MCC, and to the enthusiastic, untiring and witty vocal efforts of England's captain, Rachel Heyhoe-Flint, which had brought it all about.

I am seldom so presumptuous as to disagree with an opinion expressed by a revered England cricket captain, but I did so once. The occasion was a match on Chislehurst Green between Colin Cowdrey's XI and the Women's England XI of that time. I was keeping wicket and Len Hutton was at first slip. So I asked him what he thought of women playing cricket. He gave me a funny look and answered: 'It's just like a man trying to knit, isn't it?' But as I've said I disagreed – and incidentally the women won the match. In fact I have always supported the girls, and think that they've got quite a bit to teach us men. First-class cricket nowadays tends to be rather scientific or 'professional ' as it's so often called. The ladies bring a touch of grace into what is essentially a graceful game. Anyone who has watched women play recently will know that as bats*men* they use their feet to the slow bowlers. They have all the strokes and run like hinds between the wickets. In the old days if you wished to insult a fielder you told him that he threw like a girl. Nowadays their returns from the outfield come whistling back over the top of the stumps. Their fielding is remarkably keen and their bowling subtle and steady, though lacking in pace.

I have played quite a bit of cricket with women. At my private school the headmaster's daughter, Kitten, bowled a nifty leg-break and in the holidays we used to play a mixed match in the village of Much Marcle in Herefordshire. The star was a retired bishop's wife called Mrs Whitehead. She was a left-hander and defended dourly, and usually carried her bat. In later years I saw her exact replica in Test cricket – Slasher Mackay, the impassive Australian – though Mrs Whitehead did not chew gum!

Mothers, too, have played an important part in cricket. Perhaps the best example, as I've mentioned before, was in Australia where Vic Richardson's daughter, Mrs Chappell, coached her three sons, Ian, Greg and Trevor in the back garden with results which we in England know all too well. Penny Cowdrey, too, is another mother brought up on garden cricket, where for years her bowling tested her three sons, Christopher, Jeremy and Graham. Even more important to me personally was the fact that early in our courtship I discovered that my wife Pauline could throw a cricket ball really well. I won't pretend that it was a vital factor in our romance, but it helped!

I hope by now it is obvious that I am one hundred per cent in favour of women's cricket, and wish them success in the years ahead, though unlike the lady jockeys they will never be strong enough to compete on equal terms with men.

There is one small change which I would like to see. I wish they would wear trousers instead of those divided skirts. I'm always worried that the pad straps will chafe the back of their knees. I also think they deserve to get more coverage on radio and TV, though I can see one or two pitfalls for commentators. What girl would enjoy hearing that she had two short legs? On the other hand I suppose none of them would object if they heard that they had a very fine long leg. And finally, since they bring such glamour and a sense of chivalry and good manners into the game, isn't it about time they were called Ladies instead of Women?

Captains courageous

During my thirty-two years of broadcasting cricket, the England selectors have appointed thirteen captains for Test series in this country. In addition, Nigel Howard and Tony Lewis captained England in India only, and Ken Cranston, David Sheppard, Tom Graveney and John Edrich took over as substitute captains *during* a Test Series. I have, with one exception, been lucky enough to know them all well, either from travelling with them on tour, or from commentary and interviews. The one exception was Wally Hammond, whom strangely enough I never met until 1965 in South Africa when he was 'adopted' by Mike Smith's team and made a tremendous fuss of. This was particularly nice to see as his life in the post-war years had been sad. Anyway, for some reason, in 1946, although we televised the Lord's and Oval Tests against India, there were no interviews with the captains. So although I saw him as captain in two Tests and Lewis and Howard as captains of Glamorgan and Lancashire I cannot really claim to know at first hand their qualities as Test captains.

I am often asked who was the best Test captain of all those whom I did know, and it's an almost impossible question to answer. Each one has so many different qualities – some good, some not so good. So before trying to give an answer I think it would be helpful to give a pen picture of each one, and to analyse their strengths and weaknesses. So to start with, here are the qualities which I think are essential for the ideal captain to have, and it all adds up to an awful lot of 'musts'.

He must:
1. Be a leader whose team will respect and follow him.

2. Be absolutely fair with no favourites, and get to know each member of his team – not just the stars. He will then be able to understand their moods and problems. Cricketers are not automatons, and the good captain is one who knows when to reprimand, encourage or sympathise.

3. Know all the laws of cricket and all the many regulations which seem to get more complicated every year.

4. Be a good enough player to be in the side on playing merit alone. It makes his job so much easier.

5. Be a good tactician and study the strengths and weaknesses of his opponents. Also be prepared to listen to the advice of his senior players and judge when to act on it.

6. Be able and prepared to deal with the broadcasters and the Press and to answer their questions clearly and honestly however stupid, critical or controversial they may be, or however inconvenient the time. They all have a job to do, and a happy Press who have confidence in the captain will mean that the activities of the team are reported in the best possible light.

7. Be a reasonable speaker – to be a *good* one is a bonus.

8. Off the field be a good mixer and expect to have to suffer fools gladly.

9. Take risks to win – that is the object of the game. But when to win is impossible then ensure that the team fights to the bitter end, to draw the game. Furthermore, make sure that each member of the team knows what the tactics are, and what part he is expected to play. Far too many Test captains give no instructions to their players, saying that if they are good enough to play in a Test, they should know what to do. This is a lot of codswallop and a complete dereliction of captaincy.

10. Instruct their players to 'play the game', i.e. no gamesmanship, frivolous appeals, swearing at opponents or obvious dissent with the umpire's decision. This 'must' may well prove to be the most difficult of all to carry out!

11. Finally be LUCKY – perhaps the most essential quality of all.

Now let's see how the various captains pass on examination in all these 'musts'.

NORMAN YARDLEY

CHARACTER	LEADERSHIP	TACTICAL SKILL	PLAYING ABILITY	PR WITH MEDIA	OFF THE FIELD
Nice guy. Everyone's friend.	Too tolerant. Not tough enough.	Good and willing to take advice from senior pros. Did well v. South Africa in 1947 but was on a hiding to nothing v. Don Bradman's team of 1948 – arguably the best ever sent by Australia to England.	A schoolboy prodigy who came good. Very strong on leg side. Good field and a more than useful medium pace change bowler who got Bradman three times in Australia 1946–7.	Friendly and cooperative but did not have to cope with the pressure of TV nor the more modern down-to-earth interviews.	Never captained a touring team except when he took over from Hammond in Fifth Test in 1947. But would have been a perfect ambassador.

GEORGE MANN

CHARACTER	LEADERSHIP	TACTICAL SKILL	PLAYING ABILITY	PR WITH MEDIA	OFF THE FIELD
Product of Eton and the Guards with all their virtues and none of their vices. Friendly, straight and honest with strong principles.	A natural, undoubtedly helped by his distinguished leadership during the war with the Scots Guards.	Simple and basic, but always prepared to listen to his senior players and to take their advice.	A magnificent fielder who set a high standard. His batting not quite Test class. But for his character, would not have been worth his place.	Friendly and helpful but never under any real pressure.	Excellent. Very good mixer.

FREDDIE BROWN

CHARACTER	LEADERSHIP	TACTICAL SKILL	PLAYING ABILITY	PR WITH MEDIA	OFF THE FIELD
Bluff, blunt hale and hearty. A John Bull image!	Led by example. Lots of guts. Never gave up. Could express his wishes quite forcibly!	Sound. Based on many years of first-class cricket before and after the war. Prepared to take risks but on his Australian tour of 1950–1 never had the ammunition.	Originally a top class leg-spinner but in Australia in 1950–1 got most of his 18 test wickets with seamers. A hard-hitting batsman and a good fielder though not in the greyhound class.	Apt to be a bit impatient and suspicious (probably rightly) of certain sections of the Press. But generally friendly and informative.	Hale fellow well met but could be drawn into a fairly heated argument in which his opponent would be stabbed in the chest by a gigantic forefinger.

Animal crackers. Behind the masks are (left to right) Joanna, Cally, Ian, Clare, Barry, B.J. *and* Mini.

Down she goes! Joanna watches B.J., disguised as a golfer, sink an easy putt on the 18th green at the Isle of Purbeck Golf Club. (Copyright Pauline Johnston)

What do you think of the show so far? B.J. interviews Eric Morecambe at his home in Harpenden. (Copyright *Herts Advertiser*, St Albans)

Have you heard this one? B.J. at a cricket occasion with (left to right) Ben Brocklehurst, Managing Director of *The Cricketer*, Asif Iqbal of Kent and Pakistan, and Lord Home. (Copyright Francis-Thompson Studios Ltd)

B.J. as Chairman of *Sporting Chance* congratulates the winning team. (Copyright John Mortimer)

Cricket in Corfu – a cabbie's view.   (Copyright Pauline Johnston)

Throwing the Cricket Ball competition 1976 on Sandown racecourse. Judges Denis Compton and Godfrey Evans congratulate the 18-year-old twins from Selby, Lee and Nick Furniss – first and second in the Club cricketers section. (Copyright Foto-Call)

Two old codgers . . . the Oval 1977. B.J. with his old Australian broadcasting mate Alan McGilvray.

The BBC *Test Match Special* commentary team in the box at Headingley, August 1977. (Copyright *Daily Express*)

Cheers! B.J. (note the orange juice) at a cricket lunch with Jim Laker and Frank Butler, Sports Editor of the *News of the World*.

In windswept Scarborough B.J. presents the 1976 Man of the Match Fenner Trophy to Gordon Greenidge of Hampshire.

Are they human? The *Twenty Questions* team in 1975, with B.J., Terry Wogan, Willie Rushton and the ladies, Bettine le Beau and Anona Wynn.   (Copyright *Radio Times*)

Fiery Fred – 'the greatest living Yorkshireman' (Sir Harold Wilson) at the launching of his autobiography *Ball of Fire*.   (Copyright Studio Frankfurt Ltd)

LEN HUTTON

CHARACTER	LEADERSHIP	TACTICAL SKILL	PLAYING ABILITY	PR WITH MEDIA	OFF THE FIELD
First of the professional captains. Reserved, withdrawn and wary with a dry wit and a twinkle in the eye. Appeared slightly suspicious of everyone and everything.	Not a natural but gained respect because of his great playing skill. Outwardly calm, but inwardly felt the pressures and got easily depressed. In the end it all got too much for him – hence his early retirement.	Mainly defensive but canny and well thought out. A good judge of the game and of his opponents' strengths and weaknesses. The first captain to introduce the slow over rate as a tactic. After the battering he himself had received from Lindwall and Miller he played the game hard and knew that NO ONE likes fast bowling – hence his great faith in Tyson.	A batsman of the highest possible class and a candidate for almost anyone's World XI of all time. Of all his many strokes the cover drive was the one I savour most.	Suspicious and reserved and could give answers in double talk which not only puzzled the interviewer but possibly Len himself!	Kept to himself but did the minimum required of a captain on the social side. Not a great speaker.

PETER MAY

CHARACTER	LEADERSHIP	TACTICAL SKILL	PLAYING ABILITY	PR WITH MEDIA	OFF THE FIELD
Friendly and pleasant with a certain schoolboy charm, but undoubtedly tough under the surface.	Unobtrusive but firm and expected anyone chosen to play in a Test to know what to do without being told. Played the game hard and relied on others to do the same. Preferred the grafter to the 'fancy' stroke player.	Followed in the Hutton tradition and like most Test captains preferred not to go for victory if it meant that there was the *slightest* risk of losing.	Top class – best batsman since the war. All the strokes but the on-drive his speciality. A sound fielder and a good close catcher.	Often felt he was unfairly treated hence tended to be suspicious and guarded in his answers. Difficult to get much out of him.	Socially very good and, although he didn't enjoy it, made an amusing speech with some gentle leg pulling.

COLIN COWDREY

CHARACTER	LEADERSHIP	TACTICAL SKILL	PLAYING ABILITY	PR WITH MEDIA	OFF THE FIELD
Gentle, friendly, good mannered, polite, sensitive. Tremendous enthusiasm for life, people and cricket, aided by his strong religious beliefs.	Established good team spirit and expected high standard of behaviour. Took great trouble to look after team off the field and to make sure they enjoyed the tour. On the field not dominant nor assertive enough when the crunch came.	Great knowledge of the individual techniques required, and had a deep knowledge of the game and all its traditions. Strangely defensive at times and asked *too* many people's advice which sometimes meant postponing vital decisions.	Outstanding, might have been the greatest of all but for strange lapses of confidence in his own ability. Magnificent timer of the ball with every stroke in the book plus 'the paddle' down to fine leg. A brilliant slip-fielder – one of the best ever.	Excellent. Took infinite trouble to try to help and made a point of involving the media on the tour with his team.	Certainly the best I have seen. Nothing too much trouble – infinite patience with everyone and attended every social function: visited schools, hospitals, churches, etc. A very good speaker.

TED DEXTER

CHARACTER	LEADERSHIP	TACTICAL SKILL	PLAYING ABILITY	PR WITH MEDIA	OFF THE FIELD
Could be haughty and aloof – could be the friendliest of persons. A man of moods. Nickname of 'Lord Edward' gives a good picture of his superb bearing and physique with the suspicion of him being slightly above mere mortals.	Largely by example when either batting or fielding. A great gambler in everyday life this was not reflected in his leadership which tended to be defensive.	Too much theory mingled with pragmatic inspiration or ideas. Not always easy to follow his line of thought!	Magnificent attacking player at his best when 'seeing off' fast bowlers with brilliant strokes off the front or back foot, especially the latter. A more than useful medium fast change bowler who would have been better handled by someone else!	Tried to cooperate but one got the impression that the media was something to be tolerated with the job.	Dependent on his moods. Could be excellent and always a great party-goer.

MIKE SMITH

CHARACTER	LEADERSHIP	TACTICAL SKILL	PLAYING ABILITY	PR WITH MEDIA	OFF THE FIELD
The players' captain. Unflappable, quiet, dry wit, great debunker of conceit and pomposity. A leg-puller whose somewhat 'owlish' appearance hid a good sense of humour.	Unobtrusive. Never asked anyone to do anything he would not do himself. Chose to field in the most dangerous close positions, and to take the batting risks himself when necessary. Not afraid to go for victory, but once a lead in a series had been achieved he was apt to 'sit on it'.	Sound with a good knowledge of the game but with an instinct against using spinners, possibly because he played them so well himself. Good at pressurising new batsmen.	Not quite consistent enough to rate in the top Test class. Vulnerable against fast bowling early in his innings. Especially strong on the leg side and developed 'the lap'. A good runner between the wickets and a superb fielder at short leg in spite of his glasses.	Pretty cagey and could act dumb under pressure of questioning. Difficult to get much out of him, though he was always friendly and cooperative.	Very good at the cricketer level but not too keen on the more formal social occasions and receptions, though he tried hard!

BRIAN CLOSE

CHARACTER	LEADERSHIP	TACTICAL SKILL	PLAYING ABILITY	PR WITH MEDIA	OFF THE FIELD
Brave, tough, gutsy, determined, obstinate with a delightful sense of humour and an unexpected giggle. Great talker – on any subject.	Strong leader who didn't mince his words. Highly respected by his players. Never gave up and encouraged his team to fight to the bitter end. He always made sure everyone knew what was expected of them.	More adventurous than most and full of Yorkshire cunning. A great believer in pressurising the opposition at every opportunity.	Never really reached his true potential. A natural games player. Tremendous guts standing up to fast bowling. Was discarded by selectors too early in his career. Fine close fielder standing suicidally within reach of the bat. A useful off-spin change bowler.	Very good and prepared to answer most questions in a down to earth though somewhat lengthy manner!	Good – especially if the other person or persons were prepared to listen!

RAY ILLINGWORTH

CHARACTER	LEADERSHIP	TACTICAL SKILL	PLAYING ABILITY	PR WITH MEDIA	OFF THE FIELD
Typical Yorkshireman with slight chip on shoulder and suspicious of most Southerners and the establishment of cricket. Dry sense of humour and good business sense.	Another players' captain who looked after his men both on and off the field. Got to know their problems and their moods. Knew when to encourage or sympathise. Fought for their welfare in every way. *On the field his expertise gained their 100 per cent support.	The best tactician of all. Great understanding of the game and an unrivalled assessor of his opponents' strengths and weaknesses. A good 'reader' of a match.	Made himself into a Test all-rounder and performed many rescue acts for England batting at No. 7. Tended to underbowl himself unless conditions were ideal for his off-spin with its variation of flight and pace. A useful gully.	One of the best captains whom I ever interviewed. Never shirked a question. However awkward it was, one got a straight answer – too straight for some!	The social niceties of a tour came bottom on his list of priorities. But he enjoyed a party.

MIKE DENNESS

CHARACTER	LEADERSHIP	TACTICAL SKILL	PLAYING ABILITY	PR WITH MEDIA	OFF THE FIELD
A friendly, chirpy but determined Scot with a cheerful outlook on life. Could be obstinate. Never as popular with his own Kent side as with other people. This may possibly have been partly due to his method of team selection.	At the start of his Test captaincy was apt to be too much of a loner, and did not consult his senior players. Was in a difficult position with five or six of his side having played in far more Tests than himself. Later when he had proved himself he did take advice but after that fateful 'team' decision to put Australia in at Edgbaston, probably now wishes he hadn't.	Shrewd enough, and perfected the tactics for limited-over cricket. Strangely, often seemed not to make the best use of Underwood.	A fine player of spin but on Australian tour showed a weakness of technique against Lillee and Thomson – but he was not the *only* one! An unselfish batsman who was prepared to take risks to make up for a slow start. A magnificent fielder especially in the covers.	Friendly enough but could show a certain amount of Scottish canniness when facing a difficult question.	A good mixer and useful speaker.

TONY GREIG

CHARACTER	LEADERSHIP	TACTICAL SKILL	PLAYING ABILITY	PR WITH MEDIA	OFF THE FIELD
Blond, tall, glamorous, good looking and friendly with lots of charm. Becomes a grimmer character on the field with a fierce determination to win, though still retaining his showmanship and outsize personality so far as the crowds are concerned.	A superb leader who created tremendous team spirit on a tour. Believed in involving his *whole* team, not just those playing in the Tests. Succeeded in imparting to them his own will to win or at least to fight 100 per cent. Believed in pressurising opposing batsmen by aggressive field placing, but more questionably seemed to believe in occasional pressure by *talking* to batsmen.	The weakest part of his captaincy though he improved slightly in India. Strangely defensive for such a character. Seemed to want to establish an unassailable base before taking risks to win. Some of his bowling changes and field placings against West Indies in 1976 made even me speechless!	A fine attacking batsman, but lacking in consistency. Helped by his long reach which makes bowling to him difficult. Magnificent at driving the ball or forcing it off the back foot. His habit of holding his bat aloft 'at the ready' makes his leg stump very vulnerable to a fast yorker. A magnificent fielder anywhere and one of the finest slip catchers I have ever seen. His fast medium bowling inconsistent but always liable to take a wicket when brought on to break a stand. His off-spin too unreliable to be effective.	The best ever in answering every question as truthfully and as candidly as possible. Nothing ever too much trouble for him but in his efforts to help the interviewer and give good value sometimes overdid it – eg his 'We'll make them grovel' remark about the West Indies.	First-class rapport with everyone and always seemed to do the right thing. Created tremendous charisma by his charm and glamorous appearance.

MIKE BREARLEY

CHARACTER	LEADERSHIP	TACTICAL SKILL	PLAYING ABILITY	PR WITH MEDIA	OFF THE FIELD
Outwardly a quiet, compassionate, friendly person with a nice smile, a good sense of humour and a strong social conscience. Inside a far tougher character with strong opinions and plenty of determination. Highly intelligent he got a first at Cambridge and passed top in the Civil Service exam. Always sympathetic to the underdog, and although I don't think he is really anti-establishment he is by inclination on the side of the workers!	Quiet and unobtrusive but firm. Never raises his voice. Asks for, and takes, advice from his senior players. Inherited the team spirit originally created by Greig, but has maintained and fostered it. Genuinely liked by the players. Made a great start by winning back the Ashes in his first series as captain.	A great student of of the game. Gives it much deep thought, especially field placing. Has a happy knack of timing his bowling changes correctly.	To me he is not quite Test class but will always produce a sound innings with some stylish strokes. Nurtured on the splendid Fenner pitches when he was at Cambridge. Plenty of guts and never flinches at the fast bowlers, possibly given confidence by his plastic skull protector. Originally a wicket-keeper is now a highly competent catcher at first slip.	Absolutely first-class. Cooperative, friendly and happy to answer any reasonable question. Takes any implied criticism in good part.	Unfortunately I have never been on a tour with him. But with his basic friendly and sympathetic character I would expect him to be a great success.

And there you have my assessments of the thirteen Test captains. You may well have very different ideas as to their characters and ability. But these are *my* opinions and based on them I have chosen the one who I think has been the best *all round* captain. I will give my verdict and reasons right at the end of the book. So why don't you make *your* choice now and see whether we agree? If you want to crib, the answer is on page 220.

And as a final guide here is a table (accurate until end August 1977) showing the varying success of each captain.

	No. of times	*MATCHES*		
	Captain	*Won*	*Lost*	*Drawn*
Yardley	15	4	8	3
Mann	7	2	0	5
Brown	15	5	6	4
Hutton	20	9	3	8
May	41	21	10	10
Cowdrey	27	8	4	15
Dexter	30	9	7	14
Smith	25	5	3	17
Close	7	6	0	1
Illingworth	31	12	5	14
Denness	19	6	6	7
Greig	14	3	5	6
Brearley	5	3	0	2

Ninth Over Out of the
mouths . . .

In *It's Been A Lot of Fun* I listed quite a few of my better known gaffes which I have made during cricket commentaries. Not only do they still happen but people keep reminding me of ones which I had forgotten all about. Such as when a few years ago a mouse ran across the pitch during a Test Match at Edgbaston. Play was held up while players tried to catch it, and the poor little mouse showed up beautifully on our TV zoom lens. I was doing the commentary on TV and when describing the chase said: 'They are bound to catch it soon – it's got no hole to go down.' I then unfortunately added: 'Lucky it's not a ladies' match.' All I meant was that they would be rushing about screaming as they are always meant to do when they see a mouse. But Denis Compton especially thought it was very funny!

There was also the occasion when I evidently greeted listeners with these words: 'You join us at an interesting time. Ray Illingworth has just relieved himself at the Pavilion End!'

After the Test Match at the Oval against the West Indies I received a letter which I suspect was a leg-pull, though I am not sure. I was suspicious because it was signed by a Miss Mainpiece! She begged me to be more careful what I said because so many young boys listened to our radio commentaries. She then cited an example of what she meant by accusing me of saying at the beginning of an over bowled by the West Indian fast bowler Michael Holding to Peter Willey – 'The bowler's Holding the batsman's Willey!' If I *did* say it I swear I didn't mean it!

I also made a completely nonsensical remark at Northampton during the August match between Northants and

Worcestershire. Although it could have had an important influence on the result of the County Championship there was a disappointingly small crowd there. And I said, 'There's a disappointing crowd here today, just a few cars scattered around the boundary boards. In fact' – I went on – 'I would say that there are more cars here today than people!' Just work that one out – did the cars drive themselves in?

But even the most innocent remark can have a double meaning – *if* you have that sort of mind! Such as when on one occasion I said to Radio 2 listeners who had just joined us: 'D'Oliveira is getting badly punished by the Hampshire batsmen. A moment or two before you joined us Barry Richards hit one of Dolly's balls clean out of the ground.' A perfectly innocent remark but one that produced sniggers in the commentary box as my companions conjured up visions of this remarkable and very painful feat!

But the cricket commentators are not the only ones who drop clangers, and the Olympic Games at Montreal produced one or two good ones. During the swimming Peter Jones on the radio said: 'It's the pool that sets the spectators alight', and Alan Weekes on TV: 'If Wilkie goes on like this he'll be home and dry!' It seems uncertain whether it was David Coleman or Ron Pickering who during the 800 metres final talking about Juantorena the eventual winner commented on TV: 'Every time the big Cuban opens his legs, he shows his class!'

Frank Bough has admitted he once said as he handed over to a boxing fight, '. . . and your carpenter is Harry Commentator'. One of the most famous, of course, was John Snagge's desperate cry during the Boat Race when his launch could not keep up with the boats. 'I don't know who's ahead – it's either Oxford or Cambridge!'

But it was the golf commentators who had the biggest nightmare of all, and nightly went down on their knees and prayed that Coles would not be drawn to play against Hunt.

Two more gaffes are attributed to David Coleman. The first at the Montreal Olympic Games where he said: 'To win a gold medal you've GOT to come first.' The second was at a League match in which Manchester United were playing:

'United are buzzing around the goalmouth like a lot of red blue-bottles.'

Another good soccer one came from John Motson during the 1977 FA Cup Final. 'If Liverpool lose today it will cast grave doubts on their ability to win the treble.'

But poor Hugh Johns made a perfectly innocent remark on ITV to which some dirty-minded (!) people took exception. All he said was, 'The referee is now looking at his whistle!'

Jimmy Hill is credited with this gem – 'Over now to Nigel Starmer-Smith who has had seven craps as scum-half for England!'

And there's a delightful one which Rex Alston made many years ago, '. . . So over now to Old John Arlott at Trafford.'

I am never quite certain who was the originator of *this* remark – not much double entendre about it! Anyway, it was a cricket commentator who was talking about Cunis the New Zealand fast bowler. 'Cunis,' he said, 'a funny sort of name. Neither one thing nor the other!' I promise you it wasn't me!

Incidentally, talking of names, Bill Frindall assures me that once when referring to Asif Mahsood the Pakistan bowler I called him by mistake: 'Masif *Ahsood!*'

And appropriately, in Jubilee Year, I was reminded recently of an occasion when Henry Riddell was the commentator on some royal procession or other. After describing the Queen's carriage and escorts as they passed his commentary position, the carriage turned a corner and went out of his sight. Said Henry: 'And now the Queen's gone round the bend!'

But one of the best gaffes of all was perpetrated recently by a lady journalist when writing about our world champion motor cyclist Barry Sheene. She described him as the glamorous sportsman with that throbbing power between his legs! I think that caps anything which we broadcasters have said.

Tenth Over Sadness and joy

It was with much sadness that in September 1976 I heard of the death of Arthur Gilligan at the age of eighty-one. I had seen him at Lord's earlier in the summer, looking and sounding as well as ever, and telling me about his skiing holiday in the winter. For years he and I used to swop stories, and it was my great pleasure when one of mine was rewarded by his cheerful laugh.

Arthur was an old friend of my father-in-law in the twenties and used to stay with him when Sussex were playing Yorkshire. Just after I had married Pauline in 1948 I was looking through her family scrapbook and saw a photograph of Pauline as a very young girl sitting on Arthur's knee. So the next time I saw him I said that I had a bone to pick with him. He looked somewhat perturbed and asked me what it was.

'Arthur,' I said, 'I see that you have been dangling my wife on your knee, and I'd rather you didn't do it again.' He looked so puzzled and upset that I quickly explained to him what I was referring to.

I used to see Arthur play at the Saffrons when I was at my preparatory school at Eastbourne. He was then – in the early twenties – a very fast bowler, magnificent mid-off and a dashing hard-hitting batsman. His 1924–5 side to Australia was probably the most popular to go there this century, though admittedly they did lose and that always helps! But there is no doubt that ever after that he himself was one of the best loved Englishmen in Australia. Not just because of his sporting captaincy but because of his great popularity down under as a cricket commentator. He spoke in a natural, friendly way and even when he could bring himself to criticise, he did it kindly. He formed a famous double act with his old adversary and great friend Vic Richardson. They always backed each other up and never disagreed with what the other said. 'In my opinion he was plumb out. What do you think, Vic?' 'I quite agree Arthur.' Or, 'I'd say the pitch is taking spin now, Arthur.' 'Yes, I quite agree, Vic.'

It may sound trite now but all I can say is that it created a very friendly atmosphere and made pleasant listening. Arthur knew he tended to agree with everyone but told me how on one occasion, it had helped him out of a mess. Once on a hot day during a Headingley Test he fell asleep after lunch and as he dozed he vaguely heard Rex Alston's voice droning on without taking in what he was saying. Suddenly he woke with a start as Rex nudged him in the ribs and said: 'That's how I saw it. What do you say Arthur?'

Arthur reacted quickly for one who had only just woken up. 'I entirely agree with everything you have just said, Rex,' he replied, as his chin sunk once more into his chest. Being Arthur, no one saw anything funny in his reply.

He also swore it was true that a lady once came up to him at a Test and gave him a packet of indigestion tablets. 'Will you please give these to Brian Statham, Mr Gilligan?' 'Yes, of course I will, but why?' replied Arthur. 'Oh,' said the lady, 'I heard you say on the radio that Statham wasn't bowling as fast as usual as he was having trouble with the wind'!

Another friend of mine – and of cricket – who died in the spring of 1977 was Charles Cobham, whom we all knew at Eton as Bargy Lyttelton. He was a big man in every sense of the word, with a tremendous knowledge of cricket – its history, records and playing techniques. He was a superb raconteur and after-dinner speaker with a fund of stories about players past and present, each one accompanied by his own brand of chuckle.

At Eton he never got a cricket colour but played in Middle Club – the equivalent I suppose of the seventh or eighth XI in the school. He bowled prodigious spinners. He made them appear to be more threatening than they were by snapping the fingers of his *left* hand at the exact moment he delivered the ball with his *right*. He could always hit a cricket (and golf) ball vast distances, his most famous hit being the one which cleared the Frank Woolley Stand at Canterbury. But at Eton he suffered from the terrible pitches on which he had to play. So did my friend William Douglas-Home who was prompted to write a letter once to the *Eton College Chronicle*. In one of their recent reports of a first XI match they had said that the Eton captain had failed yet again and had obviously struck a bad patch. 'Tell him to come and play on some of our Middle Club pitches, and he'll strike a few more!' wrote William.

Charles of course rose to great heights culminating with his very successful Governor-Generalship of New Zealand. But to his immense satisfaction he ultimately became a better and more successful cricketer than most of those who had got their XI at Eton. As captain of Worcestershire in the late thirties he brought a gaiety and sense of enjoyment into county cricket which is so sadly lacking today. In spite of the many high offices he held, at Court and in the City, he was the least pompous of men and told many stories against himself.

Once, when captaining Worcestershire against Gloucestershire he had to go into bat against Charlie Parker on a sticky wicket. Off his first ball he was missed at slip by Hammond of all people – a sharp low chance to his right hand. The second ball hit the stumps without removing the bails. The third hit him on the pads and he survived a confident appeal for LBW. The fourth, believe it or not, went to Hammond's left hand and again was dropped. The fifth mercifully bowled him neck and crop. As he made his way back to the pavilion somewhat embarrassed he passed Charlie Barnett who was fielding at third man. 'Bad luck, skipper,' Charlie said. 'You were never quite in!'

Charles always used to say that his idea of heaven was to bat against his own bowling. I wouldn't know whether he will actually be able to play cricket in heaven, but I am willing to bet that even if he isn't, he'll be holding the floor, with his stories, and making them all laugh up there!

At the end of October for the first time in my life I was asked to give the address at a memorial service. It was for a unique and remarkable character called Buns Cartwright, who for forty years had been secretary of the Eton Ramblers, and their president for another twenty-one. I had known him since the early thirties when I first played for the Ramblers, and had been his friend ever since. I approached this daunting task with great trepidation because he had so many friends and acquaintances in every walk of life. They knew all about him – his many good points and the inevitable few which were not so good, which we all have.

He was an eccentric, especially in his dress, which was usually a blue pin-stripe suit with carnation and blue plimsolls, topped with a brown cap, or one of his many sombreros with the Rambler ribbon around it. He was one of a dying breed – man about town, clubman, sportsman and *bon viveur*. He never owned nor drove a car but could be seen at nearly every big sporting occasion, with cricket, tennis, golf and racing taking priority. He was irascible, gruff, critical but underneath it all was a kind man with a sharp wit and keen sense of humour. He was also an inveterate gambler and when my wife Pauline went to see him in hospital he even offered her odds of 7–4 against his own recovery.

It was obviously no good giving a solemn oration full of false praise and sentiment about such a character. So I decide to recall him as we all knew him and included one or two of the more respectable stories about him. The Guards Chapel was absolutely packed and it was the first time I had ever heard laughs at a Memorial Service. But I am certain that it was what he would have wanted, and in a strange way showed our love and friendship for him, and our gratitude for all he had done for us. But it is not a task which I want to do again.

In the New Year 1977 we went down to Windsor to the delightful Theatre Royal which is run so beautifully and efficiently by John Counsell. We went to see a new play by William Douglas-Home, one of three which eventually ran simultaneously in the West End. It was called *In the Red* and was all about a popular playwright who lived entirely on a vast overdraft at his bank – I wonder where William got all the necessary background information! I thought the play very funny and so did all the provincial audiences. But it failed when it came to London, possibly because the audiences looked on it as a fantasy, just not believing that anyone could really live like that.

There were some very good jokes in *In the Red* and I suggested another to William – I am not sure whether he put it in or not. It was the old one of the client who was being persistently pressed by his bank manager to pay off his overdraft. The client finally got fed up. 'You remember, two years ago, when I was in credit with you for five hundred pounds?' he asked the bank manager. 'Yes, I do,' replied the bank manager grudgingly. 'Well,' said the client, 'I didn't go on badgering you to pay *me* back, did I?'

Incidentally, I must try that out on *my* bank manager some time. The trouble is you have to be in credit first!

It was in February 1977 that I suffered a great disappointment. Len Maddocks – the old Australian wicketkeeper and manager of their 1977 team to England – rang me from Australia to ask me to go out there for the Centenary Test at Melbourne in March. He wanted me to make a speech at the champagne breakfast which was going to take place on the first morning of the match before play started. I couldn't really believe it. Many of my cricketing friends were already booked to go and here I was being asked to fly 13,000 miles just to make a speech. I dearly wanted to go, but, alas, the invitation came too late. I was already committed for *Down Your Way*, at least four dinners and the Boat Race, and could not cancel them all at such short notice.

I shall always be sorry that I was not able to be there at such a unique occasion – unique, because when again will there ever be such a gathering of past and present Test players spanning nearly sixty years of English and Australian Test cricket. What a fabulous opportunity it was for old and young players to meet and swop experiences. Everyone who went there was full of praise for the wonderful hospitality and organisation. Nothing seems to have gone wrong. Even the weather and the cricket matched the occasion. The gods must indeed have been on the side of the Australian organisers. Fancy arranging for the Queen to visit the match on the *fifth day* and to find that when she arrived the game was building up to a dramatic climax. The betting must have been that the match would have already finished or be heading for a dull draw. And to think that England lost by 45 runs – exactly the same margin by which they had lost that first Test in 1877. And what about Randall's brilliant and cheeky innings of 174? You can see why I was so disappointed – which reminds me of the difference between disappointment and despair. Disappointment is the first time you discover you can't do it twice. Despair is the second time you discover you can't do it once!

Jubilee Day 7 June 1977

Over the past thirty-two years I have been extremely lucky in having a grandstand seat for all the big Royal occasions during that time – and incidentally I have always been *outside* somewhere, never *inside*. First in 1947 I was on the Victoria Memorial outside Buckingham Palace for the wedding of Princess Elizabeth and Prince Philip. Then in 1952 it was Hyde Park corner for TV for King George VI's funeral, and again for TV in Hyde Park for the Coronation procession in 1953. Next I was with the TV cameras outside the garden of No. 10 Downing Street on Horse Guards Parade to describe Princess Margaret's wedding procession and, finally, thirteen years later I was commentating for radio by the Citadel on the corner of Horse Guards for Princess Anne's wedding. On all these occasions I have had superb close-up views of all the processions as they passed by, but never in my wildest dreams did I ever imagine that I would take part in one.

It happened on Jubilee Day when I was covering part of the celebrations for radio. My first position which I reached by 8 am was on Queen Anne's statue outside the steps of St Paul's Cathedral leading up to the west door. Scaffolding and a platform had been placed round the statue so that we could see right down Ludgate Hill to Ludgate Circus or behind us up the twenty-eight steps into the Cathedral itself as the congregation took their seats.

It was cool, windy and cloudy but not actually raining as we made our way through the crowds already five or six deep behind the barriers. Many had been there all night and we actually found a vicar from the Isle of Wight who, with his family, had been on the pavement since midnight on the

Sunday. Everyone was in tremendous spirits and already at this early hour there was plenty for them to watch with troops marching along the route to take up their positions. A dustman at the back of a cart which had been sprinkling sand on the wet streets acknowledged the cheers of the crowd in the Queen's best manner. There were wolf whistles from the teenage girls as some Scottish soldiers marched by, their kilts being blown up by the wind. I'm sure that at least some of the crowd now know the answer to that eternal question: 'Do they?' or 'Don't they?' An important-looking official in top hat and tails had a rather mincing gait and was greeted with cries of 'Are you free, Mr Humphries?' Some of the crowd kept singing *For She's a Jolly Good Sovereign* and others shouted the odds when a large picture hat blew off the head of a stately dowager and was pursued down Ludgate Hill by her top-hatted escort.

Between 9.30 and 10.30 am the official guests arrived, some like the Speaker and Lord Mayor in their own coaches. Then came the carriage processions with their escorts and the crowds were really getting their reward for their long wait. Princess Anne and Captain Mark Phillips came first, then the Queen Mother and her two grandsons Prince Andrew and Prince Edward. And what a cheer she got! As usual she looked superb.

And then the big moment with the clip-clop of the House-hold Cavalry coming slowly up the hill, followed by the eight Windsor Greys pulling the four-ton newly gilded Golden Coach with the Queen and the Duke of Edinburgh, waving to the crowds as the band of the Honourable Artillery Company played the National Anthem. I got a perfect view as the coach wheeled slowly round in front of the steps, and there was an anxious moment as one of the greys slipped and took fright.

Two days later I was in Goring on Thames for a *Down Your Way* and interviewed the Queen's saddler who has a saddle and harness shop there. He told me he had been up at 4 am in the Royal Mews preparing and checking all the harness. He revealed something which I don't think anyone saw – I certainly didn't and I was only a few feet away. As the Golden Coach was swinging round to the right, the off-side back wheel knocked against one of the bollards outside the Cathedral. It not only shook the coach, but the wheel might well have come off. I expect the Queen and the Duke must have realised something had gone wrong when they felt the bump.

I was able to watch the Royal party greeted on the steps by the Archbishop of Canterbury and the Lord Mayor, and then see them disappear into the brilliantly lit interior of St Paul's before the big west doors were closed. The service was relayed to the crowds outside and I was able to listen to it from my perch on Queen Anne's statue.

At the end of the service the Royal party came down the steps and then the Queen and Duke of Edinburgh, accompanied only by the Lord and Lady Mayoress, started what was to be the Queen's happiest and most successful of all her many walk-abouts. It was certainly seen by more people than all the others put together because of the worldwide TV coverage of Jubilee Day.

I said just now that the Queen was accompanied by the Lord Mayor and Lady Mayoress. That's not quite true. By some means the BBC Radio had been given permission for me to follow closely behind the Queen with a small mobile transmitter. I just couldn't believe my luck, though I felt some slight trepidation at having to walk through so many thousands of cheering people. The Queen was used to it, but I definitely wasn't! Anyway, with my producer, Roger MacDonald, and our engineer, Cedric Johnson, we set off. We followed just a few yards behind the Queen and I gave the best commentary I could manage as I walked along. It was a really fantastic experience. The Queen stopped every few yards to talk to the crowd, and accepted dozens of little posies from small children all along the route. The Lord Mayor Sir Robin Gillett did his best to act as a carrier bag!

Many people thrust their hands out for the Queen to shake, but I only saw her shake hands with one person — an old grey-haired soldier with a cluster of medals on his chest, and as she left him, there were tears pouring down his cheeks. A magnificent moment for him. We soon got a long way ahead of the Duke, who as usual had plenty to say to everyone and cracked jokes which drew roars of laughter from the crowds. We walked through the gardens on the north side of St Paul's, then out into Cheapside through the lines of spectators. The noise was deafening and as you can imagine I got quite a bit of friendly barracking from the crowd. They must have been surprised to see me coming *Down Their Way*, and amazed that I was following so closely behind the Queen apparently talking to myself.

I stopped and asked quite a few of them what the Queen had said to them and generally it seemed to be: 'Where do you come from?' and 'How long have you been waiting?' and so on. It was noticeable that when the Queen stopped to talk to someone, the cheering stopped, only to be renewed as soon as she went on her way. The Duke occasionally caught up with us and even remarked that I looked like a man from space with my headphones and the aerial on our mobile transmitter.

When we turned into the narrow King Street with high buildings on either side the noise became deafening. I was getting a bit cocky by now and so far forgot myself as to ask the Duke whether he would say something to the listeners over my microphone. With a cheerful grin he shouted, 'I can't hear myself speak!'

We finally reached the Guildhall and the walk had taken about half an hour. Even the Queen, so used to these sorts of demonstrations of love and loyalty, must have been over-whelmed by the tremendous reception she received from every-one along the route. I certainly will never forget it and it was definitely one of the highlights of my broadcasting career. I was naturally very pleased that the BBC used some of my commentary on a band of the BBC Jubilee Commemorative Record of the broadcasts of the Silver Jubilee Events, which they published in aid of the Queen's Jubilee Fund.

The day before my sixty-fifth birthday – 23 June – produced one of the happiest surprises of my life. It all started way back in March 1977 when I received a letter from my old friend Edward Halliday, the famous portrait painter who lives just down the road from us in Hamilton Terrace. He wrote that he had always wanted to paint me and would consider it a great honour if I would allow him to do so for his own enjoyment. I was naturally very surprised but thrilled. Ted is president of the Royal Society of Portrait Painters and numbers among his past sitters the Queen (goodness knows how many times), the Queen Mother, Prince Philip, Prince Charles and countless heads of state and VIPs from all walks of life. So I sat down immediately to write and say how honoured and delighted I was to join this galaxy of stars.

I imagined that he would show my portrait at the Royal Society of Portrait Painters' annual exhibition. I had to restrain myself from running as I went along to pop the letter through his letterbox. We had half a dozen sittings of about two hours a time and we thoroughly enjoyed ourselves gossiping and talking about every subject under the sun – refreshed every now and again by a glass of sherry. Ted and I had known each other from the old Television Newsreel days at Alexandra Palace. He had been the commentator and I used to go down there to do voice-overs on the cricket films. He likes cricket and knows everybody in all walks of life. So we were not short of conversation!

After the last sitting, Ted expressed himself satisfied, except for the background which he was going to make the Grandstand at Lord's with Father Time on the weather-vane on top of it. At this point I hadn't even had one glance at the picture, though Ted asked Pauline to come along and give her opinion. I was putting off the shock for as long as possible.

With the cricket season in full swing I thought no more about it, presuming that Ted would tell me when it was finished. I had heard nothing by the middle of June when Barry and Clare told me that they were going to take me out to dinner on the night before my birthday. The rendezvous would be secret, but I was to be ready in a dinner jacket by 7.15 pm when they would pick me up.

This is what I did, and at the appointed time on the day they turned up to find Pauline and me all dressed up and waiting to go. They seemed rather excited about something but refused a drink when I offered them one, which surprised me as I had put a bottle of champagne in the fridge. Anyway, the reason for their odd behaviour was soon to be revealed. The doorbell began to ring, and in streamed twenty of my closest friends, all dolled up in evening dress. Bottles of champagne and glasses soon appeared from some secret hiding place and we all went into the garden and had a splendid party.

Then came another surprise. We were all summoned indoors and there was Ted Halliday with the completed picture – a present, I was told, from Pauline with the children providing the frame. Needless to say I was very touched but pleased beyond belief. The whole party and the picture had been such a wonderfully kept secret. It has all been Pauline's idea and she had organised everything, starting her planning in January, so as to make sure my friends could reserve the date. She had also contacted Tony Smith of *Down Your Way*, Peter Baxter of *Test Match Special*, and Paddy Davis, the marvellous lady who arranges all my speaking engagements. Pauline asked them all to make sure not to ask me to do any job on that day and sure enough it remained blank in my diary. It was certainly one of the best-kept secrets of my life and I had no inkling of what was up.

But there was still more to come. After we had consumed quite a bit of champagne, I was blindfolded, put in a car, and driven off to an unknown destination. I had no idea where we were going and didn't guess even when we stopped and I was led into a building, across a thickly carpeted entrance hall and down some stairs. Then I guessed it, as I heard the tinkling piano which could be no one else except Ian Stewart. So it was the Savoy, where all my friends had already arrived and we had two tables of twelve in the restaurant. We had a wonderful evening and danced into the early hours with a huge birthday cake with a cricket match being played on top, plus of course *Happy Birthday to You* from the band. What a lucky chap I am to have such a super wife and family, and so many nice friends, who actually paid for their own suppers! They had all been at similar sorts of parties when we were all aged fifty in 1962 and sixty in 1972. It seems that all our Mums and Dads must have had a rare old time in 1911 and 1912!

Oh, I had almost forgotten about the picture. I must admit that as many people hate the sound of their own voice when they hear it recorded, so do I dislike looking at pictures of myself. But Ted had certainly got a wonderful likeness, whether *I* liked what I saw or not. One of my 'friends' said charmingly that he could tell which was me as Father Time was holding a scythe.

One of the bonuses of becoming an OAP in London is the free bus pass to which one becomes entitled. I went to collect mine from the City Hall in Victoria Street, and returned by bus for my first free ride. It was quite an exciting moment as the bus conductor came along saying: 'Fares, please.' It was, however, slightly deflating that as I reached for my brand new pass, the conductor looked at me and murmured, 'That's all right guvnor, don't bother,' and continued along the bus without waiting to see my pass. Did I look *that* old?

Eleventh Over # Dear Sir, I want to be a cricket commentator

I think this would be a good place in which to say a few words about cricket commentary. I get lots of letters from young boys who say that when they grow up they want to be cricket commentators (in my day it was engine drivers!). They usually ask how to set about it, how can they learn, and what qualifications ought they to have. It's very difficult to give a satisfactory answer, because so far as cricket is concerned, there is only ONE staff job on the BBC – that of BBC Cricket Correspondent. I was the first one appointed in 1963 and then after my retirement from the staff in 1972 I was succeeded by Christopher Martin-Jenkins. All the TV commentators are freelances and only Christopher and Don Mosey of the radio commentators are on the staff. The rest of us are freelances.

Any budding young commentator should read every book which he can get hold of about cricket. He should try to learn its history and absorb its atmosphere and do his best to understand all the laws and regulations. He should watch as much good cricket as possible and of course play it himself. If he can borrow a tape-recorder he should go to any match where he knows most of the players and practise talking about the game as far away from the other spectators as he can get. He should try to describe exactly what is going on and keep going for at least fifteen minutes without drying up. It won't be easy at first but he will find that as his confidence grows it will become easier to keep the flow going. The secret is practice and he mustn't mind if the other spectators think that he is mad chatting away to himself!

Another stepping stone to the commentary box is a job on the local paper or at the local radio station. The paper will help him put his thoughts into words and the radio will teach him the art of projecting himself into the microphone – ie broadcasting. The snag is, of course, that it's not easy to get jobs in either of these media but it is something well worth trying. In fact commentators on local radio do by far the longest stints of commentary these days except for the Test Match commentators. Another possible training ground is the hospital broadcasts which take place from so many county grounds. I'm never quite sure how the admirable people who give up so much of their spare time manage to learn to commentate in the first place. Perhaps they just practise on the poor patients right from the start!

And now for the art of cricket commentary itself. I don't think I can do better than repeat, in the rest of this chapter, what I wrote on the subject in the 1975 edition of *Armchair Cricket*, which I edited for the BBC.

It is an art for which there is no real school except experience at the microphone at the expense of the listener or the viewer. This is one reason why cricket commentators tend to be mostly in the thirty-five to sixty-five age bracket. It takes that long to learn! Nowadays, except for the ball-by-ball Test Match commentaries, there is little opportunity to practise commentary. Up to the mid-sixties there were regular broadcasts of twenty- to thirty-minute periods from county matches. Now it is usually only one- to three-minute reports, so that the budding commentator has no chance to test his ability to keep going for long periods, which is what the top commentators have to do. In addition a young voice lacks the authority of an older one and because of cricket's slower tempo this is more noticeable than with other games.

So, it's not easy to become a cricket commentator and more or less impossible without a large slice of luck, such as being available at the right place at the right time when the opportunity occurs.

Now for the qualifications:

1. Good health – 'the show must go on'.
2. A gift of the gab and the ability to keep talking.
3. A clear, strong voice which must sound confident. The accent doesn't matter, though in fact a dialect comes over

particularly well in cricket. But personality is important and can 'come through' in a voice.

4. The ability to put into words what he is seeing, which means that besides being observant he must have a varied and colourful vocabulary and a sound use of good English. The long periods of comparative inaction during a cricket match give the listeners an all too easy chance to notice imperfections in syntax or language.

5. And most important of all – for without it he can never become a cricket commentator – he must have a deep knowledge of the game, its laws and regulations, its customs, its record, its history and its players.

Acquaintance – or even better – friendship with the players is a tremendous asset and helps give an understanding of what goes on 'in the middle'. A commentator should have played the game himself, though not necessarily in the highest class. TV commentators these days are usually ex-Test cricketers whereas on the radio they are professional broadcasters supported by ex-Test players as summarisers. But then there is a great difference in the commentary techniques of TV and radio and there is no doubt in my mind that television is the more difficult.

Television Commentary

The first thing for a TV cricket commentator to realise is that he can never hope to please everybody *any* of the time. In fact he will be jolly lucky if he manages to please anybody *all* the time. Cricket, like golf, is a game played at a much slower tempo than most of the other televised sports such as football, racing, athletics, etc. There are, of course, many moments of excitement and tension but they are spread out over a whole day, and the action is anyway much slower. This means that the commentator's remarks drop like stones on a still pond. The viewer has time to listen and digest them and to weigh up their meaning and their accuracy. In the faster games a slight fluff or inaccuracy by the commentator is soon forgotten within a few seconds as a new situation develops on the screen. So the cricket commentator's comments must be concise and fit the picture exactly, and be well thought out and accurate while having to be made spontaneously at a moment's notice. This means that he must have a complete and expert knowledge of the game. He has to comment rather than give a running commentary, which is basically what happens with football or racing on TV.

So the cricket commentator always has to ask himself the vital question: 'When to talk and when not to talk?' It's easy to trot out trite instructions such as: 'Only talk when you can add to the picture', but it isn't as easy as that. First of all there is the expert viewer who plays or has played the game. He knows the laws and regulations, and all the players by sight. On switching on he only wants to hear who won the toss, the score, a report on the weather and an opinion about the pitch. After that he just wants to be kept up to date with the score and to make his own judgements on the playbacks after an appeal or a wicket has fallen.

I can understand this. A commentator on TV should, in my view, be like a knowledgeable friend who sits alongside you at a sporting event, and who fills in the details which you don't know. I enjoy watching cricket with a friend but if he starts to tell me what is happening, who so-and-so is or why the captain has moved a certain fieldsman, I feel like crowning him. I think I know and just don't want to be told.

But sitting alongside me there may well be someone who welcomes all this sort of information, and wants help with identity of the players and explanations of the laws. And so it is on TV. A large majority of the viewers are not cricket experts. I should know from some of the letters I have received in the past. What is a 'chinaman', 'silly mid-off', or a 'googly'? What is the LBW law and how many ways can a batsman be out off a no ball? Or once when I said that 'Ray Illingworth has two short legs, one of them square', a lady wrote and told me not to be so personal. Or when I said that Peter May was lucky to have made a century as 'he was dropped when two', back came a letter bemoaning the carelessness of mothers with their young children.

So, the TV cricket commentator has to try to strike the happy medium, knowing that there is really no such thing.

He will always have irate and dissatisfied viewers who will say either: 'Why on earth can't he stop talking?', or 'Why can't he tell us more?'

Radio Commentary

As he has no camera to help him the radio commentator must paint the picture himself – with words. He is the eyes of every listener and must describe in as much detail as possible everything he sees. As opportunity offers he should describe the features of the ground so that the listener who has never been there can conjure up his own idea of what it is like. It also helps if the commentator explains the exact position from which he is broadcasting in relation to the play. A brief description of the main features and characteristics of the players bring the game to life – 'he has red, curly hair, wears size 14 boots, scratches his nose before every ball . . .', etc. There is also more time on radio for details and records of players' careers.

All this information is useful to fill in the gaps which do occur during a game of cricket – when the fast bowlers are walking back to the start of their long runs, during the drinks interval or when the umpires go off to search for a new ball. But there is one cardinal rule: NEVER MISS A BALL. All this information must stop as soon as the bowler starts his run. The commentator must then describe in detail exactly what is happening until the ball becomes dead.

The art of good commentary is to get into an automatic rhythm with a description of:

The bowler running up.
His approach to the umpire and the wicket.
The delivery, the type of ball and where it has pitched.
The batsman's stroke.
Where the ball has gone.
Who is fielding or chasing it.
How many runs the batsmen are taking.
And finally when the ball has been returned to the wicket-keeper or bowler say how many runs have been added to the team's and batsman's score.

Only then is it permissible to leave the action and talk about something else, until the bowler returns to his mark. Then back to the rhythm again to describe the next ball.

Some Hints to Budding Commentators

1. Have light and shade in your voice so that during quiet periods you can talk normally and not too fast. Then when there is sudden action or excitement you can increase your tempo and raise your voice, though of course, without shouting.
2. Always think of yourself as speaking to ONE person, not to millions. You are that person's friend and guide. Tell him or her what you yourself would like to hear if you were not at that match.
3. Try not to talk over applause, especially when a batsman is returning to the pavilion after a big score. Let his reception register. This is often easier said than done, as there are many details about his innings to give to the listener before the new batsman comes out.
4. Try not to describe in too much detail how a batsman is out. Leave that to the expert summariser.
5. Remember that you are a commentator not a critic. So don't criticise an umpire's decision. Whatever you may think about it, he is in a better position to judge than you.
6. At the end of each over, give the bowler's analysis, the total and the scores of the two batsmen. Then shut up, so that the summariser can come straight in.

There is one problem which is common to both TV and radio commentators – when to give the score. The answer is as often and as unobtrusively as possible without interrupting the action, and at the very least whenever a run is scored and at the end of each over. This may be annoying to the lucky viewers or listeners who stay switched on for the whole period. But tens of thousands are switching on every minute and there's nothing more infuriating than having to wait for five or ten minutes before hearing the score. That's why in these days of an over taking up to five minutes it's a good idea to slip in the score during an over even if a run hasn't been added. In addition, of course, newcomers will want to hear details of what has happened before, so the scorecard should be shown on TV or read out on radio at least every ten minutes.

There remains one fundamental difference between the TV and radio commentators today. On TV with their galaxy of ex-Test players they nowadays concentrate solely on the cricket. They give an extremely expert and professional analysis of the play, with critical opinions on the captains' tactics and the skills of the batsmen and bowlers. But they are not encouraged to be humorous about the fringe aspects of cricket, which provide so much of the colour and fun – the fat member asleep in the pavilion, the bored blonde knitting in the crowd, the umpire's funny hat, etc. But, probably because they have more time to fill, radio commentators are given a freer rein, and indulge in more lighthearted descriptions and reminiscences, and a certain amount of friendly banter in the box.

But whatever the style of commentary one final word of warning to ALL commentators – NEVER MISS A BALL. If you do it's sure to be the one that takes a wicket.

Twelfth Over **It's the Ashes!**
It's the Ashes!

After the glorious summer of 1976, England's victory in India, and all the euphoria of the Centenary Test, it was too much to hope that cricket could continue to be so lucky. Not only did the skies open for most of May, and much of the summer, but on 11 May the Packer affair burst upon the cricketing world. I'll deal with that later but meanwhile let's take a look at the cricket which was played in spite of the rain.

As soon at the Australian team was announced most of us thought that England had a good chance of regaining the Ashes. Except for the class of Chappell and the threat of Thomson provided he was fit, the team did not appear to be up to the standard of past Australian teams. It had too many players who lacked experience of playing under English conditions, and because of the terrible May weather, this weakness was never really overcome. Match after match played by the tourists was ruined by rain, so that by the time the first Prudential match took place at the beginning of June, the whole Australian team was woefully short of practice – especially the inexperienced newcomers.

On the other hand, English supporters had a new feeling of hope and optimism. The tide seemed to have turned and there now appeared to be a nucleus of promising young batsmen round the counties. There were also more spinners, possibly due to the high over rate demanded for county cricket of 19.50 overs per hour with fines to be paid by both county and players if the target was not reached. This meant that every county captain was forced to give his spinners more bowling than in the past. England, too, had a plentiful supply of the fast medium bowlers which are so much their speciality.

The only real lack was young, fast bowlers, though for the time being Willis was in great form. His career had been marred by injuries and finally in 1976 he only bowled 238 overs and had operations on both knees. But he made a miraculous recovery and took twenty wickets in the Test series in India, a fine performance on those slow, placid pitches. His success was largely due to a change in his bowling style. He straightened out his run-up, instead of running in on a curve. The change seemed to have prevented the various back and muscular injuries which he had suffered in the past. The other big factor in favour of England was the wonderful team spirit which Tony Greig had created by his inspiring and understanding leadership.

So, except for the weather all seemed set fair for a good season's cricket, and for the first time the three Prudential Trophy matches were to precede the five Tests, instead of coming immediately after the last Test at the Oval. This was an excellent innovation, as in the past there had been danger of anti-climax following so closely on the tensions and excitement of a five-day Test. These fifty-five over games also served as useful pipe-openers, and an introduction to big match atmosphere for newcomers to international cricket on both sides.

England won the series 2–1 but not without the usual alarums and excursions. In the first match at Old Trafford, Australia batted first and after being 2 for 2, finished with 169 for 9 off their fifty-five overs. Not a very formidable total but in the end England only managed to win by 2 wickets, due to two suicidal run-outs of Barlow and Greig.

At Edgbaston, England won by 101 runs which looks easy enough but their innings of 171 was not very impressive. Six batsmen made single figures, including three noughts by the Packer trio – Greig, Knott and Underwood. The Australian bowlers responsible were surprisingly Cosier – who had not taken a wicket on the tour except in the one-day match at Arundel – and Chappell. They both took five wickets, but poor Thomson trying out his injured shoulder for the first time in a big match was wayward and expensive conceding 46 runs in nine overs and being no-balled eleven times.

When Australia batted under heavy skies Willis (2 for 14)

and Lever (4 for 29) were too much for them. Chappell was their top scorer with 19 and they were all out for 70 – the lowest-ever total in the Trophy so far.

In the third and last match the Oval pitch provided more runs. England made 242, of which Brearley (78) and Amiss (108) put on 161 for the first wicket – a record for any wicket in the seventeen Prudential matches since 1972. But again the England batting looked brittle, Old (20) being the only other player to reach double figures. Australia were going well at 181 for 1, thanks to a superb innings by Chappell. The match ended in farcical conditions, the game going on in torrential rain, which even made it impossible to identify the players from the commentary box. I have never seen cricket *of any class* continue in such a deluge. But the next day was Jubilee Day, and neither the teams nor the authorities wanted to have to come back. In spite of the appalling light and pelting rain Chappell continued to play magnificently and his 125 not out was the highest individual score in any Prudential match so far, and enabled Australia to win by 2 wickets.

There was to be no respite from the terrible weather when the First Test Match was played at Lord's in mid-June. It was one of the coldest Tests which I have ever attended and in addition most of the second day was lost because of rain and bad light. So the match was drawn with Australia still needing 112 to win with only four wickets left at the finish. This meant that England were perhaps unlucky not to win, though they really didn't deserve to after their batting in their first innings of 216. They were soon 13 for 2 and only a stand of 98 between Woolmer (79) and Randall (53) saved them from complete collapse. Underwood (11 not out) and Willis (17) in a cheerful last-wicket stand were the only other two batsmen to reach double figures. Thomson on his return to Test cricket bowled fast and for him fairly accurately and took four wickets. But Pascoe looked just as threatening and nearly as fast.

Australia replied with 296, Serjeant (81) and Chappell (66) being top scorers. In England's second innings poor Amiss (0) failed again, being bowled by Thomson in each innings. In spite of his new 'shuffling' technique he still did not look happy against speed, but his partner Brearley (49) looked fairly solid. Woolmer (120) played another fine innings and supported by Greig (91) enabled England to reach 305 – but there were still seven batsmen who failed to reach double figures, including three ducks. Australia needed 226 to win but again Willis aided by Old bowled well and with the last twenty overs to go they were 71 for 5. Young David Hookes in his first Test in England came to the rescue with a fine 50, and so they saved the match.

The England selectors must have been pleased with the bowling and fielding but a bit apprehensive about the batting. The opening partnership of Amiss and Brearley failed twice and the middle order batsmen Barlow, Knott and Old were all out of form. But Woolmer looked real Test class with plenty of time to play the fast bowlers, and he began to look more and more like Cowdrey – but without his figure! Randall batted cheerfully and as usual looked as if he was enjoying himself. Unfortunately he developed bursitis on his left elbow and should never have been sent in to bat in the second innings. Greig, deposed as captain, received a mixed reception from the crowd but played one of his typical forcing innings which have so often saved England's bacon. His successor Brearley in his first Test as captain acquitted himself well in his quiet and studious manner. He gives a lot of thought to every move and acts with authority. He was the first to admit that his task was made easier by the team spirit already existing in the side he had taken over from Greig.

The Australians had not much to cheer them up in their batting, though their new boys Serjeant and Hookes did well in their differing styles. But the bowling, with Thomson's eight wickets in the match, and the aggressive speed of Pascoe backed by the steadiness of Walker, made it certain that the England batsmen would be fully tested throughout the series.

For the benefit of my Manchester friends who resent aspersions cast at their climate, I would like to record straight away that the Second Test at Old Trafford was played in gloriously hot sunny weather throughout. England's 9-wicket victory was their first success at home since 1974 and after it Brearley was made captain for the three remaining Tests. Australia were bowled out for 297, their top scorer being Doug Walters with 88, his top Test score in England. The fact that he has never made a Test hundred over here merely emphasises the different playing conditions in England and Australia. In Australia a batsman with a good eye can get away with playing across the line. Here the first essential for success is to play straight.

It was a good all-round bowling performance by England, all the six bowlers taking wickets. In reply England got off to their usual bad start and with Amiss and Brearley both failing, were 23 for 2. But then Woolmer (137) Randall (79) and Greig (76) played splendid attacking cricket and Woolmer with his second successive Test hundred confirmed his class. Likewise Randall once again proved what a great entertainer he is. England's total reached 437, and then it was Underwood's turn, taking 6 for 66 to help dismiss Australia for 218. In this Chappell played a masterly innings of 112 but except for Hookes (28) and O'Keefe (24 not out) he could get no one to stay with him, six of the batsmen failing to reach double figures.

Brearley and Amiss put on 75 for the first wicket, of which Brearley made an impressive 44 before getting out with just 3 more runs needed. Then to the disgust of Bill Frindall, Woolmer was sent in, which meant he lost the chance of scoring three Test hundreds in successive innings. Amiss was 28 not out at the end but still looked unhappy against Thomson. With Boycott now lurking in the wings after declaring himself once again available for Test selection, it looked like curtains for Amiss, and that this would prove to be his fiftieth and final Test.

And so it turned out – for the Third Test at Trent Bridge, Boycott came into the side in place of Amiss, and with Old once again injured, and Lever surprisingly dropped, Hendrick and Botham joined England's attack.

The Test was similar to the one at Old Trafford in two ways – England again won – this time by 7 wickets, and the weather was even more perfect over all five days. It was also a sort of fairy tale with Boycott, the old boy, and Botham, the new boy, getting the welcome touch from the fairy's wand. Boycott's return was unbelievable. He batted on all five days of the match and was on the field for all but $1\frac{3}{4}$ hours. Botham, besides playing a useful innings of 25, took five wickets in the first innings he bowled for England, and proved that he really can swing the ball in the air away from the batsmen under any conditions.

Australia, although again winning the toss, once more failed to reach 300, McCosker being top scorer with 51 and O'Keefe again left undefeated with 48 not out. It was a good performance by the England bowlers to get Australia out for 243 as the pitch was a typical Trent Bridge beauty. Although Botham caught the headlines with 5–74, Hendrick with 2 for 46 bowled quite beautifully and beat the batsmen time and time again.

The new opening partnership crawled slowly to 34 before Brearley was out, and then followed one of those collapses England supporters know all too well. Woolmer made 0 (so Bill Frindall needn't have worried), Greig 11, Miller 13. Then – horror of horrors – Randall in front of his packed home crowd was run out for 13 by Boycott who hid his head in his hands as the groans from the crowd made him realise what a crime he had perpetrated. Randall can do no wrong at Trent Bridge and it was a bitter disappointment to his thousands of supporters.

It was in fact Boycott's fault. It was his call as he placed the ball towards mid-on, but Randall could not leave his crease until he saw whether the ball would be fielded. As it was Thomson swooped on it, Boycott came on and Randall, starting too late, could not reach the wicket-keeper's end in time. Boycott was genuinely upset and the whole affair must have made him even more determined to make a hundred – something I'm sure he had in mind at the start of the innings. He was greatly helped by Knott who encouraged and comforted him, nursing him back to confidence, and together they put on 215 for the sixth wicket, equalling Hutton and Hartstaff's partnership at The Oval in 1938.

Boycott (107), although dropped at slip by McCosker when 20, showed all his old skill and technique in defence, and proved how much England had missed his powers of concentration during the last three years. But to me the real hero was Knott, who batted with all his best improvisation and brilliance. His 135 was the highest of his five Test hundreds, the highest by an England wicket-keeper, and he also became the first wicket-keeper to score 4,000 runs in Tests.

So, thanks to Boycott and Knott, England made 364 and led by 121 runs. In their second innings Australia did just pass 300 by 9 runs, with McCosker again top scorer with 107. This time Willis (5 for 88) bowled with great speed and fire and once again Hendrick's figures of 2 for 56 failed to match his great accuracy and movement off the pitch which worried all the batsmen.

The partnership of Brearley (81) and Boycott (80 not out) 'came good' in England's second innings and surely – but very slowly – they put on 154 and England won easily enough by 7 wickets. To the joy of the crowd their hero Randall made the winning hit in a bright little innings of 19 not out, some slight reward to them for their wonderful behaviour throughout the match. And of course also among them were many Yorkshire supporters who had come to watch *their* hero's return to Test cricket, and had witnessed a unique display of determination and dedication. Boycott had now made ninety-eight hundreds, and even then people were saying that the fairies were saving up his final triumph for his home crowd at Headingley in the Fourth Test. A hundredth hundred in a Test *by* a Yorkshireman, *before* Yorkshiremen *in* Yorkshire. Impossible surely, pure fantasy. But now read on.

In the one match which Boycott played for Yorkshire between the Third and Fourth Tests he made the ninety-ninth first-class century he needed to set the stage for Headingley. The odds against scoring three hundreds in successive first-class matches are extremely high. The odds against a batsman reaching his hundredth first-class century with the third of these are even higher. But the odds of achieving this feat in a Test match before your own home crowd must be astronomical. And yet I am sure that the majority of that large Yorkshire crowd on the first day at Headingley *expected* Boycott to do it. He himself, in spite of all his self-confidence, must have been one of the few who felt it was virtually asking the impossible. But in spite of losing

Brearley without a run scored, Boycott proceeded slowly towards his target.

Helped by some consistent England batting for a change, it took him over five hours on the first day. For the latter part of his innings the hundred began to look inevitable, and just a question of time. He finally reached it with a classic on drive off a full pitch from Greg Chappell. Even as the ball left his bat Boycott seemed to know that it would race down the hill towards the football stand for four. He raised both his arms above his head, waving his bat on high, and just had time to do a little war dance before he was swamped by invading spectators. Headingley erupted for several minutes. This was Boycott's moment and his alone. Remarkably the fact that if England were to win this Test they would win back the Ashes seemed to fade into the background. Remembering how much had happened in the few weeks since his return to Test cricket after an absence of three years, I rank this as one of the most unlikely and emotional feats I have ever witnessed on a cricket field.

Boycott continued to dominate the match on the second day. Would he make two hundred, would he carry his bat? Well in the end he did neither and was out after tea for 191 from England's total of 436. The luck was all against Australia. In overcast weather they found the movement and swing of Hendrick (4 for 41) and Botham (5 for 21) practically unplayable. Once again McCosker – brilliantly thrown out by Randall – was top scorer with 27, and besides him only Hookes and Robinson reached double figures. When they followed on 333 runs behind, the weather was still against them and Hendrick once again (4 for 54) and Willis (3 for 32) did most of the damage. Just before tea on the fourth day, Randall caught Marsh at mid-off off Hendrick and as he did so turned a super cartwheel to signify that England had won by an innings and 85 runs and so had regained the Ashes after two and a half years in Australia's possession.

This was a great day for Brearley and the England team and needless to say there was much revelry upstairs in the English dressing-room. Also being toasted was Alan Knott, who in his eighty-eighth Test had made his two hundred and fiftieth dismissal. But even as the celebrations went on inside, there outside on the balcony was Boycott savouring and acknowledging the cheers of his supporters – cheers, which in spite of the Ashes, seemed to be for him rather than for England. The prodigal son had returned in triumph. All was forgiven. In Yorkshire at least the 1977 Test at Headingley will always be remembered as Boycott's match.

Inevitably the final Test at the Oval was an anti-climax with the Ashes no longer at stake, and to make matters worse the wet weather *before* the match prevented any play on a perfectly fine first day. The selectors after much advice for and against, decided to play the three Packer defectors and the only change was the return of Lever for Botham who was injured with a bad foot.

Despite a good start of 86 by Boycott and Brearley, England succumbed to some fine outswing bowling by Malone, belatedly selected for his first Test of the tour. His figures (47–20–63–5) are worth printing in full as his was not only great bowling but a marathon effort as well. England were all out for 214 and in spite of some lively fast bowling by Willis (5 for 102) Australia reached their highest score of the series – 385. Their most promising young batsman, left-hander David Hookes, was top scorer with a bright 85, but the most notable stand of the innings was between Walker (78 not out) and Malone (46). They put on 100 for the ninth wicket. There was only time for England to make 57 for 2, including a nice little unbroken partnership of 41 between Boycott and Randall, one feature of which was their immaculate running between the wickets! And so the match was drawn and England had won the series 3–0.

Final Thoughts on the Series

England were undoubtedly the better team. Well led by Brearley they caught and fielded better than any England side I have ever seen. A fantastic one-handed slip catch by Greig at Old Trafford, another in the gully by Hendrick at Trent Bridge, and Randall's run out of McCosker at Headingley were typical highlights. The bowling strength was ideal for this country with Willis providing the real pace, and his twenty-seven wickets was a magnificent effort, underlying his fitness and the success of his new run-up. Hendrick, Old, Lever and Botham supplied the swing and movement, and they had of course the usual economical support from Underwood, who bowled more overs than anyone. There was also the promising but underbowled off-spinner Miller and that perpetual picker-up of much needed wickets Greig.

A special word of praise for young Botham who took five wickets in his first Test innings and followed it with another five at Headingley. He is an enthusiastic cricketer who could become a great Test all-rounder. He has a prodigious out-swing, is a fine forcing batsman and a good fielder anywhere, including the slips.

The batting I am afraid still gave me the willies but there were enough plus signs to be optimistic for the future. Boycott's fairy-tale return to Test cricket after an absence of three years was the outstanding feature. He provided a touch of class and a wonderful defensive technique. He is the *bête-noire* of bowlers as he allows them so little chance and he gave a much needed solidity to the batting line-up. Whether Brearley is the right partner for him is questionable, although on occasions their opening partnerships of 34, 154, 0, 86, 5 showed a certain amount of rapport. But both are slow scorers – Boycott by design and I feel he could and should accelerate – Brearley on the other hand, although showing plenty of guts against the fast bowlers, is probably just below the real class needed for an opening Test batsman.

Woolmer – now temporarily lost – tailed off towards the end of the series, but looked the part of an England No. 3. And what about Randall? I must confess that I have gone down on my knees on some nights and prayed that he would make enough runs to justify the selectors keeping him in the side. He is a breath of fresh air – the entertainer *par excellence*. Someone who enjoys his cricket and shows it. His fielding is an inspiration to the team and he regularly goes in to bat plus twenty runs or more which he has saved in the field. He is the only Test batsman I have ever seen who *runs* out of the pavilion to bat. Then with a hop, skip and a jump he hurries

to the wicket, eager to get on with it. Note how many times he
has about three boundaries in his first twenty runs. When he
is standing at the crease I would recommend all young boys
watching to forget what they see. He does nearly everything
wrong. He fidgets, moves his head, shuffles his feet. He is
never still, like the Jack-in-the-Box he is. But in the end he
plays *straight*, his timing is sweet, and his strokes all round
the wicket – including the much neglected cut – are a joy to
watch. Test cricket needs more players like him. I am
unashamedly his fan.

For some time at least England will have to do without the
rescue acts of Greig and Knott, and the debt which England
owes them will probably only be properly appreciated when
they are not there. As I write Roope is the man in possession
at No. 5. He is a good driver of the ball but somehow does not
seem to me to quite fill the bill. But I hope that I am wrong if
only because he is such a brilliant close catcher.

But there is, as I have said, much hope for the future
– Gatting, Rose, Gower, Athey, Love, Tavaré, Cowdrey,
Hopkins, Stovold – and so I could go on. England's primary
need is for a couple of really fast young bowlers. They need
not swing the ball nor move it. But they must have pace and
the strength and physical fitness which is part and parcel of
the great fast bowler. It is a sad fact that most of our fast men
break down with alarming regularity these days – Willis,
Arnold, Old and Hendrick are recent examples. One
exception is Lever who just bowls and bowls without any
apparent after-effects. But even Botham, aged twenty-one
and strong as an ox, had to withdraw from the last Test with
foot trouble. Why *are* there so many injuries and breakdowns
in these days of expert physiotherapists, electrical massage
and new exercise techniques? Alec Bedser has a simple
answer. Young boys nowadays don't walk enough. He cites
himself – 'and the brother' – who both used to walk several
miles to school and back each day. This is the stuff to build
the frame and muscles which a fast bowler must have.

I have another theory. This breaking down has become
much more common during the last ten years or so. People
like Trueman, Statham, Bailey and Bedser seldom missed
Tests because of injuries caused by bowling. Could it be that

nowadays too much time is spent 'on the table' and too little just bowling? Exercises and massage are all very well but bowling is a contortion in itself and calls into play some otherwise unused muscles. There's one other possible cause – the constant driving up and down the motorways, often long distances on Sundays in the middle of a three-day county match. How often does one see a team arriving in their cars after sitting in cramped conditions for an hour or two, and then going straight out on to the field without any loosening up beforehand. That must be a strain on the muscles.

But I have digressed as usual. We have some good spinners today, far more than a few years ago. Miller, Cope, Carrick, Pocock, Edmonds, Emburey, Graveney, East, Childs, Southern, Arrowsmith, Savage – the list is surprisingly large. And finally Kent have done it again and produced yet another wicket-keeper/batsman to follow Ames, Evans and Knott. Paul Downton – only aged twenty – is as good as any of them were at his age. I am particularly pleased that he was picked to go to Pakistan, as at the Oval Test I implored Alec Bedser to have the courage to send him. Luckily I was preaching to the converted, because by a lucky chance when Bedser went especially to watch Downton, he was standing up to the medium pace of Asif and got a brilliant stumping on the leg side. That would have especially impressed Bedser, who always liked his wicket-keepers to stand up.

As for the Australians, I cannot believe that the Packer affair did not affect their morale and concentration. Most of them had signed, but a few had not, and that must have caused some division. At any rate they never showed the fight and determination which Australian sides have always had. It was not their fault that except for Chappell they lacked class but all too often they seemed to play careless – I don't care – sort of strokes. Hookes was the most promising of the new batsmen, and I feel that both Serjeant and Hughes will develop as a result of the experience they have gained on the tour.

Thomson, though not so menacing without Lillee, took twenty-two wickets and was undoubtedly still very fast, growing more accurate as the tour progressed. Pascoe looked nearly as quick and was sometimes livelier, while poor Malone with his outswingers was badly overlooked by his selectors. My own feeling about Walker is that he is over-estimated, hard worker though he is. He is one of those bowlers, like Statham, of whom people say: 'He should have got more wickets. His analysis does not do him credit.' But unlike Statham, Walker does not always bowl *straight*.

Except for the Packer cloud it was a pleasant series from which both captains emerged with credit. Greg Chappell – in contrast to his volatile brother Ian – was always the soul of tact and remained cool and calm on all occasions. There was some good cricket to watch, and one of the features of the series was the size and good behaviour of the crowds. What a contrast to 1976! This time there was no running on to the field, calypsos or beer cans or ruderies shouted from the terraces. Any barracking was good natured. This was so at all the grounds but my prize goes to Trent Bridge where on five days of glorious sunshine record crowds just sat back and enjoyed the cricket and applauded good play by either side impartially.

Finally, of course, England won. That made a change and gave encouragement to the many hundreds of thousands of faithful lovers of cricket who either at the grounds, or through their TV, radio or papers, follow the fortunes of their country and enjoy nothing more than seeing Australia well and truly beaten.

In the county competitions, Middlesex were the best all-round side but were perhaps lucky to finish equal top with Kent in the Schweppes County Championship. Because Middlesex's Gillette semi-final with Somerset on 17–19 August was washed out by rain – and yet had to be decided in time for the final on 3 September – they were allowed to play it instead on 24, 25 or 26 August. In the end, because of more rain, they had to settle for a fifteen overs per side match on the twenty-sixth. This meant that their *county* match against Somerset scheduled to start on 24 August had to be played a week later. It so happened that on 24, 25 and 26 August the other two contenders for the championship – Kent and Gloucestershire – both had their matches abandoned without a ball being bowled and it is likely that Middlesex and Somerset would have suffered the same fate, as Lord's was never really fit for play – even for the fifteen-over Gillette game. As it was when Middlesex *did* play Somerset a week later they were able to pick up seven very useful bonus points.

But there was no doubt about their right to claim the Gillette Cup when they beat Glamorgan by 5 wickets in the final at Lord's. My chief memory of this match was a gigantic six hit by Glamorgan's young left-hander Mike Llewellyn. He drove a ball from Emburey right up to the top of the left-hand corner of the pavilion. The ball bounced on the roof of our commentary box and was retrieved from the gutter two days later. MCC say that had there not been a trellis in the way it would have cleared the pavilion completely. I must say it was quite frightening as we saw the ball coming straight for us as if it was going to come through our window. But luckily it seemed to get a second wind and soared over our heads. It was by far the biggest hit I had ever seen at Lord's, though in 1945 Keith Miller had hit one into our old commentary box over the England dressing-room. But that was a floor lower than our present box. Anyhow, I thought it prudent to wave a white handkerchief of surrender out of our window, in case Mike tried it again.

The John Player – as it usually does – provided another nail-biting finish, all depending on the last matches. As it was at the finish Leicestershire and Essex each had the same number of points – fifty-two. But as Leicestershire had won thirteen matches to Essex's twelve, Ray Illingworth's team were the winners. Ray's cunning leadership had finally got them past the post first, but I felt sorry for Essex who once again just failed to win their first-ever trophy of any kind, although for half the season they had been top of the table.

Finally, in the Benson and Hedges final, Gloucestershire beat Kent fairly easily by 64 runs – a great personal triumph for Mike Procter. His dynamic and sympathetic captaincy had inspired the whole Gloucestershire team to play some of its best cricket for many seasons.

Here is one example of what I mean by sympathetic captaincy. David Partridge did not bat in Gloucestershire's innings of 237 (in which incidentally Andy Stovold hit a brilliant 71 and the power of his strokes must have impressed the selectors). Then in the field Partridge dropped a not too easy catch in front of the grandstand. And so, although Gloucestershire were doing well and likely to win the match without his help as a bowler, Procter called him up to bowl and kept him on in spite of two expensive overs, until he finally got his wicket. Procter then promptly took him off. But by giving him his chance he had brought Partridge into the match and emphasised that Gloucestershire were a real team in which *every* man – not just the stars – played an important part. That's what I call captaincy.

V for Victory! Derek Randall turning a cartwheel after his catch which brought the Ashes back to England at Headingley, August 1977. (Copyright Patrick Eagar)

Back to business! With Judith Chalmers at a radio and TV exhibition, listening to *Down Your Way*.

At least one joke seems to have got a laugh at a trade dinner!

Talk About! B.J. with Sound Supervisor Cedric Johnson and producer Roger Macdonald, follows the Queen and the Lord Mayor, Sir Robin Gillett on the walkabout from St Paul's to Guildhall on Jubilee Day, 7 June 1977.

(Copyright Keystone Press Agency Ltd)

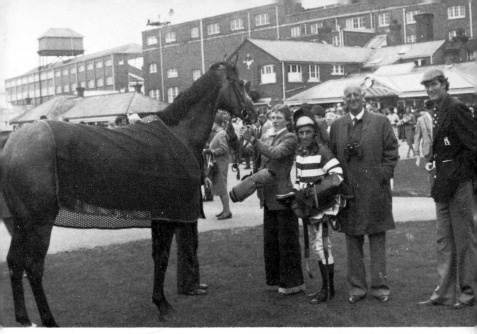

I gotta horse! W.G. Greys with B. J., co-owner David Brown and jockey Frank Morby in the paddock at Newbury.   (Copyright Pauline Johnston)

Our first win! W.G. Greys (centre with white flash) winning by a neck at Teesside in November, 1977.   (Copyright Kenneth Bright)

That's our Dad! Clare, Barry and Ian inspect the portrait with B.J. and the artist Edward Halliday after the surprise presentation.

The portrait looks down on Pauline, Mini and B.J. (Copyright *Marylebone Mercury*)

In, out. In, out. John Snagge, B.J., Humphrey Tilling and Raymond Baxter commentating at the Royal Borough of Windsor and Maidenhead Jubilee Celebrations. (Copyright Pauline Johnston)

Sixty-five years on. B.J. returns to his birthplace to open the Little Berkhamsted cricket pavilion with Barbara Cartland, introduced by Lord Orr-Ewing. (Copyright Pauline Johnston)

The family say 'Cheese!' (left to right) Andrew, Barry, Pauline, Joanna, B.J., Clare and Ian. New Year 1978.

Thirteenth Over **In the box**

The summer of 1977 was certainly a vintage one for our Radio 3 *Test Match Special*. Over the years the Press and listeners have been most kind and generous in their appreciation of our efforts. The idea, which we always try to get across – namely that cricket is fun and something to be enjoyed – seems to have caught on in a big way. In 1977 the fulsome praise which we received was really quite staggering, but none the less welcome for all that! There were big spread feature articles about us in the national dailies, Sundays and London and provincial evening papers. Some of the reporters and writers came and spent a whole day in the commentary box with us at one or two of the Tests to see exactly how it all works and what makes it tick.

The one thing which seemed to surprise them all was the friendly atmosphere, the lack of the alcoholic stimulants which cartoonists delight to show, and the apparent casualness of the whole operation. 'Just like a group of friends watching a match together and obviously enjoying themselves', said one of the writers to me. And I think he hit the nail on the head. To start with we *are* all friends and it's incredible but true that I have never had a row with anyone in the commentary box over thirty-two years. We all love cricket, enjoy watching it and talking about it – even living it. We are also all utterly different in voice, character and approach. By ringing the changes of the four commentators three times every hour the listeners are given a complete contrast.

The various boxes at the six Test grounds are basically the same in size and shape. Except at Old Trafford and Headingley they are all situated in the pavilion at balcony height directly behind the bowler's arm. Possibly because we have to make instant judgements we have always been far luckier than the Press in this respect. In only three of the Test grounds are they directly behind the stumps. At Old Trafford and Headingley the pavilions are sideways on to the pitch. So at Headingley we are high up at the back of the football stand, and at Old Trafford our box – the smallest and most cramped – is in the block which houses the main scoreboard and seats for the official guests. The boxes have glass windows which can be opened or not and ideally there is room for five people to sit comfortably in a row at a baize-covered shelf on which are four or five stand microphones. The summarisers – either Trevor Bailey or Freddie Trueman who change over every hour – sit in one corner usually with a small TV set in front of them so as to be able to study the action replays if they wish.

Next to them is the commentator, then a large space for the bearded wonder Bill Frindall, with all his books, score sheets, calculators and coloured pens and pencils, plus a thermos flask or two. On his other side will be another commentator who is 'resting' and then in the other corner a spare seat and microphone. This is used by casual visitors to the box whom we often interview – people like the manager of the touring side, Alec Bedser, chairman of the selectors, or the captains at the end of a match.

People often ask me about life in the box, its routine and what we do when not at the microphone or when it's raining. We all have our different ways of spending the day so I will only speak on my own behalf. I always try to get to the box at least an hour before play is due to start and can always rely on our producer being already there – either Peter Baxter in London, Don Mosey in the North, or Dick Maddock in the Midlands. They will have stuck a roster up on the wall and by the commentator's mike, showing our commentary times during the day – normally one twenty-minute period every hour. They will also have sorted out into piles the large number of letters which arrive for us each day. If I can, I always try to open mine and give them a cursory glance in case there is anything in them which I feel should be brought up during the day's play.

These letters are very welcome and reveal a faithful and seemingly ever-increasing band of *TMS* listeners. Some letters are just kind and say how much they enjoy the programmes. Some ask technical questions, others want information about records. Some disagree with something which we have said, or point out a mistake. But the great thing about them is that even when critical they are written in a friendly way without any of the abuse and rudeness so often posted to television commentators. Why this should be so I have never really discovered. But I do know that when I was doing television commentary I regularly received a small percentage of letters telling me to put a sock in it, or why couldn't I be like Peter West – or just simply telling me to get well and truly stuffed. Some of our radio listeners no doubt feel the same but they are either too polite to say so, or just don't bother to write. We each try to answer the more personal letters, some are answered from time to time during gaps in play, others get included in the listeners' letters session during the Monday lunch interval. The rest – as many as two thousand in 1977 – are acknowledged by Peter Baxter on behalf of the BBC.

One type of letter does create problems and that is the one asking us to get the autographs of the two teams and both commentary teams as well. Some even include autograph books or miniature bats. Others enclose treasured cuttings from old newspapers or photographs of past cricketers, which they want returned after we have seen them. If only they could see the piles of letters, small parcels and old envelopes littering the confined space of the boxes they would realise the folly of sending anything of any value which they want to be sure to get back. There is real danger of it being lost in the all inevitable chaos. As for the autographs – well, many years ago we had to make it a rule not to bother the teams. We get so many requests that we would become an intolerable nuisance were we to grant them, even if we could spare the time to keep on trailing off to the dressing-rooms. We do, however, do our best to send our own autographs though we appreciate that they are only a very poor second best. And by the way a stamped addressed envelope is the most certain way of being successful.

A word about the parcels. People are very kind and send us a varied assortment of presents. A lady from Bournemouth regularly sends us our favourite pastilles, another from Maida Vale personally delivers a bottle of wine at the London grounds. There's a lovely lady who keeps a flower shop in Hounslow who sends a beautiful bouquet at the end of each match. Other ladies send us cakes. One thing leads to another. After we had thanked someone for some sweets, the next day a dental centre sent us a toothbrush. When we thanked them for that someone followed with some toothpaste. A big sweet manufacturer sent boxes and boxes of their particular confectionery – so many that we could not possibly consume them all, and the local children's hospital benefited. On one occasion, for some reason, Greg Chappell lay on his back and kicked his legs in the air. I remarked that our Yorkshire Terrier Mini did this on our lawn as she had eczema on her back. Not only did this produce a shoal of letters, including two from Australia, but a chemical firm sent me some skin powder to put into her food. We really *are* spoilt and are most grateful to everyone for their thoughtfulness and kindness.

But I've digressed! Back to the day's routine. After looking at the letters and parcels I usually read the day's papers to see what they have to say about the game and to check in case they have got hold of a story which we have missed. Then I usually watch the players practising and get the latest news on any team injuries. After a cup of coffee it's back to the box for the start of our day's broadcasting – fifteen minutes before play on the first day and five minutes before on the other four. Once we are on the air the microphones in the box are 'live' so that those who are not commentating have to keep as quiet as possible. With about four or five extroverts this is not easy, and I'm afraid that the odd chuckle and whispered remark do sometimes come over the mike.

The lunchtime summary finishes at 1.35 pm and then we all go our separate ways. On some grounds we have a packed lunch or bring our own sandwiches. At Lord's I always picnic with my family on the lawn behind the Warner Stand. At Headingley I am lucky that Sidney Hainsworth, who

sponsors the Fenner Trophy at Scarborough and also presented the Sutcliffe Gates to Headingley, gives me a slap-up
lunch in the Taverners Tent. At Edgbaston the Warwickshire Committee generously entertains us, while at Trent
Bridge we are royally looked after by the famous old Trent
Bridge Inn. So we do pretty well but not, alas, on every day.
As I've said on Mondays we spend the lunch session answering listeners' letters, and on some Saturdays one or two
of us are needed for the phone-in programme *Call the
Commentators.*

Most of the grounds provide us with a pot of tea and
biscuits and these keep us going until close of play. Then
after Tony Lewis has given his witty, expert and informative
summary of the day's play I think that most of us feel that we
deserve a drink!

During play when I am not commentating I usually sit
watching at the back of the box. I'm still rather like a small
boy. I dread missing a ball. But occasionally I do go out to
stretch my legs and get some air, as I must admit that
Fred's cigars and Trevor's cigarettes do sometimes clog up
the box a bit! It's also quite a good thing to watch play for a
short time from a different angle and I find that by sitting
sideways on I can get a better idea of the speed of the
bowlers and the pace of the pitch. The others, some of
whom are writing for newspapers, leave the box more often
than I do. In fact John Arlott likes to come in only a minute
or two before he is due on the air, and usually leaves
immediately after it.

When it rains we do our best *not* to return to the studio for
music. We realise that people have switched on to us because
they want cricket. They can get music on at least two other
channels. So we talk about some current cricket problem or
topic, answer letters, tell stories – though these are not all
about cricket! As for instance at the Oval Freddie Trueman
asked us out of the blue if we knew what was the fastest thing
on two wheels. Naturally we didn't know. So he told us 'An
Arab riding a bicycle through Golders Green'. Last season
during one long stoppage for rain we kept talking for almost
the whole session about one thing or another. The trouble is
some people write in to say that they enjoy the chit-chat

more than the commentary! So we had better be careful or we shall do ourselves out of a job!

Only when we run out of puff or material do we hand back to the studio. But then, funnily enough, unlike the players, we never play cards. We either just gossip or tell some of the stories which were not suitable to tell on the air. When Don Mosey is one of the commentators he and I play a word game on paper which produces some ding-dong struggles and keeps us out of mischief.

Finally a word of praise for our producers and engineers, who get none of the limelight and work for very long hours with scarcely any break. As a reward we make sure they get their fair share of the sweets and cakes. There are two producers for each Test. One sits in a studio back at Broadcasting House. He opens up the transmission and is responsible for filling in with music during intervals of play and giving the lunch-time and tea-time county cricket scores. He has to listen to every ball (poor chap) and can let us know if we are off mike, not giving the score enough or making too much noise in the background. He also has a large coloured TV set and there are occasions when he can help us out by saying up the line what is happening out of our sight – eg the Queen arriving, or something going on in the pavilion below us, which *we* cannot see, but which one of the TV cameras can pick up.

In the box itself is the producer in charge of the outside broadcast at the ground. He prepares the roster and sees that we keep to it! He arranges for people to come into the box to be interviewed. He cues us with a card when we have to greet *World Service* or *Sport on Two*. He tells the summarisers how long they have got and places a stopwatch in front of them. He arranges our tea and coffee, and, as I've said, sorts out all the mail and parcels. He encourages us, reproves us gently, but always keeps us happy. He is the most indispensable person in the box including Bill Frindall. Because at a pinch our producers can also score by the Frindall method. By the end of the day he must be exhausted, as he does not even get a break during the intervals, when he has to produce *Listeners' Letters, Call the Commentators*, etc.

I hope now that you have got some sort of picture of what

goes on behind the scenes in the box. It may all sound a bit chaotic – and so at times perhaps it is. But so long as you enjoy your radio visit to the Test Match as much as we enjoy being there, then we are all happy.

So that is how I see a typical day in the box. Others see it differently! We were much amused by an article in *The Times* in which Michael Leapman gave *his* impression of the way we carry on.

Now over to Brian Johnston at Lord's:

BRIAN Good morning. I'm afraid the news from here isn't too good. Play has been delayed because of picketing outside the Grace Gate by dozens of the less successful county players, who are complaining that they haven't been made offers by Kerry Packer's cricket circus. It's fairly nasty out there. None of the Test players has yet crossed the picket line except Mike Brearley, the English captain, whose fetching crash helmet is standing him in good stead at last. Now you know I don't like to get involved in politics, but this unfortunate incident does reinforce my view that the game isn't what it was. What would some of the all-time greats have made of a picket line, I wonder? I remember old 'Goofy' Grunwick, that great Essex wicket-keeper/batsman – the greatest player of underarm full tosses of his generation I should say, wouldn't you Fred? Anyway, I remember a policeman once tried to stop him getting into Lord's on the grounds that it was three in the morning and he was trying to climb in over the Tavern roof. He happened to have his stainless steel groin protector on at the time, so he just thrust his midriff into the policeman's face and knocked him flying. The policeman was fined for indecent assault. Pickets, I don't think he would have given much time to them. But here's Trevor and he's panting, as though he's hot from the fray. Good morning, Trevor, what's the latest?

TREVOR Good morning, Brian. Well it's looking pretty ugly out there. I was just on my way in when I happened to meet this old friend of mine that I hadn't seen since late last night and we decided to go to the Tavern for our first of the day. It was ugly, very ugly – that's the only word I can think of to describe it. It took us several minutes to fight our way through to the bar. 'Blacklegs!' they shouted at us, which was doubly unfortunate since my friend happened to be a West Indian. I think you know him – 'Fingers' St Paul, surely the fastest left-handed

scoreboard operator of his generation. He and I were wondering
what the old-timers would have made of all the fuss. Do you
remember 'Goofy' Grunwick, the great Somerset leg-break
bowler, who could make the ball turn on a sixpence, but lost his
touch when they barred the use of coins on the field of play?

BRIAN   Yes, we were just talking about him. Let's ask Bill if he
can look through his record books to see if there's ever been a
picket at a cricket match before. (Pause and sound of record
books being riffled through). Ah, here we are. He says no,
there's never been one, but there was once a strike at a cricket
ball manufacturer's in Peshawar, where the workers were cam-
paigning for bigger stumps to be used. This would have shortened each innings, so you could have matches of four innings
each instead of two, doubling the number of balls you needed.

TREVOR   Never came off, did it Brian?

BRIAN   It didn't, no. And now while we're waiting for the umpires
to sort things out, I'd like to thank those listeners who've sent me
little favours, as they always do. A listener in Glastonbury has
sent me some wine gums packed in a pair of stout gumboots.
She says I'm to suck the gums, wear the boots when rain stops
play and fill them with champagne if England win. 'And if
you're ever in Glastonbury', she writes . . . no, I don't think
I'll read that, but it does sound a lot more fun than sitting here
droning away about cricket. And another young woman from
Bayswater has sent me a pair of undergarments to warm
myself during the cold spell we've been having, though I must
say they don't look too practical. She's sent me a limerick to go
with them, which again I can't read to a family audience but
I'll tell you the last line. It goes: 'Oh no, they're not mine,
they're the vicars.' But let's get back to talking about the
all-time greats. John has just struggled up here. What have
you got to tell us, John?

JOHN   Well Brian you were talking just now about 'Goofy' Grunwick that great Worcester opening bat who still, I think, holds
the record for scoring the fastest single in Test matches against
New Zealand. I was just wondering if you remembered how his
brilliant career was ruined in that famous Lord's Test against
Pakistan. He went off to get another sweater and when he hadn't
come back after an hour they went looking for him and found
him *in flagrante* . . .

BRIAN   Really. I thought it was in the Long Room.

JOHN   Anyway, they caught him with the wife of one of the
selectors and it was clear that he'd managed several times to get
past her perhaps rather half-hearted defensive prods. Her hus-

band did him a terrible injury with the groundsman's turf cutting implement.

BRIAN   Never played again did he, John? He took up female impersonation, I remember. In fact I saw him in action a year or so afterwards in a drag pub near the Oval, doing an amazingly intricate exotic dance with a bat and a set of stumps. Fred, you come in now, who was the greatest performer you ever came in contact with?

FRED   Funny you should ask me that, Brian, because I once came up against the wife of that selector myself. It was at a charity game down at Little Filandering on behalf of Prince Charles's fund for arthritic coachmen.

BRIAN   Marvellously worthwhile cause, that.

FRED   Yes, but unfortunately it rained most of the day and I was sent to help this lady make the teas and the upshot was that nobody got any tea and I remember coming away thinking that maybe Grunwick wasn't as goofy as people thought.

BRIAN   That wasn't quite what I meant, Fred. Who had the biggest feet of anyone you can remember?

FRED   Funny you should ask that because the wife of that selector I was mentioning had the most colossal pair you've ever seen. She played once in a women's Test and was the only player ever to have been warned by the umpires for wearing down the pitch when she was fielding at slip.

BRIAN   Well, while we've been rabbiting on here, play has actually got under way and the Australians have lost a couple of quick wickets. But, John, you were going to tell us something?

JOHN   Yes, Brian, it was about 'Goofy' Grunwick, the Surrey left-hander, who was certainly the finest extra cover of his generation . . .

Among the many hundreds of letters which we receive during a season, there is always a lot of poetry. I never knew there were so many budding poets and poetesses. This reminds me that a cricketing friend of mine once told me the difference between poetry and prose. He quoted the lines:

> *There was a young batsman called Walls*
> *Who was hit a terrible blow on the thigh*

My friend explained that these two lines are prose. 'But,' he added, 'had the blow been four inches higher, that would have been poetry'!

Anyway, after we had won the Ashes at Headingley, a

lady sent me this splendid parody on the famous Crispin's Day speech by Henry V before the Battle of Agincourt from Shakespeare's Henry V, *Act 4, Scene 3*. I was able to read it out at the end of the Fifth Test at the Oval, when we had some time to spare. I wish we had had Lord Olivier in the box with us so that he could have given it the rendering it deserved.

> *This day we won the Ashes*
> *He that lived this day and came safe home*
> *Will stand a tiptoe when this day is mentioned*
> *And rouse him at the word 'Ashes'.*
> *He that lived this day and sees old age*
> *Will yearly on the vigil feast his neighbours*
> *And say 'Tomorrow is Ashes day'.*
> *Old men forget, yet all shall be forgot*
> *Then will he open* Wisden *and show his record,*
> *And say 'These wickets I had on Ashes day'.*
> *But he'll remember with advantages*
> *What feats he did that day, then shall our names*
> *Familiar in his mouth as household words*
> *Brearley the Captain, Boycott and Willis*
> *Hendrick and Botham, Randall and Greig*
> *Be in their flowing cups freshly rememb'red*
> *This story shall the good man teach his son*
> *And Ashes day shall ne'er go by*
> *From this day to the ending of the world*
> *But we in it shall be remembered*
> *We few, we happy few, we Band of brothers*
> *For he today that won the Ashes with me*
> *Shall be my brother*
> *While others think themselves*
> *Accurs'd they were not there*
> *At Headingley on Ashes day.*

One of the most amusing packages contained two imaginary sleeves for a cricketing LP entitled *Bumper Hits for Six* or *When the Mighty Compton played*. Some of the suggested titles were:

> Hello *Dolly*
> Little *Dolly* Daydream
> The *Third Man* Theme
> John *Boles* and Gracie *Fields* Medley
> After the *Ball*

Ashes of Roses
Amazing *Grace*
I *Cover* the Waterfront
Run, Rabbit, *Run*
Bye, Bye, Blackbird
The Little White *Duck*
Oh, *Maiden*, my *Maiden*
Over and *Over* again
Kanhai Forget You?
Little Miss *Bouncer*
Close to you
May I?
High *Wide* and Handsome
Life is Just a *Bowl* of Cherries
Follow On
You're *Driving* me Crazy
Lords of the Air
Changing of the *Guard*
I Lift up My Finger and I say . . .
Varsity *Drag*

All these were sent in to us in two colourfully painted sleeves
by Brian Orchard. We read them out on the air and this
must have inspired a Mr D. B. Gardner who sent us these:

Try a little ton, *Denness*
Is *Younis* or is you ain't my baby
Thank *Evans* for little girls
Happy Days *Zaheer* again
Huttons and *Bowes*
Keep *Bright* on till the end of the road
Walters, Walters, take me to the altar
My funny *Valentine*

I was especially pleased to receive the above because it was
nice to know that there is someone else who makes as bad
puns as I do!

It might amuse you to see whether you can think up any
more – the punnier the better!

And talking of puns there was one I actually missed and
immediately received letters from two different people pointing out what I *should* have said. It all started with a man who
wrote in to say that he was in trouble. He said his Afghan
hound had chewed up the inside of his *Wisden*, and eaten all

the records! What should he do? I didn't really see what *I* was expected to do about it but remember making one or two rather wet suggestions such as that he should build higher shelves or get a smaller dog. But as my two correspondents so rightly pointed out the obvious reply I should have given was that the Afghan hound should have his Wisden teeth taken out!

Another piece of poetry was sent to me the previous summer by Mr Alan Hamilton of Torquay. He called it *The Cricketer's 'If'* – (with apologies to Rudyard Kipling). I think it sums up quite beautifully exactly what cricket is all about, and explains just why it means so much to so many of us. Mr Hamilton, who was eighty-five, sent a copy of the poem to his old school, Wellington, where it was hung up on the notice-board of the pavilion. Alas he died in 1977 but his widow has kindly given me permission to use it.

THE CRICKETER'S 'IF'
(with apologies to the late Mr Rudyard Kipling)

> *If you can keep your head when bowlers skittle*
> *Both opening batsmen with the score at three –*
> *When, knowing that your later batting's brittle,*
> *You grimly think 'It all depends on me!'*
> *If you can play defensive, watchful cricket,*
> *Leaving alone out-swingers on the off,*
> *(Knowing full well that, if you grope, you'll snick it)*
> *However much frustrated watchers scoff!*
>
> *If you can overcome unsure beginnings,*
> *And start to push the score along a bit –*
> *If you can play a really sterling innings*
> *And play your natural game, which is to H!T*
> *If you can score a hundred, and be master,*
> *Yet shield your partner while he settles in –*
> *If you can wrest a triumph from disaster,*
> *And lead your side to a noteworthy win.*
>
> *Or, if outwitted by a paceman's terror,*
> *You see your middle stump shot out for 'duck'*
> *If, still unruffled, you can note your error*
> *And not just put it down to rotten luck!*
> *If you can bowl a 'long hop' and get pasted*
> *Yet keep direction and your length as well –*

If you can think 'That lesson won't be wasted –
I'll serve him up some teasers for a spell!'
If you can bear to hear, though sorely shaken
The umpire's 'No' to your assured appeal –
And realise you might have been mistaken
And show no outward sign of what you feel!

And if you can, when mid-off drops a sitter,
Curb your impatience and still play the game.
Reflecting that the poor chap's feeling bitter
And think 'Ah, well! I might have done the same'
And when, at length, you ache in every sinew
Your limbs feel leaden and your fingers sore.
If, when your Captain asks: 'Can you continue?'
You can still rise to just one over more.

If you can field with keen determination
Watching the stroke and ever on alert
Stopping the hard ones with anticipation
And never make complaint although it hurt.
If you, at slip, can hold an awkward flyer
Or run the batsman out from deep third man.
If in the deep, you catch a swirling skyer
And keep your head from swelling – if you can!

If you can mix with cricketers as brothers
And mingle with both teams at close of play –
And pass the spirit of the game to others
Wherever you may meet them day by day –
Although you hold no County Member's ticket,
And play your local matches just for fun:
You will have done a mighty lot for cricket
E'en though you never play for England, Son!

ALAN F. HAMILTON

Fourteenth Over # Horse d'oeuvres

Towards the end of 1976 I had become slightly involved in a new sport for me – horse racing. I became part owner of a flat racehorse. And for those of you, who like me, know very little about racing let me hasten to explain that flat is not the shape of the horse, but records the fact that he runs *on* the flat and not over hurdles or fences.

I had done something fairly similar about ten years earlier when I owned one leg of a greyhound with Colin Cowdrey, John Woodcock and Michael Melford. As it was trained and ran in Kent and because of Colin's nickname, we called it Kentish Kipper. It used to run at Catford and won two or three races, though we were never there to see them. That's the trouble about owning a greyhound. It's not a very satisfying business. The owners have no say when it will run – that is arranged between the trainer and the stadium. They cannot see it *before* a race like you can a horse in the paddock, though they are very generously allowed to give it a gentle pat afterwards. We did once visit its training quarters but somewhat naturally the dog did not recognise us as his owners. We also went to watch it run once or twice, and it was amusing to see the way its price shortened when the bookies realised that we were there. They assumed we had come especially to back it – as if our measly £1 to win would make any difference to them. Another thing against greyhound racing is that the races are over so quickly you hardly have time to read the race, and even if your dog runs well, the pleasure is so fleeting.

So in the end we were quite pleased when Arthur Milton, the Gloucestershire cricketer and double England international at cricket and soccer, made an offer for Kentish

Kipper. Arthur said that he knew of a lonely little old lady down in Bristol who wanted a greyhound as a pet. He said he would give us what we had paid for him. So thinking that we were doing both ourselves and the lonely little old lady a good turn, we sold Kentish Kipper to Arthur for a hundred pounds. We thought no more about it for some time until a friend showed me a cutting from a Bristol newspaper, reporting the greyhound races down there. 'Kentish Kipper wins again!' was the headline. Arthur has always been a bit cagey about it and I still don't know how many races the dog won down in the West Country. But I strongly suspect that the lonely little old lady was none other than a stylish opening batsman, a brilliant close fielder and an England right-winger!

My entry into horse racing came about through David Brown the England and Warwickshire fast bowler. I suppose it started in 1967 during the MCC tour of West Indies. David met and fell in love with a very attractive girl called Tricia Norman. They met in Kingston at some sportsmen's gathering when Tricia was in Jamaica with her father, a well-known gynaecologist. She had always been a good point to point rider in England and while in the West Indies rode as a jockette in flat races against men jockeys. In fact we saw her come in second in a race at Georgetown, Guyana. It was a case of love at first sight and Big Dave – as he's called – had definitely bowled a maiden over. And to continue with cricket jargon, he soon got *hooked* on horses after they were married.

For some years, the Browns lived just outside Worcester where they raised a family and bred ponies. Dave had always wanted a farm and in the winters when not on tour used to study pigs and their breeding, so after a very successful benefit in 1973 they began looking round for a farm, which they eventually found near Kidderminster. They turned it into a stud and sort of livery stable, with masses of loose-boxes transformed from the old cowsheds. There they started to breed and break horses. They owned a mare called Santa Marta and sent her to a stallion called Grey Mirage. He was a class horse and among other races had won the Two Thousand Guineas trial at Kempton and had also broken the track record for two-year-olds over seven furlongs at Newbury.

The happy result was a strapping roan colt which Tricia brought up and broke and was the first person to get on his back. Dave asked me whether I would like a share in him and for a bit of fun I said I would. I brought in Martin Gilliat, and Dave already had the two Warwickshire cricketers Jack Bannister and Big Jim Stewart, and three others. We started as eight partners, but one fell by the wayside, so now we each own one-seventh of the horse – though which part has never been specified! And now for his name – and I'm afraid you are in for a bit of PUNishment. In order to keep the Grey of Grey Mirage and the cricketing connection I suggested that we might call him W. G. Greys, and surprisingly this was accepted by Wetherbys. He is trained by the well-known Midlands trainer Reg Hollinshead, who had his best season ever in 1977 with fifty winners.

W.G. ran in six races – he had a few weeks off with a damaged muscle and a cough – and he finished 'in the frame' twice. The other four times he ran well and never let us down, usually finishing about sixth or seventh out of big two-year-old fields with over twenty runners, after leading for most of the race. He is a big colt and stands 16.2 and the experts say that he won't be fully developed until he's a three-year-old, and we then hope his distance will be a mile. In 1977 he ran one 5-furlong, three 6-furlong and two 7-furlong races. At York in October we had our first thrill when he finished third in a 5-furlong race and then came our first taste of victory in November during the last week of the flat racing season. He won a 6-furlong race at Teesside Park by a neck but alas I was not able to see him win.

But Dave and Tricia were there to celebrate with Reg Hollinshead and his admirable stable jockey, Tony Ives, both of whom think highly of W.G. So do we all, and hope that by the time you read this, he will have proved as successful as the famous bearded Doctor after whom he has been nearly named. At this stage I am not quite sure what happens if he wins a really big race. Do we get a long leading rein so that all seven of us can lead him in? But after just one victory I mustn't get too cocky. Anyhow, it never pays to boast, as an American once found when visiting a small farm somewhere in England. The English farmer took him on a tour round the three hundred acres or so and when they returned to the farm after walking a couple of hours, the American said: 'You know, way back home in America it takes me two days in my car to go round my farm.' 'Yes,' replied the Englishman, 'I once had a car like that too!'

During the winter when not doing *Down Your Way* or writing books like this, much of my time is taken up by speaking at lunches, dinners, or even at business conferences. Besides bringing in some useful lolly, it satisfies my urge to stand up in front of an audience and tell stories and jokes. This all stems from my admiration of the old stand-up comics whom I used to enjoy so much when I went to the music halls.

In the days before radio and TV a comic would tour the country using virtually the same act, year in year out. He might occasionally add to it, give it a bit of polish, or adjust it slightly to suit a particular audience. But basically it didn't change and I do much the same with my speeches. I have about three, which I normally use. One completely on cricket, one based on my overall BBC experiences over thirty-two years, and the third just an after-dinner speech, with jokes and stories – some true, some not. I have this absurd hankering to make people laugh, and get tremendous satisfaction from hearing the laughter after telling a tale.

There are virtually no new stories – just old ones in a different wrapping. It all depends on the way they are told and more or less everything depends on timing. I learnt a lot by studying the methods of the great stand-up comics like Max Miller, Ted Ray and Tommy Trinder. My wife Pauline often asks me how I can go on doing the same old speeches.

The answer is that each audience is different, and reacts differently to the same story. So that each performance is a new challenge. One thing I learnt from the comics was how important it is to win over your audience right from the word go. This is especially so with the Round Table dinners. The Tablers are a boisterous lot and very appreciative, but unless you do 'get' them at the start, they are inclined to barrack or interrupt. But another thing I learnt was to keep going at a good pace, so if one joke falls a bit flat, you are soon on to the next one, and hope for better luck!

I find the Tablers most stimulating and thoroughly enjoy my evenings with them. They are all under forty years of age, so are lively and quick to see a joke. They must be pretty near to what used to be a typical music hall audience. I treasure the memory of one of their chairmen who announced after the loyal toast: 'You may smoke now the Queen's drunk!'

I was told of one Round Table who thought up a most ingenious idea which amused me, though I know it shouldn't have done. During one of their more boisterous dinners it was reported to them that two Panda cars were waiting outside in the car park, obviously hoping to catch one or two of the diners with the breathaliser. So at the end of the evening their chairman found a teetotal Tabler (a rare bird!) and told him to go out into the car park and pretend to be roaring drunk, and then to get into his car and drive away. This the t.t. did, singing at the top of his voice, and swaying and lurching all over the place. He staggered into his car, and drove off very very slowly as if he was having difficulty in seeing. Sure enough the Pandas, thinking that they had a certain victim, followed him slowly out on to the road. They let him go about a mile, then one of them passed him, and signalled for him to stop. They asked him to blow into the bag and were amazed when it did not turn green. Nor could they smell any drink on his breath. However, since he had done nothing wrong, they just asked him for his name and address and then let him drive off. They realised that they had been 'had', and were not surprised on returning to the car partk, to find that, thanks to the decoy, it was empty.

I am also occasionally asked to propose the health of the bride and bridegroom at a wedding. Here I have quite a good tip for anyone asked to do the same thing. You inevitably have to start with a number of 'in' family jokes, but after that I recommend that you read out what the stars foretell for the young couple. You will find by just reading out what the astrologer has to say, that there are quite a few innocuous innuendos which should amuse the wedding guests – especially when they have had some champagne.

I recently had to do the honours at a wedding of the daughter of great friends of mine in Yorkshire. By scanning the London evening papers for a week or so I was able to read out one or two appropriate forecasts. Things like:

'You'll now be able to start on a job you've been too busy to deal with earlier in the week.'

'Probably the quietest day of the week — favours those of you who want to be left in seclusion to get on with what you want to do.'

'You'll be putting spare time this evening to practical purposes.'

And one especially for the bride:

'Be careful today if handling any electrical gadgets or tools.'

And for the bridegroom:

'There's nothing to be afraid of — it's just that you must be prepared to mark time and not burn up too much physical energy!'

In November 1977 I was asked to go back to my old private school, Temple Grove, to open a new gymnasium. The school used to be at Eastbourne when I was there in the twenties, but it moved to Uckfield during the thirties, and has been there ever since. There was a big audience of parents and boys, as after the opening the boys were going off for their half term. I remember the speech days which we used to have, when an Old Boy, who usually seemed to be a general or admiral, got up and waffled away for about twenty minutes. They normally boasted complacently that they had been no good at work or exams, and implied that it did not seem to have handicapped them in after life.

I hope I did not fall into the same trap. I kept my speech as short as possible and included a few jokes which were so old that they were fresh to this new generation of boys. The headmaster did a great job in introducing me to the parents, masters and boys, and never seemed stuck for a name. This was unlike a headmaster I once knew who was getting on in years, and becoming more and more absent-minded. At one speech day he was going round talking to the old boys, and said to one of them with a note of triumph in his voice: 'Ah, it's Smith major, isn't it?' 'Yes sir,' replied Smith. 'Well, tell me Smith,' said the headmaster, 'I can never remember. Was it you or your brother who was killed in the war?'!

Luckily I did not have to give away any prizes, or I might have had an embarrassing experience such as the actor Gerald Harper once had. He was presenting the prizes at the speech day of a girls' day-school and shook hands with all the winners as they came up to receive their books. Each time he murmured some innocuous remark like 'Well done', 'Congratulations', or 'I hope you'll enjoy this book'. After a while he got a bit fed up with this, and thought he would try something different, and more interesting. So when the next girl – an attractive blonde aged about fifteen – stepped up on to the dais, he shook her by the hand, gave her the book and said confidentially: 'And what are you going to do when you leave school?' 'Oh,' replied the girl somewhat taken aback, 'I *was* going straight back home to have tea with Mum.'!

Talking of embarrassment I like the story of the three middle-aged businessmen who were lunching together. They were discussing the most embarrassing moment in their lives. One said it was when he had forgotten to lock the bathroom door, and the *au pair* girl walked in, and saw him naked in the bath. The second said it was when his shorts fell down around his ankles as he was serving in a tennis tournament. The third man thought for a bit and then said: 'Well, I must admit my most embarrassing moment was when my mother caught me masturbating.' The other two were surprised. 'I cannot see why that should embarrass you. We all used to do it as boys. There was nothing to be ashamed of.' 'Yes, I know that,' said the third man, 'but unfortunately she caught me at it last night!'

This business of masturbation was of course always a problem at schools where they used to regard it as a terrible crime. At Eton quite a long time ago a boy was caught by his housemaster, who after giving him a lecture, sent him down to see the school doctor. In those days even doctors used to say it would make you go mad if you went on doing it. But this particular doctor tried a new tack. He asked the boy why he did it, and the boy honestly replied that he did it because he enjoyed it. 'Well,' said the doctor, 'I must warn you that if you continue you will go blind.' The boy thought for a moment. 'In that case,' he said, 'would it be all right if I went on doing it until I have to wear spectacles?'

Besides Jubilee Day I did quite a number of one-off broadcasts during 1977. There was my usual Boat Race commentary from Chiswick Bridge with interviews with the crews afterwards. Then came a telephone broadcast with Australia from the Oliver Messel room at the Dorchester Hotel in London. This was organised by Diana Fisher, one-time secretary in our Outside Broadcasts Department. Now she is one of the best-known voices and faces on Australian radio and television. She was over here on one of her hectic world tours, when, wherever she is, she has a hook-up each night with Australia and interviews stars of the entertainment and sporting world. On this occasion she wanted a couple of sportsmen so Ted Dexter and Denis Compton kindly obliged, with myself humbly representing the entertainment world.

We were royally entertained by Diana but received no fee, though come to think of it, Denis did make something out of the evening. When he got into the lift to come up to the suite he was joined by an Arab in flowing robes who somehow seemed lost. Denis is nothing if not friendly and was soon chatting up the Arab, and managed to direct him to the floor where his room was. The Arab was profoundly grateful and as they parted slipped a one pound note into Denis' hand. Better than nothing of course, and presumably free of tax. But on present Arab form it could so easily have been a thousand pounds or a diamond watch.

I took part twice in *Games People Play*, a light-hearted sporting quiz chaired by Peter West. There are two teams, each consisting of a sportsman and an entertainer, and my two partners were Rachel Heyhoe-Flint, who has an inexhaustible fund of sporting knowledge, and Pete Murray, Arsenal supporter and keen cricket and tennis player. I cannot remember whether we won – I rather think we did, but the result did not matter. It was just fun to do.

Mike Craig, an amusing Yorkshireman from Dewsbury, produces a programme *It's a Funny Business* in which he talks

to people about the funny side of their careers. He kindly did
me the honour of including me among such stars as
Morecambe and Wise, the late Ted Ray, Arthur Askey, etc,
and used quite a few of my old recordings from *In Town
Tonight* days.

Then there was the *Archive Auction* in which Phyllis Robinson invited me to choose about half a dozen records or tapes
for which I might bid if ever there was an archive auction. It
was a sort of *Desert Island Discs* except that the choice was
limited to material which had been recorded by the BBC
since it started. Needless to say it is a fantastic and quite
unique collection and one could have chosen enough records
to make a hundred programmes. However I tried to make it
as personal to my own tastes as possible and this was my
selection:

1. *Tommy Handley, Jack Train (Colonel Chinstrap) and Diana
    Morrison (Miss Hotchkiss)* in an excerpt from *ITMA*
    recorded just after the end of the war. I chose it because
    Jack and Diana had been great friends of mine, and I
    have always considered Tommy Handley by far the
    greatest *radio* comedian, thanks to the brilliant way he
    could read a comedy script.

2. *A recording of the occasion in September 1938 when Neville
    Chamberlain left Heston Airport to go to meet Hitler in Munich.*
    At the time I was sharing rooms with William Douglas-
    Home and one evening his brother Lord Home rang up.
    He was then Lord Dunglass, parliamentary secretary to
    Mr Chamberlain, and had been told suddenly he too was
    to go to Munich. He wanted us to lend him a shirt as all
    his clothes were up in Scotland. He actually borrowed
    one of mine, so we thought we had better see them off.

    I can still remember Mr Chamberlain with black hom-
    burg and umbrella standing by his (by modern stan-
    dards) ridiculously small two-engined plane. He made
    the following little speech: 'When I was a boy I was
    always taught to be an optimist. When I return from
    seeing Herr Hitler I hope I shall be able to say – as
    Hotspur did in Shakespeare's *King Henry IV* – "Out of
    this nettle danger, we pluck this flower safety".' This

received a sympathetic cheer from the small crowd who had gathered to see him.

On listening to the recording it is amusing to see how broadcasting has improved. Before he makes his little speech you can hear Mr Chamberlain say in a hoarse whisper: 'Let me know when to start,' and then the engineer's voice saying: 'O.K. Go ahead.' Imagine that happening at London Airport today.

3. *Peter Bromley's commentary on the finish of the 1977 Grand National when Red Rum created a record by winning for the third time.* Red Rum has always been one of my heroes and I think he is a fabulous horse. But I really wanted to pay tribute to what is in my opinion the most difficult of all forms of commentating. And I chose Peter Bromley because I think he is the best of them all. A racing commentator has to know and remember so many things, and be able to produce these facts while giving the fastest commentary of any sport, with the possible exception of ice hockey.

Often at places like Newmarket there may be a field of thirty comparatively unknown horses charging straight towards him in a line, and often to make it even more difficult, with the field split, half on one side of the course, half on the other. The commentator has to know the colours, owner, jockey, trainer of each horse and put the right name of the horse to them, and at the same time read the race and make sure to call the first three horses home in the right order. How racing commentators do it I don't know except that it does involve endless hours of homework, juggling the colours and the names around until you get them right. So far as I know Peter himself has never called the wrong horse home, and what's more, if a photo finish is asked for by the judges, Peter is always prepared to stick his neck out and say who *he* thinks has won. I take off my hat to the racing commentators.

4. Next came a nostalgic pre-war memory of *Harry Roy and his Band from the Mayfair Hotel*. In the thirties after a visit to the Palladium or Holborn Empire we often used to go along to hear them, sitting at a table close to the band so

that we got to know them well. The piece I chose was 'Somebody Stole my Gal' with clarinet and a touch of singing from Harry himself, and plenty of that magnificent pair at two pianos – Ivor Moreton who did the twiddly bits in the treble, and Dave Kaye who provided the vital rhythm and accompaniment.

5. *The famous speech by Gerard Hoffnung which the BBC recorded at the Oxford Union after the war.* It describes his adventures with a bucket on a pulley at a building site, and with his high-pitched voice, gives me hysterics every time I hear it.

6. *Alan Gibson's commentary on the last over of the 1963 Test Match at Lord's between England and West Indies.* I had to have something to do with cricket and this was one of the most exciting Tests I have ever watched, not just because of the finish, but because throughout the five days fortunes had swung first one way, then the other. I was doing the TV commentary during the exciting last moments when with two balls left of the match to be bowled by Wes Hall, England needed 6 runs to win, with only one wicket to fall. David Allen was the batsman and he had just been joined by Colin Cowdrey whose broken left arm was in plaster. Had he had to bat he was going to stand as a left-hander and play with his sound right arm. But luckily David Allen resisted the temptation to hit a six for victory and kept out the last two balls safely. A draw was the fairest result to both teams.

7. *'Scorn not his simplicity' – sung by Adrian Hardy.* When *Down Your Way* visited Kilkeel in County Down during the summer of 1977 I interviewed a young teenage student artist who not only painted but also sang in a group. His name was Adrian Hardy and at the end of the interview instead of choosing a piece of music for us to play later, we recorded him there and then. The song he chose to sing was a haunting ballad composed by Phil Coulter, who among other things had composed 'Puppet on a String' for Sandie Shaw when she won the European Song Contest. Phil has a mentally-handicapped son and the title of the song explains exactly what it is about. I, for very

personal reasons, found it terribly moving, and just had to include it for my final choice.

My appearances on TV are practically nil these days, but for the last six years I have done the TV commentary on the Lord Mayor's Show. As in 1976 we were part of *Swop Shop* and before the procession started I was persuaded to offer a miniature cricket bat as a swop. The Lord Mayor was again wired up under his robes with a small transmitter and microphone so that he could give a message to viewers as the coach passed our cameras opposite St Pauls. When he had made his little speech the Lord Mayor – Air Commodore the Hon. Sir Peter Vanneck – thought he would make a professional handback to me, but unfortunately cued back to Raymond instead of Brian! Raymond Baxter had helped him at his Press conference about the show, and he must somehow have got Raymond's name stuck in his mind. But he immediately realised his mistake because our sound engineers heard him say as he sat back in his coach – 'Blast it! I should have said Brian.' Luckily, though, they had already switched back to my microphone, so his remark did not go out over the air.

The one other TV appearance I made was in Bruce Forsyth's *Generation Game*. This is a tremendous *tour de force* by Bruce and I can think of no one else who could anywhere near match his bubbling audience-winning personality. He makes wonderful use of the camera, and his various facial expressions after cracking a corny gag, which has either gone well or flopped, are real television. But no matter how great an artiste he is, much of his success is due to his professional preparation beforehand and all the hard work which goes with it.

It was fascinating to watch the rehearsal with Bruce putting stand-in contestants through the various games. He even read through the cards about each contestant and as he did so I kept thinking of what gags I would make about the various items on the cards. For instance one man had just been promoted to be superintendent of a cemetery. I thought my comment might have been – 'Well, you're *dead* lucky, aren't you?' As it turned out during the actual show Bruce remarked 'Oh, so you've got a lot of people under you!' His great skill is in making these gags appear to be spontaneous, though of course with the help of a scriptwriter, they have been worked out carefully beforehand.

After a daylong rehearsal Bruce has a two-hour break before the show. Then he goes out to warm up the audience just before the recording starts. The show is recorded on the Thursday evening before the Saturday it goes out, and ideally many of the audience are in parties and Bruce gains an immediate rapport with them. Incidentally, he does not meet the real contestants until they appear in the show, nor have they any idea of what the various games will be.

My small part was in No. 3 game called *Name the Commentator*. Five of us, John Snagge, Dan Maskell, Peter Alliss, John Motson and myself each in turn read out a bit of doggerel giving clues about the game on which we usually commentate. The contestants had then to write down who they thought each commentator was. One team guessed me, the other said 'Robertson of *Down Your Way*'; the male partner apologised afterwards and said his mind went blank. John Snagge and John Motson were each guessed by one team, but Peter Alliss and Dan Maskell stumped everyone. Remarkable really, when you consider how regularly they are on TV during the summer. One team in fact gave the hilarious answer of Virginia Wade when trying to guess Dan! Anyhow, it was all a lot of fun, and meeting the contestants afterwards cleared away any doubts I might have had about them being made to look fools. They had all thoroughly enjoyed themselves and would not have missed it for the world.

Oh, and by the way, the answer is definitely YES – Anthea *is* as gorgeous to meet as she is to see on the TV. If Bruce's stage musical activities prevent him doing any more *Generation Games*, millions of people of *all* ages throughout the country will greatly miss his delightful frolics.

Fifteenth Over Packer up your troubles!

And now, reluctantly, I must say something about the Packer affair. I have put off doing so for as long as possible because I personally feel it is all so very sad. Coming out of the blue as it did, it split cricket down the middle, put a severe strain on old friendships and introduced argument, resentment and rancour into the dressing-rooms.

Cricket was made the whipping boy and the cricketers the pawns (albeit well paid!) in what was essentially an Australian television battle. It all started because Mr Packer was refused exclusive TV rights for Test Matches in Australia by the Australian Cricket Board. Mr Packer – possibly out of pique, possibly to give himself a bargaining weapon – promptly set about signing up over fifty of the world's top players to play in a series of 'Super Tests' in direct opposition to the official Tests already arranged between Australia and India in Australia in 1977–8 and between Australia and England in 1978–9.

He did this in complete secrecy and I think what stuck in the gullets of old squares like myself was the underhand and deceitful way in which it was all carried out. That Tony Greig, captain of England, straight from the successful tour of India and the euphoria of the Centenary Test, could play a leading part in these signings, passed my comprehension.

Maybe because of the way it was done, the establishment overreacted. But if someone suddenly points a pistol at your head, your first instinct is to defend yourself and that is precisely what the ICC and TCCB set out to do.

All this has been particularly sad for me because nearly all the players concerned have been my friends for many years. Because of the clever way in which Mr Packer insisted on secrecy and silence as part of the contract, none of the first players to sign were allowed to consult their solicitors, their cricket employers or just friends like myself, before signing. Had they done so, there are so many things I would have wanted to put to them.

First and foremost, there is the question of job satisfaction. This to me is a vital column in the balance sheet of a job. All one read about in the law case were the moans from the players about too much travel, dysentery, separation from wives, the dole, etc, etc. *Why*, if they were so unhappy, did they go on playing? It was of course a very false picture. I have been on ten tours and have shared the players' enjoyment and thrills in playing cricket round the world, seeing new places and meeting friendly and hospitable people. I *know* they have enjoyed themselves and have considered themselves lucky compared with the nine to five commuter, the miner, the bus driver and so on.

Of course, hotels are sometimes tatty, aeroplanes break down, some food is lousy and one misses one's family. But this happens to thousands of businessmen, merchant seamen and members of the Forces as well as cricketers. In general the hotel and travel arrangements on tours are absolutely first class.

Much was made by their counsel of the fact that some cricketers have had to go on the dole during the winter. What did not come out in the papers was that the player who complained in the courts that he, an England cricketer who had had to go on the dole, was in fact writing a book at the time for which he had received a fat advance! But of course most cricketers do find winter employment, many of them going to coach in sunny climes, and others having part-time jobs with firms in this country. Ironically, in the old days cricketers were paid a salary spread over the year. But this was changed to an April to September engagement, so that they *could* qualify for the winter dole if they wanted it.

Anyhow, my point is that a cricketer's lot is a happy one compared with so many other professions and jobs, and that this *must* count when weighing up its value. I would also have tried to remind my friends of that seemingly old-fashioned word loyalty – to those who discovered them, coached them and developed their skills and techniques by advice or playing alongside them. They also owe a very special loyalty to their faithful supporters who either subscribed to or worked so hard to organise the many fund-raising schemes for their tax-free benefits.

And now for perhaps the most important thing of all. What about pride in playing for one's country or county and trying to win the Ashes or the County Championship? Surely this must be worth *something* even in these commercial days? Did they really stop to think what it would be like to play on vast rough football grounds on a dummy pitch in a concrete tray before huge empty stands? Did they really want floodlights, white balls, black sightscreens, microphones dug into the grass around the stumps, or someone asking them what they thought of the umpire's decision as they returned to the pavilion? I doubt it, if they were honest. But nevertheless whenever they were asked to comment on their signing, time and time again out came the phrase: 'It's an offer I couldn't refuse.'

So let's look at the money side, and here the players are on a better wicket. I don't think there is anyone who would deny that the average county cricketer has for years been underpaid, even taking into account the pleasing nature of his job. This is especially evident when comparisons are made with the average soccer player. A county cricketer who does not play for England earns anything between three to four thousand pounds for five months, depending on his county and his share of the various competition money prizes. In other words, a player from a top county will probably earn not only a higher basic salary but be more likely to pick up bigger perks by appearing in more semi-finals and finals. On average the successful soccer player in the first division earns about ten thousand pounds a year and again the player in a successful club gets more in bonuses and win money.

But there are several things to remember. A soccer season is for eleven months, not five, and it is a more physical game (loud boos from anyone who has had to face Lillee and Thomson!). So the playing life of a soccer player is generally much shorter than a cricketer, nor does he get one – or even two – *tax-free* benefits worth nowadays anything from twenty-five to fifty thousand pounds. Which of us can save that sort of money these days? But just a word about these benefits. They are tax free because of a case won by J. Seymour of Kent in the 1920s. This case established that benefits are not guaranteed nor part of a cricketer's contract. They are just gifts given by a grateful county and its supporters after no specific time, though it is usual for them to be granted to a player after he has been capped for ten years. The soccer benefits, however, are part of the player's contract and so become taxable.

Cricket benefits and testimonials have been granted since well before the end of the last century. But I do agree with the modern cricketers who find them degrading. Public appeals, collections and getting your friends and supporters to help, must be embarrassing. I know I should loathe it. The final reward undoubtedly makes it worthwhile in the end. But in principle cricketers should be paid sufficient for the job they do, and not have to rely on charity.

Cricketers who represent their countries have of course done much better. Test Match fees (in 1977 two hundred and ten pounds per Test plus a win bonus of two hundred and fifty pounds) have been laughably low compared with money earned by top players in other sports. Things, though, are now much brighter with one thousand pounds for each Test and five thousand pounds for an overseas tour. But the regular Test cricketers – say about fifteen in England – do get considerable spin-offs like writing books or articles, TV and radio interviews and quizzes, sponsorship of cricket equipment, private tours, and top coaching jobs. Many firms too give them quite lucrative jobs in order to cash in on their names. I would be surprised if over twelve months these top England players have not been earning either side of five figures with one or two considerably more. Not great money people may say compared to sportsmen like tennis players, golfers, boxers, racing drivers and speedway riders.

True enough, but these are in the main individual sports and the really big money is associated with a sport that takes place in America where the huge prizes are. That is where our own tennis players and golfers go in order to get into the big time. But even so it is still only the *top* players who earn the gigantic sums we read about. Ask the professional golfer how he does if he fails to finish in the prize money. He has to find his own travel and subsistence expenses himself.

If only America would take up cricket! But the truth is that cricket in England has always had to be subsidised. In the old days there were rich private patrons, then came the pools and now sponsorships, even including the County Championship and Test Matches. Cricket has for too long been run by badly paid secretaries – many of them retired officers. Each club also has many hard working volunteers who devote all their free time to cricket. So there are no bureaucratic administrators in cricket who are paid money which otherwise would go to the players.

I would certainly agree that cricket should have become more businesslike and more understanding of the economic difficulties of the players. For instance, I think that membership subscriptions are absurdly low for counties with Test Match grounds where their members can see the Tests for nothing. The Packer affair would probably never have happened if the players had been given more businesslike contracts offering more long-term security.

It's no secret, I believe, that up to 1977 Alan Knott had no contract with Kent whatsoever. It was done on a basis of saying in September – 'Goodbye – see you next April.' So perhaps you cannot really blame the players for snatching at a lifeline which offered untold gold and some short-term security. 'It's an offer I couldn't refuse. I've got my wife and children to consider.' They have all said it and meant it – and yet.

If the Packer 'Super' Tests succeed what will be the effect on our cricket? So far the signings have undoubtedly nudged the authorities to hasten the Cornhill Insurance Sponsorship for Tests (it was already being discussed before Mr Packer came along) and the counties to try and be more professional and realistic with their contracts. But if the Super Tests succeed then official Tests are bound to suffer. There cannot be two Test series competing side by side for public support. If the official Tests lose, then the rich Packer players will get richer and the ordinary first-class cricketer will get poorer – because the living of the average county cricketer comes from Test Match profits. It is as simple as that. That is why the players themselves voted FOR the ban against Packer players at the Cricketers' Association meeting.

So where do we go from here? I am sure that eventually there must be a compromise. There has to be, or top cricket as we know it will slowly strangle itself to death. Who will hold the cards at the end of the winter season is anyone's guess. But I would think that when each side has taken stock there will be some sort of suggestion to hold the Packer series in October and November and so leave his players free to play for their countries on winter tours. In return I suppose that the Packer matches might be given first-class status and allowed to be played on Test grounds, so long as they keep to the laws of cricket.

But there are two snags here. Will Mr Packer abandon his demand for exclusive Test coverage and how will the players react to playing eleven months of the year? For a long time now they have been complaining of too much cricket and calling for shorter tours – rightly in my opinion. If this compromise came about they would only have a few weeks off in September and March. But of course money does help! Though pity the poor fast bowlers. How *will* their feet stand up to it?

As I write it is too early to judge who is winning. Mr Packer's five-day 'Tests' have got off to a bad start so far as attendances at the grounds are concerned. He has, so we are told, even had to use dubbed applause to cover up the embarrassingly small crowds. As I had suspected – and hoped – matches between the world's top cricket players, however good they are, will not draw spectators if it does not matter to *them* who wins. They can admire the superb techniques, the magnificent stroke play and the fastest bowling in the world. But this soon begins to pall unless there is the necessary tension. The players on the other hand *are* trying hard enough, since there is an extra thousand pounds or so for each member of the winning team which CANNOT be shared with the losers, as it is recorded for income tax.

Due to the holiday period in Australia most of the TV ratings have been inconclusive, though on the evidence seen they must have been a disappointment to Packer, as has also been the support of the vital advertisers.

But he must certainly be encouraged by two things. The TV camera coverage has by all accounts been superb – eight cameras giving pictures and re-plays in various degrees of slow motion and magnification from all parts of the ground. And undoubtedly limited-over cricket under floodlight has caught on and provided thrilling finishes in front of crowds of twenty thousand.

So I suspect that this will be the Packer future – night cricket with the stars on the field as well as in the sky. He *may* try to compete with the Australia–England series in 1978–9 but I doubt whether it will succeed if he does. I suspect that unless spectators can become involved over five days, his 'Tests' will slowly die the death.

And now a final word about the ICC and TCCB ban on the Packer players from playing for their countries and counties. In the thirty-one-day court case brought by Mr Packer, Mr Justice Slade declared this ban illegal and to be an incitement to the players to break their contracts with Mr Packer. Ironically, if the cricket authorities had done absolutely nothing until next summer and then just not have picked the players all would apparently have been legal. If the judgement was based on such a simple point of law it makes me wonder why the trial was allowed to meander along for thirty-one days, with witness after witness just giving his opinion of the whole affair. I may be wrong but I would say that the only opinion that matters is that of the Judge. Could it not have been given sooner and so have saved the huge costs of two hundred and fifty thousand pounds which the cricket authorities now have to pay.

So what *will* happen about the ban? I must say that without being vindictive I was always in favour of it – I just could not see how the players could serve two masters – especially when their Packer series next winter would clash with the Australia v. England Tests. I think that the countries and counties will now go their own way. Australia did not choose *their* players for their West Indies tour – the West Indies did choose theirs, and now Pakistan – after some dithering – have left their Packer players out of their team touring England.

My bet is that England will not choose her Packer players again for England. I may well be wrong but there is no way that the law can force the selectors to choose them. The selectors will want to build up the side that has toured during the winter and prepare it for the Australia series in 1978–9. I myself believe this is only fair to the players who went to Pakistan and New Zealand, and that they would not welcome the return of the Packermen. The counties are in a different position. Those with Packer players who have contracts will have to honour those contracts – not necessarily by *playing* the players but by *paying* them.

Gloucestershire, I am sure, will be delighted to welcome back Procter, who achieved so much for them in 1977. What Kent will do is more problematical.

As I said at the start it is all very sad, and poor old cricket faces some difficult days ahead. But no matter if TV ratings do give victory to Mr Packer, I'm sure that cricket will get over it, and that in the years ahead we shall see a number of bright new stars playing for England. It's a great opportunity for them – thanks to Mr Packer.

Sixteenth Over I can't help laughing

(If you don't like corny jokes – skip this chapter!)

A man had just returned from his honeymoon and was asked by a friend whether he had enjoyed it.

'Yes, I certainly did,' he replied. 'I never knew you could have so much fun without laughing.'

I can see what he meant and of course it *is* possible to have fun without making a noise to prove it. But most of us, when hearing, seeing or experiencing something funny, do usually show our approval or enjoyment by a guffaw, chuckle, chortle, giggle, snigger or at least a gentle titter. I have been lucky in that throughout my life I have spent a lot of time laughing. So much so that I have often been accused of not taking anything seriously. Not true really, but I know what people mean. I have been blessed(?) with a sense of the ridiculous and a vivid imagination, plus a mind which is automatically tuned to trying to make a pun or joke at every possible opportunity.

There are so many different types of humour and I'm afraid that most of the things which make us laugh are usually jokes against or about other people. There are the usual things that happen to them such as slipping on a banana skin or falling accidentally fully-clothed into a swimming pool. There are the physical characteristics like a funny walk, a stutter or a comic face. I suppose one of the biggest laughter-makers is the pricking of pomposity or the humbling of authority. Try not to laugh if someone like a bishop or a schoolmaster sits on a well-placed whoopee bag! Hardest of all, of course, is the ability to laugh at yourself when things happen to *you* – then somehow it doesn't seem quite so amusing!

There is perhaps an even greater variety of *verbal* humour. Wit, satire and sarcasm come lowest on my list. Farce, slapstick, jokes, cross-talk, shaggy dog stories and quick-fire gags make me laugh the most. At the end of my last book *It's Been a Lot of Fun* I included six stories which always make me laugh. This time I will mix some jokes with the stories and place them all under various headings. Once again I hope some of them will tickle your particular sense of humour and anyway they could always come in useful for that speech you are due to make at your niece's wedding or at the village cricket or football club dinner. There are also – I hope – one or two which would be suitable for an old girls' gathering!

Animal

A man was telling a friend about the two elephants which were walking up Bond Street. One of the elephants told the other that he wanted to fart. 'Oh,' said the other elephant, 'you can't do that here. It will make far too much noise in a narrow street like this. You will have to go and do it in Hyde Park.' So the two elephants set off up Piccadilly towards Hyde Park. The man then asked his friend: 'Have you heard it?' to which his friend replied: 'No.' 'Well,' said the man, 'you would have done if you had been in Hyde Park.'

A lady had a pet dog which was one of those tiny chihuahuas. Its hair began to fall out so she went to her local chemist and asked him if he had anything to stop hair falling out. He went to a shelf and produced a pot of ointment. 'Rub this in twice daily, but there must be no friction, so don't wear a hat for a week.' 'Oh,' said the lady, 'it's not for my head, it's for my chihuahua.' 'In that case,' said the chemist, 'I would advise you not to ride a bike for a fortnight!'

Two flies were sitting on Robinson Crusoe. One of them flew off and called out to the other, 'Bye Bye. See you on Friday!'

Courts

JUDGE (to the accused who had just been found guilty by the
   Jury): Before I sentence you, what would you like to say?
ACCUSED: F—— all, m'lord.
JUDGE (to his clerk): What did he say?
CLERK (in a whisper): F—— all, m'lord.
JUDGE (to clerk): Oh, no. He definitely said something. I saw
   his lips move.

It was a hot summer's day in court and getting on for
lunchtime. In the witness-box was a girl who had been raped
and she was being cross-examined by counsel.
COUNSEL: . . . And what happened then?
GIRL WITNESS: He drove into a field, stopped the car and put
   his hand inside my dress.
JUDGE (looking at his watch): And there I think we will leave
   it until after lunch.

Three magistrates were trying a case of suspected rape. One
of them was a retired colonel who had fallen asleep after a
good lunch. Another was the local grocer, and the chairman
was a somewhat prim ex-headmistress. The bashful young
girl in the box was giving details of what had happened. The
lady chairman asked her how it all started and what the man
had said to her. The girl blushed. 'I'd rather not say it in
public,' she pleaded. 'Very well,' said the chairman, 'write it
down then on a piece of paper.'

   This the girl did and the piece of paper was handed up to
the bench. The chairman read it and then handed it to the
grocer who glanced at it and nodded. The chairman then
turned to the colonel who was still asleep, snoring fitfully.
She nudged him and whispered into his ear, 'Wake up
colonel, I've got something for you to read,' and thrust the
note under his nose.

   He woke with a start, saw the piece of paper and quickly
put on his specs and read: 'I am feeling randy. What about a
poke?' The colonel looked at the lady chairman for a second
or two in amazement and disbelief. 'Madam,' he said in a
hoarse whisper, 'you must have gone out of your mind!'

Doctors

A man went to see a doctor in a terrible panic.

'Doctor,' he said, 'please examine me at once. I think I'm going to have a baby.'

The doctor examined him and said, 'By God, you're right. This will cause a great sensation when I tell my colleagues in Harley Street.'

'So it will back home in Laburnam Crescent,' said the man. 'I'm not even married.'

A man went to the doctor with a very bad cough. The doctor gave him a large dose of cascara. The man was very surprised. 'Cascara doesn't cure a cough,' he said. 'No, I know it doesn't,' said the doctor. 'But it will stop you coughing. After a dose like that you won't dare to.'

A doctor was telling a friend about a nun who had terrible hiccoughs which she couldn't stop. So in desperation she went to the doctor, who, after a short examination, told her she was pregnant. 'Goodness me,' said his friend, 'was she really?' 'No,' said the doctor, 'of course not. But it cured her hiccoughs!'

A woman went to her doctor with a bad cough. After examining her throat he asked her, 'Do you ever get a tickle in the morning?' 'Well, I used to, Doctor,' she replied, 'but not now. We've changed the milkman.'

A man had that very painful 'universal complaint'. The doctor examined his backside and said he would like to try out a new cure he had just heard about. The man agreed and the doctor inserted a lot of tea leaves in the appropriate place, saying it would take two or three weeks to effect the cure. But after a week the pain was still there so the man became impatient and decided to go to a more orthodox doctor in the next town. He told him what was wrong and after the examination the doctor said: 'Well, I'm afraid there's nothing I can do for you except to give you some ointment. But I'll tell you one thing. You are going on a long journey with a strange lady!'

Food and wine

A man attended a club dinner and was disgusted at the quality of the food. So he wrote to the secretary to complain about it, and received the following reply: 'Thank you for your letter and I am so sorry that you did not enjoy the food at our dinner the other night. Will you please bring it up at the annual general meeting?'

A guest sitting at the top table at a dinner got only one glass of wine to drink the whole evening. But he got his own back on his hosts. It was his task to propose the toast of 'Absent Friends' – and he coupled it with the name of the wine waiter!

Football

A team of elephants was playing a team of mice. One of the elephants trod on a mouse and killed it. The referee took the elephant's name and gave a penalty. The elephant was very apologetic. 'I'm sorry, ref,' he said. 'I didn't mean to do it. I was only trying to trip him up.'

A team of insects were playing and for most of the first half they were a man short. The missing player was a centipede who ran on to the field thirty-five minutes late. 'I'm sorry,' he said to his captain, 'it took me longer than I thought it would to do up all my boots.'

A little boy was lost in the vast crowd at a football match. A policeman saw him crying so went up to him and asked him what was wrong. 'I've lost my Dad.' The policeman looked about him and asked, 'What's he like, son?' 'Beer and women,' replied the small boy.

A league side was doing very badly and languishing at the bottom of the table. Needless to say their gates were very poor and attendances had dwindled to a few hundreds. A man rang up the manager one Friday and asked: 'What time does the match start tomorrow?' Back came the immediate reply: 'What time can you get here?'

Another side had such poor crowds that before each match the public address announcer used to announce the names of the crowd to the two teams!

Good news – Bad news

An officer out with a patrol in the desert called his men together at an oasis one night. 'Men,' he said, 'we have been out in the desert for six weeks, we are miles from anywhere and quite frankly we are lost. But I have two bits of news for you, one bad, one good. I'll give you the bad first. We have run out of rations and from now on we will have to live on camel dung.' There was a groan of disgust from the men. 'But, wait for it,' the officer said, 'here's the good news. There's plenty of it.'

The slave driver on a ship went down into the hold to address the slaves who were all sitting manacled together rowing as hard as they could. 'Slaves,' he said, 'I've got some good news for you. You may have half an hour's rest.' The slaves sank exhausted at their oars. 'But, listen,' said the slave driver, 'here's the bad news. When you have had your rest the Captain wants to go water-skiing.'

Honeymoons

The newly married young couple had arrived at their hotel late in the afternoon, and had been shown up to their luxurious honeymoon suite. At long last they were alone. The bridegroom put his arms round his wife and said expectantly: 'Shall we go to bed now? Or would you rather stay up late and watch the 5.40 pm news on BBC 1?'

Hospitals

A man woke up after an operation and through a mist saw a

figure standing by his bed. 'Was my operation a success, doctor?' he whispered. 'I don't know old chap,' said the figure. 'I'm St Peter.'

A young couple got married and nine months later the wife went into hospital to have their baby. The young husband was pacing anxiously up and down in the hospital waiting-room when a nurse rushed in. 'Mr Jones,' she cried, 'many congratulations. You have got a son.' 'Amazing,' said Mr Jones looking at his watch, 'nine months exactly to the minute.'

Half an hour later the same nurse rushed in again. 'Mr Jones, Mr Jones, wonderful news. You have also got a daughter.' 'Amazing,' said Mr Jones again looking at his watch which now showed 9.45 pm. 'Nine months exactly to the minute.'

Another half an hour went by when the excited nurse ran into the room shouting: 'It's triplets and this time, it's another boy.' 'Amazing,' said Mr Jones looking at his watch, 'nine months to the exact minute.' So saying he picked up his hat and coat and made for the door. 'Where are you going?' asked the nurse. 'I'm off to have a quick drink,' he replied. 'There's nothing more due now until 11.15 pm!'

Hotel

The driver of one of those huge juggernauts was driving through the night and thought he would stop off somewhere for a few hours sleep. He tried one or two lodgings he knew in a town through which he was passing but there were no vacancies. He then tried the various pubs and small hotels but they too were full up. Finally, in desperation he decided to try a large luxurious five-star hotel, although he knew he could not afford their usual high prices. So he plucked up courage and walked up to the receptionist – a smart young man in black coat and striped trousers. 'Excuse me,' said the lorry driver, 'but do you have any special terms for long-distance drivers?' 'Yes,' replied the young man without any hesitation. 'F . . . Off!'

Irish stories

My stepfather was an Irishman from Tipperary and was I suppose fairly typical – genial and friendly but with an explosive temper, easily aroused. I'm not sure what he would have thought of the modern spate of Irish stories. I suspect he would have enjoyed telling them himself but resented being told them – at any rate by an Englishman. I must say they do make me laugh though I take care not to tell them to any of my Irish friends. I suppose with all the horrors being perpetrated in Northern Ireland they are rather 'sick'. But ridicule can act as useful anti-propaganda. Remember how as soon as war was declared Tommy Handley unleashed a series of anti-Hitler jokes which would never have been allowed by the BBC against a foreign statesman in time of peace. One good thing about the Irish stories is that they are short. I cannot resist telling one or two, all of which start with: 'Did you hear about the Irishman who . . .'

1. Was told to take his car in for a service, but got it stuck in the church door.
2. Drove his car into a river and when asked why, said a policeman had stopped him and told him to dip his headlights.
3. Thought that a Royal Enfield was a place where the Queen kept her chickens.
4. Was ordered to blow up a car and burnt his lips on the exhaust pipe.
5. Was found drinking a glass of beer on the roof of a pub. When asked why, he said he had been told that drinks were on the house.
6. Was accused of raping a girl and was lined up in an identity parade. The girl was then brought into the yard where the row of men were standing and the Irishman pointed to her and said: 'That's her!'
7. Had his right ear cut off in an accident on a building site. He and his mate Paddy were looking for it in all the rubble when Paddy picked up an ear. 'Here it is,' he called out. 'No,' said the Irishman who had lost the ear, 'that's not it. Mine had a cigarette behind it!'

8. Was playing in a game of soccer which was being televised. He scored a penalty for his side, but missed it on the
   action replay.
9. Came home unexpectedly from work and found his wife
   in the arms of his best friend. He rushed to a drawer, took
   out a revolver, and pointed it at his own head. 'This is too
   much,' he cried, 'I am going to shoot myself.' At this his
   wife began to laugh. 'I don't know what you are laughing
   at,' he said to her. 'You're next.'

And finally, there was the world champion tobogganist
hurtling down the Cresta Run at over 60 mph. At one of the
worst corners he had a terrible accident. He met an Irishman
Coming up!

Marriage

A husband and wife were arguing as so many do about
money – or the lack of it. 'We've simply got to economise,'
said the husband. 'If only you could learn about food we
could sack the cook.' 'In that case,' said the wife, 'learn
about making love and we can sack the chauffeur.'

On most Sundays when I am at home I take our Yorkshire
terrier Mini for a walk in Regent's Park. We usually go
alongside the zoo and see the elephants swaying from side to
side and sniff the pungent smell of the foxes. It always makes
me think of the man and wife who went one day to the zoo.
The wife got too close to the bars of the gorilla's cage, and the
gorilla dragged her screaming through the bars. He began to
rip off her clothing with the obvious intention of raping her.
'Help, help,' she cried to her husband, as she stood starkers
in the gorilla's arms. 'What shall I do?' 'Tell him you've got a
headache as you always do to me!' replied the husband
unsympathetically!

Misprints

Under a picture of the late Sir Francis Chichester was the
following caption: 'The great yachtsman Sir Francis
Chichester who with his 24-foot cutter *circumcised* the world.'

The treasurer of a cricket club sent out a notice to members at the beginning of a new season. It regretted that due to inflation the annual subscription would have to go up by two pounds per anum. (His secretary evidently could not spell.) A few days later came a letter from one of the members who said that he would prefer to go on paying through the *nose*.

Political

Mrs Thatcher was addressing the annual Conservative Ladies' Conference at the Royal Albert Hall. She emphasised that difficult times lay ahead and that the Tories would have a real fight on their hands. 'Ladies,' she cried, 'we have taken it lying down long enough. From now on we must stand with our backs to the wall.'

While Harold Wilson was Prime Minister the Queen discussed with him the question of giving him a State funeral were he to die suddenly. 'No, thank you, Mam,' he replied, 'the vast expense and trouble would not be justified. You see, Mam, I shall only be there for three days.'

Mrs Gandhi went on a State visit to Singapore and with the Prime Minister Lee Kwan Yew was watching a military parade. They were sitting together under a canopy, when suddenly the skies darkened, there was a clap of thunder and down came a tropical storm. The parade ground was soon flooded and the rain was so heavy that it came through the canopy under which Mrs Gandhi was sitting and she got drenched. Remarkably the Prime Minister was lucky and no rain fell on him, although he was only a few feet from her. So he apologised profusely to Mrs Gandhi for the fact that he was dry and she was sopping wet. 'Thank you,' she replied, as servants rushed forward to help dry her, 'but I still don't understand why it didn't Lee Kwan Yew!'

Quickies

What was the nickname given to a well-known judge who had no thumb – Justice fingers.

A man rang up the rodent officer at the local town hall to complain that his house was overrun by homosexual mice. 'What shall I do to dispose of them?' he asked. 'Get a pouffy cat,' was the reply.

A man always told people that his Cockney wife was really a Scandinavian. When they expressed surprise he explained that 'She eats like a Norse.'

What would you call a Frenchman at a circus whose act was to be shot out of a canon?
Napoleon Blownapart.

What's got six eyes and can't see?
Three blind mice.

What do you call a deaf elephant?
Anything you like. He won't hear you.

Religion

A Protestant vicar, a Catholic priest and a Rabbi were all having an argument as to which of them was the better person and nearest to God. 'Nearest to God, you say,' said the Rabbi, 'I *am* God.' At this the other two roared with laughter. 'All right,' said the Rabbi, 'come with me and I'll prove it.' So curiously they went with him down to the red light district of the town. The Rabbi knocked on a door and a luscious blonde opened it. '*God*,' she said, 'Are you here again?'

School

A public school is a place where you make friends for life and this is one of the reasons why I am so grateful to Eton. Almost anywhere I go I seem to run into an old friend or acquaintance, and most of my very close friends have lasted forty-five years or so since we were at Eton together. Of course you can also make enemies, though these don't often last for life. Unlike the two very distinguished Old Boys who had hated each other at school, and had made a point of avoiding each other ever since. Over the years they rose to the top in their respective professions – one becoming an Admiral, the other a Bishop.

As bad luck would have it they both had to attend an official ceremony at Windsor which required full ceremonial dress. There was a special train from Paddington and they were both pacing up and down the platform. The Bishop, an extremely portly figure was in his apron and gaiters, and the Admiral in full dress uniform. The Bishop spotted the Admiral and was surprised to recognise his old enemy. Determined to continue the feud and score off the Admiral, he approached him and said: 'Excuse me, Station Master, but could you tell me what time this train leaves for Windsor?' The Admiral was taken aback for a moment but suddenly realised who the Bishop was. 'Yes, madam,' he replied 'it goes at 11.15 but in your present state I would advise you not to travel!'

Race

I know that some people dislike racial stories and consider that they do harm to race relations. But there always have been stories about Jews, Scotsmen, Irishmen and so on. So, provided they are not malicious and are funny I can see no real harm in them. For instance I was told this story up in Bradford where they have a very large Pakistani community. A young Yorkshire boy arrived late at school one morning. 'I am sorry I am late teacher,' he said, 'But I had to get my own breakfast.' 'All right, Johnny,' said his teacher. 'Sit down. We are doing geography this morning, and have been talking about the division of India and Pakistan. Can you tell me where the Pakistan border is?' 'Yes, Miss,' said Johnny. 'He's in bed with Mum. That's why I had to get my own breakfast!'

Shaggy dog stories

A circus was doing very badly. Audiences were dwindling and the proprietor was losing so much money that he realised that unless drastic action were taken he would have to close down. So he summoned all his staff and asked them to think up some publicity gimmick which would bring the crowds in. After a lot of discussion the elephant trainer came up with this idea. 'My old elephant Jumbo is very obstinate and won't obey anyone except me. Why don't we offer a prize of fifty pounds to anyone who can make him sit down in the ring. I guarantee he will just stand there and refuse to budge unless *I* tell him to do it.' The proprietor thought this was a great stunt so plastered the town with leaflets and handbills announcing that on Saturday night there would be this sensational competition to see who could make Jumbo sit down. Prize fifty pounds.

On Saturday night the circus was packed out. There was standing room only. The proprietor was delighted as he counted his takings. After the interval the ringmaster announced the competition and Jumbo was brought into the ring by his trainer. He stood in the middle of the ring and the audience were invited to step in one by one and see if they could make him sit down in thirty minutes. There was a rush to try and people tried everything. They pulled his trunk, twisted his tail and shouted various words of command. But to no avail. Jumbo just stood there. So after twenty-nine minutes the ringmaster announced that with one minute to go there was just time for one more person to try. A small man stepped into the ring carrying a ladder. This he placed against the elephant's hind quarters and climbed up. When he got to the top, he lifted up the elephants's tail, and gave him a tremendous kick up the arse. The elephant with a scream of pain immediately sat down. So the small man climbed down his ladder, collected fifty pounds from the ringmaster and left the ring to uproarious applause from the audience.

Although he had had to fork out fifty pounds the proprietor had made a killing on the night. He was so pleased in fact that he asked the elephant trainer to think out another scheme for the following Saturday. The trainer said he had an absolute certainty which no one could possibly win. The task would be to make Jumbo nod his head up and down, and then shake it sideways. 'He'll never do that for anyone,' said the trainer. 'He wouldn't even do it for me. Your fifty pounds will be quite safe.'

So the same procedure was adopted the next Saturday night and once again the circus tent was packed. At the interval the audience were again told what they had to do, and were invited to try their hand for half an hour. Hundreds of them came into the ring and tried everything to make Jumbo nod his head, then shake it. But he just stood there, ignoring all their efforts.

Finally, with one minute to go the ringmaster announced there was only time for one more person to try. Once again the same small man stepped into the ring with his ladder. This time he placed it against Jumbo's shoulder and climbed up. He took hold of Jumbo's ear and whispered into it: 'Do you remember what I did to you last Saturday?' Jumbo nodded his head up and down. The audience were amazed. The small man then whispered into Jumbo's ear: 'Do you want me to do it again?' At this Jumbo shook his head vigorously from side to side. The audience cheered, the small man climbed down the ladder, pocketed another fifty pounds and left the ring. A just reward for his remembering that simple adage: 'An elephant never forgets'.

Before the start of a needle village match, the home captain found he was one short. In desperation he was looking round the ground for someone he could rope in to play when he spotted an old horse grazing quietly in the field next door. So he went up to him and asked him if he would like to make up the side. The horse stopped eating and said: 'Well, I haven't played for some time and am a bit out of practice but if you're pushed, I'll certainly help you out', and so saying jumped over the fence and sat down in a deckchair in front of the pavilion.

The visitors lost the toss and the home side batted first, the horse being put in last. They were soon 23 for 9 and the horse made his way to the wicket wearing those sort of leather shoes horses have on when they are pulling a roller or a mower. He soon showed his eye was well in and hit the bowling all over the field. When he wasn't hitting sixes he was galloping for quick singles and never once said 'neigh' when his partner called him for a run. Finally he was out hoof before wicket for a brilliant 68, and the home side had made 99.

When the visitors batted the home captain put the horse in the deep and he saved many runs by galloping round the boundary and hoofing the ball back to the wicket-keeper. However the visitors were not losing any wickets and were soon 50 for 0. The home captain had tried all his regular bowlers in vain when he suddenly thought of the horse. He had batted brilliantly and now was fielding better than anyone. At least he could do no worse than the other bowlers. So he called out to him: 'Horse, would you like to take the next over at the vicarage end?' The horse looked surprised. 'Of course I wouldn't,' he replied. 'Whoever heard of a horse who could BOWL?'

Transport

A man was motoring along a main road when he saw a very attractive blonde by the side of the road thumbing a lift. So he stopped and asked her to get into his car. As they were going along, in order to make conversation, he asked her what she did. 'Oh, I'm a witch,' she replied casually. The motorist was surprised to say the least. 'I just don't believe it,' he said. 'Can you prove it?' Saying nothing the blonde put her hand on his knee, then slowly started to run her fingers up the inside of his thigh. AND HE IMMEDIATELY TURNED INTO A LAY-BY!

The wife of a keen motorist was a terrible 'back seat driver'. She used to keep up a running commentary on what she thought her husband should and should not do. 'Mind that lorry; there's a girl coming out of that turning; look out for that child,' etc etc. It used to go on non-stop, and drove the poor man crazy. One day they were out in the car and the usual advice was coming from the back. After a while the driver noticed that there was silence and gratefully drove on in peace. Suddenly a policeman on a motorbike drew alongside and signalled him to pull into the side of the road. When he had stopped he unwound his window, and the policeman got off his bike and said breathlessly. 'Excuse me, sir, your back door swung open a few miles back and a lady fell out on to the road. I'm glad to say she's not hurt.' 'Oh,' said the driver, 'that must be my wife. She must have leant against the door and fallen out. Thank goodness for that. I thought for a moment I had gone deaf.'

It was a very foggy night in London and all the traffic was crawling along at about five miles an hour. For safety's sake a man thought he would walk right behind a bus which he knew was going his way, and so be protected from oncoming traffic. When he got home he told his wife what he had done and added . . . 'at least I saved my usual 15p bus fare.' 'Why didn't you walk behind a taxi,' said the wife, 'and save £2.50?'

A man was belting along a main road at about eighty miles per hour, when just ahead of him he saw a tractor with two men on it coming slowly out of a gate and on to the road. Realising that if he went straight on he would hit the tractor, he swung violently to his left and shot through the gate into the field from which the tractor had come. He bumped along the field parallel to the road for several yards then noticed a gap in the hedge. So he drove through it back on to the road and continued his journey at speed, as if nothing had happened. 'You know George,' said one of the men on the tractor to the other, 'we only just got out of that field in time!'

A Mini had broken down and its owner was standing disconsolately by the side of the road. A very posh new Jaguar drew up and its driver asked if he could help. The Mini-owner said he did not know what was wrong, so the man in the Jaguar said: 'OK, I'll give you a tow – I've got a thin nylon rope in my boot. I'll go along slowly but if anything is wrong blow your horn like mad.' So they set off slowly and were cruising along at about 30 mph when a big red Mercedes passed them at great speed.

This nettled the Jaguar driver who thought that for the sake of Queen and Country he should show that British was best. So forgetting he had the Mini in tow he set off in pursuit and soon reached 100 mph and was gaining on the Mercedes. The poor man in the Mini wondered what on earth was happening. From the sedate speed of 30 mph he was suddenly hurtling along at an incredible pace, and his small car was swaying and jumping all over the place. Remembering what he had been told he started to hoot like mad.

As he did so, they shot past a police car parked in a lay-by. The police driver was amazed and quickly got on to the radio to speak to another police car three miles up the road. 'Look out,' he said, 'there's a crazy road race going on and they're coming towards you very fast. There's a big red Mercedes doing well over 100 mph. Close behind and just about to pass him is a man in a Jaguar. And believe it or not in a Mini nearly touching the Jaguar's rear bumper is a frightened looking man sounding his horn like mad, trying to pass them both!'

Ted Moult is a lovely character and was a most amusing companion on the various tours or series we did together with the *Treble Chance Quiz*. We always used to do a warm-up session for the audience before the recording of the show began. In his slow lazy drawl he used to tell some splendid stories and this one was my particular favourite.

A man was driving his car through a country village when it suddenly spluttered and came to a halt. He looked at his fuel gauge and realised that he had run out of petrol. He spotted a man sitting on a bench outside a pub so went up to him and asked him if he would be very kind and give the car a push to the village garage about two hundred yards up the street. The man very decently agreed to help and with much puffing and blowing managed to push the car to the garage.

The driver, who had remained in his seat in order to steer the car, gave the petrol attendant a five pound note and asked him to fill the car up with five pounds' worth of petrol. When he had done so, the driver turned to the man who had helped him and who was standing close by looking quite exhausted.

'I'm sorry,' said the driver, 'but I have spent all the money

I had with me on the petrol, so I have none to give you. But do you smoke by any chance?' 'Yes, I do,' gasped the man between breaths. 'Well,' said the driver, 'I should give it up if I were you. You look half-knackered!' And so saying he wound up his window and drove off!

A little girl kept biting her nails and her mother told her that if she didn't stop doing it she would grow very fat. The next day she and her mother were on a bus, and sitting opposite them was a very pregnant blonde. The little girl kept staring at her. After a while the blonde got fed up and said to the girl: 'What are you staring at me for? Do you know me?' 'No,' said the little girl, 'but I know what you've been doing!'

A motorist was lost near Guildford and stopped to ask a passer-by the way. Motorist: 'Do you know the Hog's Back?' Passer-by: 'No. I didn't know he'd been away!'

Last Over or Who's been a lucky boy, then?

As the time came for me to bowl this last 'over' I began reflecting on my past – always a dangerous occupation. But I am glad that I did so, because once again it was brought home to me how very lucky I have been all through my life. The last two months especially have constantly reminded me of the variety of my life, and the different cross-sections of people whom I have met and been able to call my friends.

I must admit that when checking through my diary for November and December it looks rather like a gastronomic orgy. Take cricket. There were two excellent lunches organised by firms who give great help to cricket, the Wrigley Company and John Haig. The former give generous financial support to young cricketers, the latter sponsor those excellent competitions for clubs and villages.

It is at gatherings such as these that one realises how cricket seems to bring out the best in people. Why *are* cricketers – and even cricket writers and broadcasters – so nice? There can surely be no other game in the world that so enriches the lives of those who are connected with it or play it.

There was another evening reception for the official opening of the Lord's Cricket School by Gubby Allen. As the gossip writers would say 'anyone who is anyone in cricket' was there to see Derek Shackleton bowl the first ball to Colin Cowdrey. It is quite easily the best cricket school I have ever seen. It has superb lighting and six nets with varying degrees of pace and spin. And vital in our search for fast bowlers, there is a long run-up for the bowlers of at least seventeen yards, which many people would consider to be the maximum necessary for *any* fast bowler even in a Test Match.

The school was paid for by members of MCC with some help from commerce and a magnificent contribution from that lover and patron of cricket Jack Hayward. In recognition of this the playing area is known as the Hayward Hall. Jack told me he was off that week back to his home in the Bahamas to rehearse for the annual pantomime out there. He was going to play one of the Ugly Sisters in *Cinderella* and I was able to give him two gags to use in the 'dressing for the ball' scene. One ugly sister to the other:

'How do you like my religious dress?'

'Religious dress?'

'Yes – lo(w) and behold.'

'Well, I call *mine* a barbed wire dress – it protects the property without obscuring the view.'

I wonder if he used them!

I have always acknowledged how lucky I was to go to Eton, which to me has proved to be the best trade union in the world. Wherever I go on my job I always seem to run into an Old Etonian and on numerous occasions this has broken the ice or gained an *entrée* – especially if he is a highly respected official and I greet him as 'Fruity' or 'Jumbo' or whatever I used to call him at Eton.

Anyhow, in November I was invited to speak at the annual dinner of the Eton Rackets Club which brought me into contact with a lot of my Etonian friends. Luckily many of them were quite young so quite a few of my hoary jokes were new to them. Like the old one of the housemaster's wife who attended a concert at which the headmaster's wife recited a piece of French poetry. When she had finished the housemaster's wife applauded loudly and turned to her companion. 'Didn't she recite that well? And how wise not to attempt the French accent!'

The biggest occasion during the autumn was a theatrical one – the lunch for one thousand guests given by Peter Saunders at the Savoy to celebrate the twenty-fifth year of *The Mousetrap*. It was a marvellous opportunity to meet again so many of the stage personalities with whom I have worked from time to time in the last thirty-two years. Pauline and I gave a lift home to Evelyn Laye and Anna Neagle – how's that for three beautiful ladies in one taxi?

Then there were Jack and Cis Courtneidge holding court in a corner, Cis as vivacious as ever, and Jack with that lazy drawl of his asking me about the Packer business. Another mad cricket enthusiast was Celia Johnson and Dinah Sheridan too, though she admitted that she was not *quite* as keen as Celia. She said that Celia stops to watch every village cricket match which she comes across in the summer. Vera Lynn, and Tommy Trinder – for once without his hat, and in spite of Fulham in his usual good form – represented variety. It seems impossible to keep cricket out of this because Andrew Cruickshank unexpectedly is a fan and so of course is Michael Denison who is a regular at Lord's. Dulcie Gray was with him, though I don't know how she finds time to be social with her acting, her radio part in *Waggoners' Walk* and writing her thrillers. There were two regular Arsenal supporters there – impresario Peter Bridge and Ian Wallace. I always enjoy meeting them so that I can reel off the Arsenal side which I used to watch in the thirties:

Bastin, James, Drake, Jack, Hulme,

Copping, Roberts, Crayston,

Hapgood, Male,

Moss

That was the line-up as far as I can remember, and unlike today they remained in that formation right through the match. It must have made George Allison's job as commentator so much easier than that of the modern commentators.

Two of the best of our light comedy actors are as amusing off the stage as on, Donald Sinden with his delicious fruity voice and Leslie Phillips with that wicked leer in his eyes. And then someone we had not seen for a long time but looking just as young and beautiful – Sally Anne Howes, whose father Bobby was a great friend of Pauline's father. And of course tinkling his white piano as an accompaniment to the champagne and smoked salmon was Ian Stewart, whom I remember playing the second piano opposite Carroll Gibbons *before* the war!

And finally, the host himself Peter Saunders, another

cricket enthusiast and a kind, generous person completely unspoilt by his great success. He is the only one of my friends who has a telephone in his car. But unlike Lew Grade he only has *one*. So if you ring him up you can't be asked to hold on 'as he is on the *other* line'. I am afraid all this has read rather like a mixture of *Jennifer's Diary* and Nigel Dempster. But it is an illustration of how lucky I have been to know so many fascinating people in the world of showbusiness.

This lunch also emphasised the strong link which exists between the stage and cricket. Perhaps it is not so surprising as they are both forms of the arts requiring great skill and technique, utter dedication and hard work. At the same time they both offer the individual the chance of showing off his talents, while remaining the member of a team. The affiliation goes back a long way. I suppose the most famous actor cricketer of all was Sir C. Aubrey Smith, that grand old film actor, who actually captained England in the first ever Test against South Africa in 1889. He was a fine fast medium bowler, whose slanting run-up earned him the nickname of Round-the-corner Smith. He founded the Hollywood Cricket Club and ran a flourishing cricket team which included such actors as Nigel Bruce, Ronald Coleman and Boris Karloff.

Sir George Robey was a member of MCC and in the twenties Old Harrovian Sir Gerald Du Maurier was a regular attendant at the Eton and Harrow match at Lord's. Other frequent watchers at Lord's over the past forty years or so have been Clifford Mollison, Arthur Askey, Richard Attenborough, Michael Denison, Ian Carmichael, David Tomlinson and of course Trevor Howard – a good all-round club cricketer who always insists that any film contract which he signs gives him time off to see the Lord's Test. He has watched MCC and England teams all over the world, as has that remarkable nonagenarian writer of farces Ben Travers. Another writer who adored cricket was the late Terence Rattigan, who was himself good enough to play for Harrow.

The Stage Cricket Society has always produced an enthusiastic side and I remember playing against them shortly after the war for the Cross Arrows at Lord's. They were captained by that ace 'villain' Garry Marsh who was a determined left-handed bat and they could also call on the slow left arm wiles of Lauri Lupino Lane, and the batting skills of Cyril Luckham.

But of course nowadays it is the Lord's Taverners who give the actors a chance to perform before large crowds on Sundays throughout the summer. I wouldn't dare to attempt to grade them in any particular order, but there are some pretty useful actor-cricketers playing today. As batsmen there are John Alderton, Tim Rice, Willie Rushton and David Frost. The bowlers include Brian Rix, Roy Castle, Tom Baker, Michael Jayston, William-Sccchhh-Franklyn and Harry Secombe. The latter is in fact an all-rounder in more senses than one, and in spite of being so shortsighted can give the ball an almighty tonk. To guard the timbers today there are Ian Lavender and Ed Stewart, but some years back now there were the two bravest wicket-keepers whom I have ever seen, Eric Sykes and the late John Slater. Both of them took far more balls on the chest than they ever did in their gloves!

Then there are the mad keen cricketers who are always ready to turn up and play in these charity games. Their skills may vary but their enthusiasm and light-hearted approach make the Lord's Taverners' matches the fun and success that they always are. People like Bernard Cribbens, Gerald Harper, Michael Aspel, Pete Murray, Tim Brook-Taylor, Ronnie Corbett, Leslie Crowther and Nicholas Parsons. What a cast.

There is just one other player I must mention – Norman Wisdom – whose son incidentally has played for Sussex. Some years ago Norman was playing for the Taverners against an Old England XI at Lord's. He was batting, and making the crowd roar with laughter at his antics, doing his falls and funny walks. An old MCC member who had been dozing peacefully in the sun, was suddenly awoken by an extra loud burst of laughter. He looked up to see Norman falling about all over the place, and turned to his neighbour and said: 'I don't know how good a cricketer that chap is, but he ought to be a comedian!'

My post has also brought back some memories including

an invitation to dinner with the Junior Common Room at New College, Oxford, where I had spent three such happy years in the thirties. So far as I know I still hold two records there. First, I am the only rugger player to have scored a try for the college in a macintosh, which a spectator had lent me to cover my confusion when my shorts had been ripped off. And secondly, I must still be the only person to have had his trousers removed and thrown through the window of the senior common room, where they landed on a table round which the dons were sitting drinking port.

And of course there is the wonderful variety of Christmas cards. Like those from some of my old Grenadier staff when I was Technical Adjutant in the 2nd Battalion Grenadiers from 1941 to 1945. The nice thing is that they still sign themselves with the nicknames which I bestowed on them. My scout car driver Hengist, my chief clerk Honest Joe, the driver of the store truck Tremble – so called because it was the name of a decrepit old butler whom he played in a sketch in one of our battalion revues. And my soldier servant (as the Brigade of Guards called a batman) Pasha whose surname was Ruston. One ex-guardsman sent me an old programme of the revue we did at Seigburg in Germany in the autumn of 1945. It was called *What About It Then?*, and to show you the standard of its humour, here is one of the jokes which I remember.

'What's the difference between funny and fanny?'

'Well you can feel funny without feeling fanny, but you can't feel fanny without feeling funny.'

And a card from an old friend Frank Copping took me back to my few years as a city gent, disguised in a bowler hat, with a rolled umbrella, and in a pinstripe suit too tight under the armpits. Frank ran the cable department where I started when I joined our family coffee business. He nursed me and tried to teach me business methods without, I fear, a great deal of success. But I did enjoy ringing him up from the next office and pretending to be an irate Italian agent of ours called Enrico Colombino; not that my Italian accent was all that hot.

And always most welcome are the cards from all the friends I have made in the cricketing countries round the world, including this year one from Mike Brearley and Ken Barrington in Pakistan. I got to know Brearlers well when he toured South Africa with Mike Smith's MCC team in 1964, straight from his triumphs on the Fenners pitch at Cambridge. For some strange reason he hardly made a run on the tour and indeed looked a complete novice. But I shall always remember how well he took it, and never showed the terrific disappointment which he must have felt – fortified perhaps by his triumphs at the bridge table with Charles Fortune, David Brown and myself.

Barrers was on at least six of the MCC tours which I went on, and he was always a tremendous influence for good both on and off the field. A one hundred per cent fighter on it, and a great mimic and joker off it. His take-off of W. G. Grace in the nets is a classic – complete with MCC cap with a button on top, beard and towels stuffed inside his shirt to give him the necessary girth! I would say that he and Brearley should make an ideal partnership.

And this is perhaps the best place for me to give you my selection of the best all-round captain of England during my years of commentating since the war. As you have probably discovered, it has been a very difficult task. They all – inevitably, since they are human – have their good and bad points. The circumstances in which they played and the quality of the teams which they led, also varied considerably. For instance I have a feeling that with the material of the Hutton/May teams in the mid-fifties under his command, Freddie Brown might well have proved the best captain of them all. In fact, it's rather fun to create the perfect captain made up of the best characteristics of some of the others. How about a captain with:

> the fighting qualities and leadership of Freddie Brown
> the unflappable character of Mike Smith
> the tactical ability of Ray Illingworth
> the playing skill of Len Hutton
> the magic PR touch with the media and the crowds of Tony Greig
> the off-the-field charisma of Colin Cowdrey.

I reckon he would have been *some* captain, though I

suspect its perfectly possible to mingle some of the other characteristics and produce an equally fine specimen.

But sticking to one man, I have given pride of place to Ray Illingworth. He may not have been the establishment's favourite man, but he does possess most of the essential qualities. A determined character with a dry sense of humour, leadership, tactical skill, playing ability and excellent public relations with the media. He loses a few marks for his off-the-field image, but as I have said he went out to Australia with one thing only in mind – to win back the Ashes – and he did so. Two other tough and single-minded captains did likewise – Douglas Jardine and Len Hutton. The nice guys of this world like the Gilligans, Allens, Mays and Smiths perhaps lack the killer instinct that a captain must have to win. Anyway I am sure that some of you have made out equally good cases for people like May, Cowdrey or possibly Brearley on his initial but successful record so far.

The BBC always have lots of parties at Christmas time and this year in December the director-general, Ian Trethowan, gave a delightful dinner party at the Television Centre in honour of Antony Craxton, who was retiring from the Corporation.

'Crackers' was brought up near Lord's in a musical family, but his first love was always cricket. We used to play a lot in charity matches and for all I know he may have been a very good leg-spinner. Unfortunately the ball never pitched, so I shall never find out! For years he was our TV cricket producer and we had much fun and enjoyment. Like me he thinks there is more to cricket than what goes on out in the middle, and he was always on the lookout for the unusual shot of off-the-field activities. He produced some of the best leg-pulls on Jim Swanton, like the time when the election of a Pope coincided with a Test Match at Lord's, where Jim and I were the commentators.

In St Peter's Square, Rome, the crowds were massed waiting for the tell-tale puff of white smoke from one of the Vatican chimneys which would be the sign that the Cardinals had made their decision. At the same time at Lord's a chimney in the old Lord's Tavern caught fire and black smoke belched out. Quick as a flash Crackers had a camera pointing at the black smoke. 'There you are,' I was able to say, 'Jim Swanton has been elected Pope.' Or the occasion when one of his cameras spotted John Warr and his fiancée Valerie sitting together in the grandstand – Warr and Piece!

When he left cricket, Crackers became the Royal Producer, culminating in his triumphant broadcast of the Jubilee Service in St Paul's, which by coincidence was his two hundredth Royal TV occasion. Many of his friends were at the dinner, John Snagge, Michael Standing, Peter West, Cliff Morgan, Richard Baker, Robert Hudson and myself all representing the commentators. As you can imagine there was much reminiscing and Crackers actually told an announcer's gaffe which I had not heard before – I thought I knew them all!

Here it is: An announcer was introducing a concert. 'Tonight's concert,' he said, 'will be given by the Ceffield Shity Police Band' . . . After he had finished the rest of the announcement his producer told him what he had said, and that listeners were already ringing up to complain. The producer advised him not to apologise as it would only draw attention to his mistake. But he ordered the poor announcer to be sure to get the name of the band right in the closing announcement. So when the end of the programme arrived the announcer – now a bag of nerves – steeled himself and came out with: 'You have just been listening to a concert given by the Sheffield City Police Band. The concert was broadcast from the Ceffield Shity Hall.'

But, in spite of all my friends, the true foundation of my happiness has been my wife, my family and my home. By the time you read this Pauline and I will, I hope, have celebrated our Pearl wedding. I would just like to thank her for her continued love and understanding. Also for her patience with my jokes, my many absences from home, and my possible over-indulgence in work. My family, thank goodness, have given me few problems, only boundless joy and amusement. Barry and Clare live in their own homes in London, and Andrew is still working in Sydney, so that Ian and Joanna are the only ones still at home. But almost every weekend we have a family reunion for Sunday lunch when we laugh, quarrel, play cards and table tennis, and tuck in to roast beef and Yorkshire pudding (when the housekeeping account is not too heavily overdrawn). So thanks too to them for making me so happy and I forgive them for trying to get their own back on me – they now tell *me* far worse jokes than I ever told *them*.

It is interesting that my way of life and connections with the entertainment world have obviously influenced their choice of jobs and careers. Not one of them is a member of any of the professions. Nor do any of them do nine to five humdrum office jobs. Barry's pop group 'Design' broke up amicably in 1976. He now has a small music publishing business, records the odd single or jingle and does a first-class cabaret act which includes all the well-known Noël Coward songs which he delivers crisply and clearly just like the Master. He also still composes songs full of melody and is just waiting for one of them to 'take off'. It is as a composer that I see his future. Don't forget the name, Barry Alexander, so called, as I have mentioned earlier, because there is already a Barry Johnston in Equity.

Clare after three years in Australia now works as a PR executive in London, and one of her accounts is a famous TV and recording company. She is much travelled and she and I have a 'visited the most countries' contest. Since her return from Australia via South, Central and North America she has edged ahead and her total is now fifty-three against my forty-four.

Andrew worked in Foyles Book Shop over here and then three years ago left for Sydney where he now works for a worldwide English publishing firm. And to keep up the entertainment theme Ian – after a year's varied experience in Australia as a messenger for ABC, a jackaroo on an estate, a 'showie' on bumper cars and a researcher for a mining firm – now has a job with a large group of record shops. The nice thing about all their jobs is that they got them on their own merits without any help or influence from Dad. Incidentally, whenever she has time off from running the house, looking after Joanna or her charities like the Life-Boats and the Mentally Handicapped Children, Pauline does a spot of photography at which she is highly trained and expert.

And finally our home in St John's Wood where we are so marvellously looked after by our wonderful housekeeper Cally. What we would do without her I don't know. She and Pauline between them continue to look after Joanna with loving care and devotion. As a result Joanna – now aged twelve – is a happy pupil at the Gatehouse Learning Centre in Bethnal Green, which is so efficiently and kindly run by its remarkable founder Mrs Wallbank. We have been in St John's Wood now for thirty years and I could wish for no more friendly nor delightful place in which to live – remarkably peaceful and still with a village atmosphere, although only ten minutes away from Piccadilly Circus by car. The large garden is an added joy, not just for us but also for our Yorkshire terrier, Mini, who spends her life chasing (but never catching) grey squirrels. I am the destroyer in the garden – I weed, mow and light the bonfire. Pauline and our faithful friend Mr Webber do the creative work. The colourful result of their labours is enjoyed as much by our neighbours as by ourselves.

So there we are. I hope you have stayed with me until close of play, and have enjoyed, or at least tolerated, the meanderings of a remarkably happy and lucky person, to whom life – like cricket – is a funny game and still A LOT OF FUN.

St John's Wood
Christmas 1977

Index

Abbas, Zakeer, 21
Adair, General Sir Allan, 28–9
Adamson, Joy 66
Adelaide, 71
Alderton, John, 217
Alexander, Barry, 15; *and see* Johnston, Barry
Allen, David, 184
Allen Gubby, 214, 220
Alley, Bill, 96
Allis, Peter, 186
Allison, George, 215
Alston, Rex, 126, 128
Ames, Les, 104, 157
Amiss, Dennis, 17, 19, 21, 32, 71, 72, 75, 78, 101, 102, 148–9, 150
Andrew, Prince, 133
Anne, Princess, 13–14, 132, 133
Any Questions, 39, 40
Archive Auction, 182–4
Arlott, John, 126, 165
Armchair Cricket, 140
Arnold, G. G., 19, 20, 33, 70, 156
Arrowsmith, Robert, 157
Arsenal, 181, 215
Asif, Mahsood, 103, 126, 157
Askey, Arthur, 182, 216
Aspel, Michael, 217
Asquith, Lady, 26
Astill, Ewart, 34
Athey, Bill, 156
Attenborough, Richard, 216
Attlee, Clement, 58
Auckland, 70
Australia, 31–3, 34, 49, 69, 70–6, 78–82, 110, 112, 120, 131–2, 146, 147–58, 187, 193
Australian Cricket Board, 187

Bailey, Jack, 20

Bailey, Les, 28, 76
Bailey, Trevor, 28, 82, 156, 162, 165
Baker, Richard, 221
Baker, Tom, 217
Balderstone, Chris, 100
Balfour, Lord, 54–5
Bannister, Jack, 176
Barlow, Eddie, 27, 149
Barlow, Graham, 147
Barnett, Charlie, 129
Baroda, Maharajah of, 21
Barrington, Ken, 219
Baxter, Peter, 22, 137, 162, 163
Baxter, Raymond, 185
Be My Guest, 15
Beard, Anthony, 53–4
Bedi, 19
Bedser, Alec, 103, 104, 156, 157, 162
Benaud, Richie, 72, 103
Benson and Hedges Cricket, 83, 94, 159–60
Bird, Dicky, 82
Birkett, Lord Justice, 49–50
Blofeld, Henry, 21–2, 64–5
Boat Race, 18, 125, 131, 181
Booth, Richard, 60–1
Botham, Ian, 150, 151, 153, 154, 155, 156
Bough, Frank, 125
Bowen, Michael, 40
Boyce, Keith, 76
Boycott, Geoff, 150–1, 152–3, 154, 155
Bradman, Don, 33, 34, 110
Brearley, Mike, 96, 97, 98, 122, 123, 148, 149–50, 151, 152, 153, 154, 155, 219, 220
Brewster, Mrs Emma, 52
Bridge, Peter, 215
Bridgetown, 16
Brind, Harry, 81

Brisbane, 28, 31, 71
BBC, 11, 12, 14, 15, 19, 23, 25, 38–51,
    62, 77, 134, 135, 139, 140, 163, 177,
    182–4, 202, 220
Brocklehurst, Belinda, 85
Brocklehurst, Ben, 85
Bromley, Peter, 183
Brooke-Taylor, Tim, 217
Brown, Christopher, 86
Brown, David, 175, 176, 219
Brown, Freddie, 86, 112, 123, 219
Bruce, Nigel, 216
Burwood, Richard, 38, 40, 46

Call My Bluff, 12
Call the Commentators, 165, 166
Cally, 88, 223
Campbell, Patrick, 12
Cardiff, 94
Carmichael, Ian, 216
Carpenter, Harry, 125
Carrick, Phil, 157
Carrington, Lord, 29–30
Cartwright, 'Buns', 129–30
Cassandra, 11
Castle, Roy, 217
Celebration, 38
Chamberlain, Neville, 182–3
Chandrasekar, 19
Chappell, Greg, 33, 73, 106, 146, 147,
    148, 150, 153, 167, 158, 164
Chappell, Ian, 73, 79, 80, 81, 106, 158
Chappell, Mrs, 81, 106
Chappell, Trevor, 73, 106
Charles, Prince, 136
Charlie Girl, 17
Chichester, Sir Francis, 203
Childs, John, 157
Churchill, Winston, 57, 58
Close, Brian, 25, 96, 97, 98, 99, 118, 123
Cobham, Charles, 128–9
Coleman, David, 125–6
Coleman, Ronald, 216
Collingwood, 59–60
Compton, Denis, 124, 181
Cook, Captain, 35
Cope, Geoff, 157
Copping, Frank, 218
Corbett, Ronnie, 217
Corfu, 85–6
Cosier, Gary, 147
Coulter, Phil, 184
Counsell, John, 130

County Cricket Championship, 94, 95,
    125
Courtneidge, Cecily, 215
Cowdrey, Christopher, 106, 156
Cowdrey, Colin, 73, 80, 82, 105, 115,
    123, 149, 174, 184, 214, 219, 220
Cowdrey, Graham, 73, 106
Cowdrey, Jeremy, 106
Cowdrey, Penny, 73, 106
Cowper, Bob, 16
Craig, Michael, 61, 181–2
Cranston, Ken, 108
Craxton, Anthony, 220–1
Cribbens, Bernard, 217
Cricketer, 85, 86
Cricketer's Association, 192
Crisp, Mr and Mrs, 26
Cruickshank, Andrew, 215
Cross Arrows, 217
Cunis, Bob, 126
Curran, Sir Charles, 38

Daily Mail, 39
Daily Mirror, 11
Daniel, Wayne, 96, 99
Datsun International Double Wicket
    Competition, 26–7
Davies, John, 52–3
Davis, Paddy, 137
Denison, Michael, 215, 216
Denness, Mike, 17, 18–19, 31–2 34, 70,
    71, 72, 100, 120, 123
Desert Island Discs, 15–16, 182
Dexter, Ted, 34, 116, 123, 181
Dimbleby, David, 41
Dimbleby, Richard, 41, 42, 43, 47, 49
Dixon, Alan, 12
D'Oliveira, Basil, 103, 125
Douglas, J. W. H. T., 71
Douglas-Home, George, 59
Douglas-Home, Henry, 58–9
Douglas-Home, William, 27, 59, 60,
    129, 130–1, 182
Down Your Way, 12, 14, 16, 18, 31,
    38–51, 52–63, 66, 87, 131, 133, 135,
    137, 177, 184, 186
Downton, Paul, 157
Dredge, Colin, 94
Du Maurier, Sir Gerald, 216
Duckworth, George, 34

East, Ray, 157
East Africa, 69

Easter Parade, 18
Edgbaston, 21, 70–1, 72, 73, 78, 81, 120, 124, 147, 165
Edmonds, Phil, 78, 79, 157
Edrich, John, 19, 33, 70, 74–5, 78, 81, 96, 97, 99, 108
Edward, Prince, 133
Edwards, Percy, 58
Eisenhower, General, 57
Elizabeth II, 131, 133–5 136, 204
Elizabeth, Queen Mother, 14–15, 133, 136
Ellison, John, 77–8
Emburey, John, 157, 159
Engineer, Farooq, 103
England, 16–17, 18–19, 20–1, 31–3, 34, 69, 70–2, 74–6, 78–82, 95–104, 146–58, 175, 187, 193, 194, 216
Englemann, Franklin ('Jingle'), 41–2, 43, 47–8
Essex, 95, 159
Eton, 26, 128, 129, 180, 205, 214
Eton and Harrow Match, 216
Eton College Chronicle, 129
Eton Rackets Club, 214
Eton Ramblers, 130
Evans, Dai, 52
Evans, Godfrey, 103, 104, 105, 157
Evers-Swindell, Patricia, 55

FA Cup Final, 126
Fenney, Paddy, 42
Fenner Trophy, 165
Festival of Remembrance, 13
Fisher, Diana, 181
Fisher, John, 16
Fleming, Chris, 61
Fletcher, Keith, 17, 19, 20, 21, 72, 78, 79, 80
Fordham, Michael, 74
Forsyth, Bruce, 185–6
Fortune, Charles, 26, 219
Franklin, William, 217
Fredericks, Roy, 95, 99, 102, 104
Frindall, Bill, 126, 150, 151, 162, 166
Frost, David, 217
Funny Way to be a Hero, 16

Games People Play, 181
Gamlin, Lionel, 41
Gandhi, Mrs, 204
Gardner, D. B., 171
Gatehouse Learning Centre, 222

Gatting, Mike, 156
Generation Game, 185–6
George VI, 14, 132
Gibbons, Carroll, 215
Gibson, Alan, 184
Gillett, Sir Robin, 134
Gillette Cup, 70, 83, 95, 158–9
Gilliat, Martin, 18, 176
Gilligan, Arthur, 127–8, 220
Gilmour, Gary, 69
Glamorgan, 94, 108, 159
Gloucestershire, 70, 129, 159–60, 194
Gooch, Graham, 72, 75, 78, 79
Gower, David, 156
Grace, W. G., 71, 72, 219
Grade, Lew, 216
Grand National, 183
Graveney, Tom, 108, 157
Gray, Dulcie, 215
Greenidge, Gordon, 95, 97, 99, 102
Greig, Tony, 16, 17, 19, 32, 71, 72, 74, 75, 78, 96, 98, 100, 102, 121, 123, 147, 149, 150, 151, 154, 155, 156, 187, 219
Grey Mirage, 175–6
Grimmond, Jo, 26
Grout, Wally, 103
Guinness throwing the cricket ball competition, 76–7
Guyana, 17

Hackforth, Norman, 66
Hainsworth, Sidney, 164–5
Hall, Wes, 184
Halliday, Edward, 135–8
Hamilton, Alan, 172–3
Hammond, Wally, 108, 110, 129
Hampshire, 74, 125
Hampshire, John, 78, 79, 80
Handley, Tommy, 182, 202
Hardy, Adrian, 184
Harper, Gerald, 180, 217
Harris, Sir Arthur, 57–8
Harrow, 216
Hart, Syd, 55
Hartstaff, Joe, 151
Hassett, Lindsay, 49
Hayward, Jack, 214
Headingley, 20, 78–80, 81, 99–100, 128, 152–4, 155, 161, 162, 164–5, 169
Henderson, Dickie, 39
Hendrick, Mike, 19, 20, 32, 96, 150, 151, 152, 153, 154, 155, 156
Heyhoe-Flint, Rachel, 37, 105, 181

Hibberd, Stuart, 56–7
Hill, Jimmy, 17, 126
Hill, Lord, 62
Hitler, Adolf, 182, 202
Hoffnung, Gerald, 184
Holder, Vanburn, 96
Holding, Michael, 96, 99, 101–102, 124
Holiday Hour, 43
Hollinshead, Reg, 176
Hollywood Cricket Club, 216
Home, Lord (Alec Douglas-Home), 58, 59, 182
Home, Lord, 59
Hookes, David, 149, 150, 153, 157
Hopkins, John, 156
Horne, Kenneth, 34
Horton, Henry, 74
Howard, Nigel, 108
Howard, Trevor, 216
Howes, Bobby, 215
Howes, Sally Anne, 215
Hudson, Robert, 221
Hughes, Kim, 157
Hulbert, Jack, 215
Hutton, Len, 28, 71, 80, 105, 113, 114, 123, 151, 219, 220

Illingworth, Ray, 33, 80, 119, 123, 124, 142, 159, 219, 220
In the Red, 130–1
In Town Tonight, 77, 182
India, 18–20, 21, 108, 121, 146, 187
International Cricket Conference, 69, 187, 193
ITMA, 182
It's A Funny Business, 61, 181–2
It's Been a Lot of Fun, 11, 15–16, 124, 196
ITA, 62
ITV, 126
Ives, Tony, 176

Jack de Manio Precisely, 15
Jardine, Douglas, 220
Jayston, Michael, 217
Jeffries, Colonel, 29
John Player League, 83, 94, 95, 159
Johns, Hugh, 126
Johnson, Cedric, 134
Johnson, Celia, 215
Johnston, Andrew, 88, 221, 222
Johnston, Barry, 88, 136, 221, 222
Johnston, Brian, retires from BBC, 11; covers Princess Margaret's wedding,

13–14; autobiography, 15–16, 124, 196; tucks in ears, 17–18; covers Indian tour, 1974, 18–19, 21; leg pulled by Wadekar, 19–20; and golf, 23–5; covers Datsun competition, 26–7; wins Denzil Batchelor award, 27–8; and Grenadiers, 28–31, 218; visits Australia, 1975, 31–4; and *Down Your Way*, 38–40, 42–4, 46–9, 50–1, 52–63, 66; and *Twenty Questions*, 66–8; covers Prudential Cup, 69–70; and 1975 Test matches in England, 70–6, 78–82; and *In Town Tonight*, 77–8; in Corfu, 85–6; and pets, 91–3; on captaincy, 108–23, 219–20; commentating gaffes, 124–6; and old friends, 127–30; and Jubilee Day, 132–5; has portrait painted, 135–8; on commentating, 139–45; and *Test Match Special*, 161–7; and horse racing, 174–6; speech making, 177–9; 'one off' broadcasts, 180–4; TV appearances, 185–6; on Packer cricket, 187–94; sense of humour, 196–7; and *Mousetrap* lunch, 214–16; and Oxford, 218; family life, 221–3
Johnston, Clare, 14, 31, 35, 88, 136, 221, 222
Johnston, Ian, 88, 221
Johnston, Joanna, 87, 88, 90–1, 221
Johnston, Pauline, 14, 16, 85, 87–90, 106, 127, 130, 136–7, 177, 214, 221, 222, 223
Jones, Peter, 66, 125
Juantorena, 125
Jumadeen, 98
Just a Nimmo, 17

Kallicharran, Alvin, 69, 95, 96
Kanhai, Rohan, 16, 97–8
Karachi, 80
Karloff, Boris, 216
Kaye, Dave, 184
Kempton Park, 175
Kent, 94, 95, 103, 120, 158, 159, 191, 194
Kentish Kipper, 174–5
Khan, Majid, 76
King, Collis, 95, 97
Kipling, Rudyard, 172
Knott, Alan, 16, 21, 33, 34, 71, 74, 76, 80, 81, 95, 96, 100, 102, 103, 104–5, 147, 149, 151–2, 153–4, 156, 157, 191

Kureishi, Omar, 20

Lancashire, 19, 70, 108
Lancashire League, 73
Lane, Lauri Lupino, 217
Langley, Gil, 103
Larwood, Harold, 33
Lavender, Ian, 217
Lawson-Dick, Clare, 40
Laye, Evelyn, 214
Le Beau, Bettine, 66, 67
Leapman, Michael, 167
Lee Kwan Yew, 204
Leeds, 20
Leicestershire, 159
Let's Go Somewhere, 77
Lever, John, 76, 78, 148, 150, 154, 155, 156
Lewis, Tony, 108, 165
Lillee, Dennis, 31, 32, 33–4, 69, 70, 71, 72, 74, 75, 78, 81, 100, 101, 120, 157, 189
Lindwall, Ray, 113
Listeners' Letters, 166
Liverpool, 126
Llewellyn, Mike, 159
Lloyd, Clive, 70, 95, 96, 100, 102
Lloyd, David, 19
London Weekend, 76
Lord Mayor's Show, 12–13, 87, 185
Lord's, 20, 21, 31, 70, 72, 73, 74–6, 78, 79–80, 94, 95, 98, 99, 105, 127, 136, 148, 159, 164, 215, 216, 217, 220
Lord's Cricket School, 214–15
Lord's Taverners, 217
Love, Jim, 156
Lynn, Vera, 215
Luckham, Cyril, 217

McCosker, Rick, 33, 79, 81, 151, 152, 153, 154
MacDonald, Roger, 134
MacGilvray, Alan, 73, 74
Mackintosh, Alex, 42
McIntyre, Arthur, 104
Mackay, Ken, 103
Mackay, Slasher, 106
Macmillan, Harold, 29–30
Macpherson, Stewart, 40–1
Maddock, Dick, 162
Maddocks, Len, 131
Mallett, Ashley, 79
Malone, Mick, 154, 158

Manchester United, 125–6
Mann, George, 111, 123
Margaret, Princess, 14, 15, 132
Marsh, Gary, 217
Marsh, Rodney, 32, 33–4, 71, 72, 153
Martin-Jenkins, Christopher, 31, 139
Maskell, Dan, 186
May, Peter, 71, 80, 97–8 114, 123, 142, 219, 220
MCC, 20 23, 31, 34–5, 102, 105, 159, 175, 214, 216, 217, 219
Melbourne, 16, 32, 70, 71, 72, 80, 131
Melford, Michael, 174
Miandad, Javed, 70
Middlesex, 94, 158–9
Milburn, Colin, 75
Miller, Geoff, 151, 155, 157
Miller, Keith, 113, 159
Miller, Max, 177
Milton, Arthur, 174–5
Mollison, Clifford, 216
Morecambe, Eric, 62, 182
Moreton, Ivor, 184
Morgan, Cliff, 17, 221
Morrison, Diana, 182
Mosey, Don, 73, 74, 87, 139, 162, 166
Motson, John, 126, 186
Moult, Ted, 212
Mousetrap, The, 214
Muir, Frank, 12
Murdoch, Richard, 34
Murray, Deryck, 98
Murray, Pete, 77, 181, 217

Neagle, Anna, 214
New Caledonia, 35–7
New Zealand, 69–70, 126, 194
Newbury, 176
Newmarket, 183
Nimmo, Derek, 17
Niven, David, 16
Noble, Monty, 72
Norman, Tricia, 175, 176
Northampton, 124
Northants, 95, 124–5

O'Connor, Des, 62
O'Keefe, Kerry, 150, 151
Old, Chris, 19, 20, 21, 72, 78, 148, 149, 150, 156
Old Trafford, 16, 21, 70, 98–9, 126, 147, 149–50, 154, 155, 161, 162
Oldfield, Bertie, 104

Olympic Games, 125
Open House, 15
Orchard, Brian, 171
Oval, 18, 21, 80–2, 100–2, 124, 147, 148, 151, 154, 157, 165, 170
Oxford, 26, 218

Packer, Kerry, 146, 147, 154, 157, 158, 187–94, 215
Pakistan, 18, 20–2, 69, 157, 193, 194
Parker, Charlie, 129
Parkinson, Sir Kenneth, 27–8
Parks, Jim, 103
Parsons, Nicholas, 217
Partridge, David, 160
Pascoe, Len, 148, 149, 158
Pataudi, Nawab of, 19
Pebble Mill, 15
Percival, Richard, 76
Perowne, Leslie, 40
Perth, 31
Pharaoh, Jack, 61–2
Philip, Prince, 70, 132, 133, 134–5, 136
Phillips, Leslie, 215
Phillips, Mark, 14, 133
Pickering, Ron, 125
Plomley, Roy, 15
Pocock, Pat, 98, 157
Pollard, Dick, 34
Port of Spain, 17
Prasana, 19
Procter, Mike, 159–60, 194
Prudential Cup, 69–70, 95, 96, 146, 147–8

Randall, Derek, 132, 148, 149, 150, 151, 152, 153, 154, 155–6
Rattigan, Terence, 216
Ray, Ted, 177, 181
Red Rum, 183
Redhead, Brian, 26
Redpath, Ian, 33
Reunion, 25–6
Rice, Tim, 217
Richards, Barry, 27, 101, 125
Richards, Viv, 95, 96, 97, 99, 100, 101
Richardson, Vic, 73, 81, 106, 128
Ridell, Henry, 126
Rix, Brian, 217
Roberts, Andy, 96, 99, 101, 102
Robertson, Fyfe, 42
Robey, Sir George, 216
Robins, Derek, 42

Robinson, Richie, 153
Robinson, Phyllis, 40, 41, 46, 47, 182
Roland, Arthur, 55
Roope, Graham, 80, 81, 156
Rose, Brian, 156
Rowe, Lance, 16, 95
Roy, Harry, 183–4
Royal Society of Portrait Painters, 136
Rushton, William, 66–7, 217

Sabina Park, 80
Santa Marta, 175
Saunders, Peter, 214, 215–16
Savage, Richard, 157
Sayers, Ben, 54–5
Schweppes County Championship, 158
Scott-Johnston, Alastair, 67
Secombe, Harry, 217
Selvey, Mike, 99
Serjeant, Craig, 148, 149, 157
Seymour, J., 190
Shackleton, Derek, 214
Sharpe, Phil, 78
Shaw, Sandie, 184
Sheene, Barry, 126
Sheffield Cricket Lovers' Society, 87
Shepherd, John, 103
Sheppard, David, 108
Sheridan, Dinah, 215
Shuter, John, 40
Simon, Sir John, 54
Simpson, Bobby, 16
Sinden, Donald, 215
Slade, Mr Justice, 193
Slater, John, 217
Smith, Anthony, 40, 46, 48, 137
Smith, Sir C. Aubrey, 216
Smith, Desmond, 19
Smith, Mike, 108, 117, 123, 219, 220
Snagge, John, 125
Snow, John, 70, 74, 82, 96, 98, 100
Sobers, Gary, 101
Somerset, 94, 95, 158, 159
South Africa, 108, 110, 216, 219
Southern, John, 157
Southport, 19
Spencer, Tom, 82
Sport on Two, 166
Sporting Chance, 13
Sri Lanka, 69
Stage Cricket Society, 216–17
Standing, Michael, 221
Starmer-Smith, Nigel, 126